Wicked Holiday

SOPHIA SNOWE

Copyright © 2022 by Sophia Snowe

All rights reserved.

No part of this book may be reproduced in any form or by any electronic or mechanical means, including information storage and retrieval systems, without written permission from the author, except for the use of brief quotations in a book review.

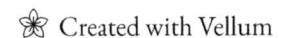

❀ Created with Vellum

Collection info

This is a special, exclusive collection of steamy holiday romances released in the last year. For a limited time only, this hardback is offered EXCLUSIVELY via direct purchase and not available on any other retailer site.

The Wicked Holiday collection includes "Ready to Jingle," "Consumed," "Halloween Games," and all the extra bonus scenes for each book. All Sophia Snowe novels are connected across series, no matter the trope or genre.

Content Warning

These books are only for age 18+ readers due to graphic sexual content, including bondage, bullying, multiple partners, age gap, Daddy king, rape and graphic language. If you are triggered by any of this or are even remotely unsure, please heed this note and refrain from reading this book.

Ready to Jingle

Chapter One

HO, HO, HO!

Merry

"I'm not sure about this, Merry. Who puts an exclusive sex club out in the open like this? It's gotta be full of creeps," my friend Tasha said with a shudder as we got out of the Uber. In front of a place that looked like it might have once been a gym located uncomfortably close to Skid Row in Los Angeles.

Not like me to be in a place like this, but bear with me for a moment. I will explain.

I sighed as I regarded my roommate and best friend's deep frown and pursed lips. Even annoyed, she managed to look dainty and sweet—blond hair tied up in a ponytail, big blue eyes, angelic features. Totally a wolf in sheep's clothing, but what would I do without her? She was loyal, bold, funny, and a certified crackpot. "We're gonna have to see. But we made it all the way here… Maybe we can try?"

Okay, maybe I was the crackpot this time around.

We stood staring at the building for a while. All the windows were blacked out, so at least anyone scrolling by couldn't see inside. People fucking in front of the whole wide world just wouldn't cut it for me unless they were performing on SXTube and I had my trusty ten-speed rabbit with me—but then, what did I really know about sex clubs? Did people still value their privacy when they had their candy canes and nether tinsel exposed for everyone to see?

I heard this place was infamous for its New Year's Eve orgy bash, but I was a get-naked-in-private kind of girl, and that's what I hoped to get tonight.

And I will say this again: the 'I' in this case had to be batshit crazy to even entertain this idea. I truly was desperate.

I rubbed my hands together, having seconds thoughts. I was supposed to be in the library, studying for my last exam before the holidays, but here I was, doing something completely insane —although I wouldn't say impulsive. I had been thinking about it for months, fantasizing about a sexy holiday present to myself.

Of course, no one except Tasha, the one person who'd seen me at my worst since we first shared a dorm room three years ago, had a clue what I was up to.

No one but she knew I had never done anything like this.

I also had never had an orgasm with a guy, period. Never had anyone made my hoo-ha play Vivaldi's four seasons by angels on harpsichords. And I wouldn't count a climax achieved with my battery-operated BFF—everyone knew it wasn't the same.

Pathetic.

So, I might as well have called myself a fucking virgin,

considering that no penis had ever played an Oscar-worthy role in this penis fly trap. No stiff pole had ever made the muff happy. You get my drift. A few robotic strokes—imagine C-3PO awkwardly jerking back and forth, lost in a vast, unknown landscape—doesn't a lover make (sending this PSA to all my exes).

Yep, none of this ass had been kicked, touched, poked, teased, licked by anyone experienced enough to claim a mere quarter-notch in his belt. For the most part, Netflix dates came cheap but the chill part consisted more of a dartboard game where no one had *ever, ever, ever* hit the bull's eye.

I reckon there's no more doubt at this point about the seriousness of my situation.

Sounds unbelievable, I know. But as I said, I'd never gotten my best jollies.

In short, I was a ball of nerves ready to pop. A complete mess.

My sexual encounters with the few boyfriends I'd gone to third base with had been brief and forgettable. So much so, I tended to avoid dating in general. And the only thing that had ever caressed my ass in a pleasing, satisfying manner was my Victoria's Secret and Fruit of the Loom underwear, depending on my mood.

I had no idea why it had been hard to find someone who could actually get me off and convince me there was nothing wrong with me. That I wasn't just a walking piece of ice with limbs and clothes on. Maybe the boys I'd met in my folks' world had been too afraid of them to truly be themselves with me—it was like asking Little Red's grandma to get her groove on with the wolf, like that would be normal. Yeah, more on that a little later.

Fact was, after meeting too many clueless frogs who seemed to permanently glitch after a clumsy fumble that never got me anywhere near a sliver of anticipation, I decided I had to do something about it. Besides, nobody here knew who I really was—including Tasha—and I wanted it that way.

In truth, I'd made it through almost all of pre-law without sowing one measly wild oat. I could run for office and for once, a candidate's record would be squeaky clean. I'd probably reduce any of my rivals' campaign managers to snotty tears on the election trail.

But you know what I really wanted to do? I wanted to ruin all my chances at an unblemished political career. I wanted to do what any other self-respecting student went to college for: get laid good and proper—with all the off-the-chain sexy bells and whistles—and come screaming like a Valkyrie woman leading her warriors to battle.

Merry, Merry. Might as well live up to my name now.

I looked up at the huge poster hanging on the wall next to the door of the building: "Merry Balls ... Jingle all the way! Come inside and suck your way to Santa's naughty list." Bold as you please.

Merry Balls ... you might say it sounds tacky and ridiculous but I say it had to be a sign and I was supposed to be here.

I looked above the arched doorway at the establishment's name: *TOP D*. Again, I sighed.

"But I see your point, you know," I told Tasha.

Because who in the hell would call their club 'TOP D'? Is it someone's initial? Top Dog? Dick? And in that case, what if the owner had a small pecker? The irony...

Still, I was ready to jump in with my arms, legs, and everything in between. Heart clearly trumped head, for I was ready to walk through those doors and stroll out hours later a changed—blissful—woman.

It was just after six, so the night was at its youngest. A few people had walked inside already. I counted two women and an older guy who looked like a male version of Dame Judi Dench, without the class.

Did I say I was desperate?

Enough to rope Tasha into this craziness. She'd been to a sex club before of course, freaky as she was, so she felt somewhat responsible for me. She made me sick...

I had to nip this in the bud.

"Fine, this sucks, I agree," I continued, "but it's one of these places where no one will know who we are. If we go somewhere else, like that other famous club downtown, Tasters, I dunno, your mother might find out somehow," I warned her. *And other people might recognize me, which would be an entirely other layer of fucked-up.*

Tasha stared at me as though I'd forever lost my ever-loving mind and suddenly sprouted pustules on my face. She clicked her tongue.

"As traditional as she is, Mama would rather burn a Bible than go to a sex club," she stated, and then laughed. "And how on earth would she know we went to a sex club, huh? Or even where the sex clubs are located in this city. She lives in rural Idaho, for God's sake."

I rolled my eyes but couldn't help a laugh, for what she said was true. I'd met the woman once when I joined Tasha on summer break and stayed with her people on the farm. Her mother was the type who would feel compelled to go to confession if she ever accidentally ran a red light. That said, she was a lovely lady who loved her family, and I didn't want Tasha to get in trouble because of me. I didn't have anyone to shock—my mom had passed years ago after a long battle with cancer, and my dad ... well ... he was gone too, but that was another story.

So back to what I said about my family. I was somehow glad Tasha didn't know much about them or the fact my father used to be the head of a Maltese mafia family in LA. No lie. Admittedly, such a thing as a Maltese mafia family hardly existed in California or elsewhere in this country until Dad had put it on the map. He was pioneering like that. A veritable Elon Musk of the city's underbelly. After his sudden death not too long ago, my stepmother, Elaine, had taken over.

Until now, I'd been afforded some freedom to follow my career aspirations until it was time for me to be married off to some stuffy old boss who couldn't tell a clit from a bullet. Luckily for me, my stepmother believed a woman should be educated and above all, shrewd.

So you see, my friend didn't need to know just how 'different' my upbringing had been—at least for the time being. Miraculously, I'd managed to spend years living low-key, away from the glitz I'd been around all my life. One could afford a small degree of anonymity in a big city inhabited by people from all over the world. Not everyone would have heard of the Camilleri name and what it entailed.

Time, however, was running out, for when I was done with my studies in a few years—something my family begrudgingly tolerated me doing—I'd have to go back into the fold, and I'd risk losing Tasha, who might or might not understand why I kept her in the dark.

So now that you have the picture, you must think me pretty sick, and not in a good way. If you only knew…

So here I was, standing fifty feet from some junkyard, searching for a clue to the mystery between my legs. This was the time for me to see what all the fuss was about. Bullshit, or truth? I had to find out.

Also, it was painfully embarrassing to be in my position at age twenty-one—a freshman in the orgasm department, and not much better in the down-and-dirty sex department, either. I mean, while other girls giggled at each other's stories about carnal adventures and discussed how often they squirted, I was the one who sat listening, with nothing to contribute. Before you start wondering if I look like one of Cinderella's ugly sisters or am covered in scales or something—just no, okay? Don't go there. Tasha often told me I was pretty, with my dark hair, green eyes, curves and height, and she was a blunt bitch so I had no doubt she wouldn't lie to me.

Tonight didn't have to be difficult. The goal was for me to be with someone who knew his way around a woman's private parts without need of an instruction manual and achieve my first ever orgasm with a man. This is why Merry *Frey*—a fake last name as a nod to one of my favorite Norse goddesses—had reserved a special session with not one, but *two*, studs. Better safe than sorry wasn't just a phrase. Apparently, this deed could be a hundred times better if freaky shit was involved, so I was doubling my chances at a great outcome.

Tasha shifted on her feet, arms crossed, obviously still not quite convinced. I knew she'd cave though. Decked as she was in a schoolgirl skirt and a Santa hat, she was as ready to jingle with some random hot hunk as I was. Only, she didn't book a 'Jingling Trifecta Package Experience' like I had. She'd pretty much wing it, as she did with everything in life. Including her sudden, mid-year, three-hundred-sixty-degree switch from pre-med to a Bachelor's program in Mythology, when she got fed up with her first choice.

I stared at her, wondering if I should have put on a naughty Mrs. Claus costume, but instead I'd gone for a body-hugging short black dress that showed off my curves and long legs.

When I took a hesitant step forward, a tiny voice in my head reminded me who I was, that I was still the daughter of a man who'd been one of the most notorious mobsters in Los Angeles, so I had to be careful. People might be watching me at random times, but I had been careful to cover my tracks. I was usually so well-behaved, and so absent from family drama, they often forgot about me.

Mostly though, I was so done with dating losers—they were everywhere. I had started to wonder if I was cursed.

Suddenly, the door of the club opened, the sound making me jump, and a guy walked outside. About as tall as my five-foot-ten and built like a brick house, he wore a black t-shirt with tattoo sleeves on his arm. I trailed my gaze over his strong jaw, down his wide chest, to his large hands. He had a ruggedly dark, attractive vibe to him that made my pulse quicken and my belly flop. You know, like when you see your favorite hot actor on your favorite streaming service and you feel your vajayjay tingle. Then you need to squeeze your thighs together because you suddenly imagine his sexy butt in full Loki costume lying there between your legs, feasting on the goods, licking around your clit and sucking on the nub like a ravenous beast. *Yeah, you know who I'm thinking about...*

From the symbols this man had tattooed on his neck, I pegged him to be part of the Bulgarian mafia. I didn't really know much about that world. Before he married my stepmother during my middle school years, Father had always told me how this life wasn't for me, but over the years I did pick up a few things about it.

The man put a cigarette into his mouth and lit it. He inhaled deeply, then released the smoke, all the while staring at both of us.

His gaze rested on Tasha for a moment before he shifted it to me, slowly scanning my body, then stopping on my lips while my heart began fluttering uncontrollably inside my chest.

"Are you ladies going in or are you just going to stand there?" he finally asked.

He had a perfect American accent, so he was probably born here. Tasha yanked on my arm, giving me that look again. I tossed my mahogany hair behind me and straightened my back. *Fuck it.*

Besides, I knew my stepmother was already scouring for a potential husband for me. I was my father's eldest and I should have been married to some hot shot family ally long ago. It was surprising I'd held off this long, but each day of borrowed freedom brought me closer to my destiny. Would they even allow me to finish law school before they sold me off to some geezer? And if not, would my new husband let me continue my studies?

The thought made me both sad and pissed off. It wasn't like

my stepmother hadn't been fucking her way through the LA male population already, yet for some reason everyone closed an eye because her people were so powerful. Really, thanks to her we could continue living a good life.

Besides, to be honest, I also craved a family of my own. Babies to hold. A stable life. Partying and sleeping around wasn't for me. I wanted more.

"Yes, we are coming in," I said to the stranger.

I grabbed Tasha's hand and proceeded to drag her inside. The guy nodded, smirking, and then opened the door for us. Another huge man built like an even bigger brick house, came outside as we entered and stood there like a statue, hands together in front of him. When the door closed behind us, he was chatting with guy number one.

Soon, we found ourselves in a large open space. The red lights and Christmas music were a bit of a distraction, but after a tough year, everyone wanted to get into the holiday spirit again.

"Welcome to "Top D," a fake-boobed, fake-smiling hostess dressed in a Mrs. Claus costume welcomed us by the stairs. I was suddenly glad I hadn't opted for that getup. I wanted to laugh when I read her name tag: Candy. Could this have been any more cliché? "We have a naughty elf strip show that starts in about an hour and if you would like to watch it then please let me know as soon as possible. Are you ladies looking for a male or female companion tonight?"

"Neither for me. I like to do my own hunting. For her now..." Tasha hitched a thumb at me, "you gotta ask her."

I kicked her in the shin for I was already uncomfortable as it is. She didn't have to announce our plans to the whole fucking block. Sweat tickled my brow as I spoke in as low a tone as I could muster, and still have her hear me.

"Er ... I reserved the 'Jingling Trifecta Package Experience' for two men and maybe one who could ... possibly watch us." I quickly rubbed on my belly, which now felt like a warzone.

"Name?"

I coughed into my hand. "Merry," I said, wondering now if my real name was common enough. "Merry ... Frey," I stated my assumed last name. Better safe than sorry—I had to protect myself, just in case. "I said I'd pay in cash." I handed her the exact amount and she thanked me. Oh boy. This was really happening.

"I see your details here," she said sweetly, reading through my booking page where I'd explained about my 'problem.' Heat rose to my face as everything was becoming very, very real. "Hmmm ... okay. You explained well what you wish to get from the experience, and our job here at Top D is to make your fantasies come true." She grinned way too hard and my stomach roiled. *Oh boy, oh boy, oh boy.* "Go and have a seat at the bar and you will be notified as soon as everything's ready for you."

Then she was off, disappearing somewhere down the dark corridor and I took that moment to gather my wits. I convinced myself that this would be way easier and more fun than climbing Mt. Everest in sub-zero conditions, but I wasn't so sure.

Tasha snickered and dropped a kiss on my cheek. "You'll be fine," she said, then grabbed my arm and dragged me to the bar.

"Come on, let's get you a drink to loosen you up a little. If you get any more tense, I could snap you like peppermint brittle," Tasha coaxed me.

"All right, but please let's be a little discreet. I don't want to attract more attention than necessary. I just need to get in some room, do the deed, get off and get out. That's it."

"...Leaving me here alone with all the sharks."

I snorted. "As if. I'm more worried about everyone else in here with you around, roaming the place."

"Nah. I'll just sit here at the bar. How long is it gonna take you, anyway?"

I bit on my lip, no idea what to expect.

"Oh, okay," she added. "Just for fuck's sake don't start talking about nerdy shit on law and history if you want to blend in. All you have to do is be someone else for a minute, get outside of yourself. Not that there's anything wrong with the real you, but this is different. Just relax! You'll be fine!" She jiggled my arm and affectionately flicked my chin with her forefinger.

"Okay," I said as we sat down. We were the only two women in this area. I wondered where that guy with the two women had gone off to. This place had to be huge with private rooms and even a massive orgy room in the back, according to what I'd read. The barman smiled at us. He looked quite in his element wearing nothing but red shorts and a Santa hat. He was handsome, clean and nice looking, but not my type. Probably gay, too. "Can we have two vodkas with orange, please," Tasha ordered. "Make both double."

"Coming right up," he said, giving Tasha a wink. Her face turned red and I rolled my eyes, wondering if she'd end up banging the bartender by the end of the night. She was such a worldly woman and I couldn't think of a better person to bring with me here. I needed all the encouragement I could get.

Oddly enough, despite a bit of nervousness and apprehension, I was more than ready.

Ready to jingle.

I knew I gave people an odd vibe sometimes, especially since I had photographic memory and loved nerdy stuff. I enjoyed living in my own predictable world of facts, textbooks, and various causes, where I had a degree of control. Still, despite what people thought, I could let my hair down like the best of them. Although in these times, being a nerd was the height of badassery, too, so I wore that badge proudly.

Still, tonight, I'd just have fun, for the sake of the Elusive Orgasm with a Sentient Being—that's what I was calling it these days. Only not aloud, or Tasha would hit me upside the head with a pan.

We both had our drinks and I ordered another double round because the first wasn't enough to calm my nerves.

That made me a bit tipsy, so when Candy eventually returned, I inexplicably wanted to hug her.

"Ladies, I hope you're enjoying yourselves." She turned to me. I smiled big at her. "Ms. Frey, your room is prepared so if you will follow me…" Before she started heading back with me in tow, she added, "Will you both be going in together? It wasn't in the booking…"

"Oh, no, no. I'm only here for moral support," Tasha said. "I will just have a looksie right—"

"She's going to find someone out here," I said boldly. "I'll be alone."

"Certainly, Ms. Frey. Let us proceed." Another over-the-top grin made her face look like the Cheshire Cat's.

I looked at Tasha and she gave me a reassuring nod. "Go

have fun. I'll be okay out here." She grabbed my hand then leaned over for a hug. "Call me if you need me, is that a deal?"

"Deal," I said, swallowing. "I should be back soon."

"Dammit, girl. Take all the time you need! You earned this. Off you go."

After doing some research late last night, I calculated that normally woman needed an hour to fulfil all her needs in a sex club, but since I had never had a proper orgasm, I didn't know if this applied to me. On the other hand, I wanted to believe it could.

I followed Candy through another long corridor bathed in dim lighting, with doors on each side. Whoever owned the club really enjoyed Mariah Carey as her Christmas album had been playing on repeat since we'd entered. As we walked, we were flanked by large Nutcracker soldier figurines lining the walls, and reindeer shaped decorations trimmed with small LED lights. It could have seemed too much, but it really wasn't. I'd have described it as cute, actually, and rather tasteful, considering we were in one of the underground jizz palaces of LA, as I liked to call them, in a spot bordering one of the dodgiest neighborhoods in the city.

"This way. The guys in there will explain everything to you. Wishing you the best," she said, sounding genuine.

My stomach made a funny jolt, but I kept going until I walked inside a large room with black walls and red furnishings. I mean, there was literally no other color anywhere. Not even a decoration or light fixture on the wall or piece of furniture that wasn't black, and no furnishing or upholstery that wasn't a rich red—in either velvet or damask. This included the black and red

Christmas tree and garlands framing the windows covered in heavy curtains.

Everything looked like I might have imagined if I'd thought about it long enough. There was a large bed in the middle that could fit an entire family of giants and some long chains hanging above it that would make the Ghost of Christmas Past green with envy. Several sexual toys, lube, and other accessories sat on a small table nearby. There was also a large black leather sofa facing the bed—currently occupied by two of the hottest men I'd ever seen.

My throat went dry, and I found myself rooted to the spot. This was it.

These two men sat waiting for me. I recognized the one from the outside with his smoldering gaze. Both had familiar features, but the second seemed like the opposite as he was a blond with amber eyes and slightly longer hair. The first, who I'd met, had much darker eyes and hair, cropped close to his head. He gave me one of those intense looks that cut through skin, but his expression remained impassive—a man of a few words, apparently. They were both dressed in a black t-shirt and red pants, matching the room.

Damn, they had this planned to a T, with uniforms and everything.

"It's you," I said, feeling overwhelmed by the alcohol that ran through my system and my nerves. I'd paid a ridiculous fee for this experience, so I hoped I wouldn't blow it. Although money wasn't really an issue, I hated to waste it, and more importantly, I didn't want to have to explain how I'd spent several thousand dollars.

My stepmother would be furious, I was sure. Not because

she cared about what I did, but she was banking on me making a good match. When she'd taken charge of the estate and the business, everyone thought she wouldn't be capable enough, but she proved them wrong. She was tough, ruthless sometimes, but she treated me and my little sister well, so I couldn't complain.

Still, I didn't want to find out what she'd do if she learned about my shenanigans. She might see it as a slight, a blemish on my reputation, which might affect her plans for me. My world was not for the faint of heart.

"Hi," I finally found my voice and met their gazes. "I'm Merry Frey. I imagine you read my notes about … what I'm looking for." The tall, blond one curved his lips in response. "You two look like you could be related?"

"Yes, Merry. This is my brother Emilio and I'm Gregory," he finally introduced himself. "And we're here for you." A lopsided smile exposed a dimple on his left cheek, then he stood from the sofa and walked up to me.

He brushed my hair away from my face and caught my chin between his thumb and forefinger. "Would you like a drink? We have wine, or anything you could possibly want." The meaningful look in his eyes told me that indeed, he—they—did have what I want, thank you very much. He caught a strand of my hair and played with it. "You are so beautiful. This is going to be fun.

And then, taking advantage of my distraction—I mean, Brad Pitt had nothing on this guy—he leaned down and kissed me, his lush, full lips incredibly soft and hard at the same time.

I froze for a moment because what's a woman to do when one of the sexiest men alive walks up to her and shoves his tongue down her throat? Pull back? Mumble a muffled thank you? Jump his bones and hope he's as well-endowed down there as he is out here? I left out the 'slap him' option because hell, I'd sort of asked for this.

I mean, take that movie—When Harry Met Sally. Hadn't Harry deserved to be blindsided by his friend Sally's fake loud orgasm in that infamous diner scene?

At least, that character had a point of reference.

Which I did not. But as he pulled me close and I felt his huge hard-on press against my stomach, his muscled arms snake around me, my panties got soaked on the spot and I wanted to scream out loud all right.

Jingle holy amazeballs!

I'll take door number three, please. Bone-jumping it is.

Heat rushed through my toes when his hand cupped my ass cheeks and squeezed. His kiss was sensual and unhurried, exploring, urging me to trail my palms up his chiseled pecs and wrap them around his neck. He brought a hand up leisurely to the underside of my breasts and my nipples peaked from the touch. I moaned against his mouth when his tongue danced around mine. He tasted like mint and bourbon—such an intoxicating mix.

As I started to let go, kissing him back, he pulled away from me. Panting, I stared at him in confusion and considered hanging him over the flaming pit of Hell simply for stopping what he had been doing.

Why? The word hung on the tip of my tongue.

He pressed his forehead to mine, which was strangely comforting. "Don't worry, sweetheart. I'm going to make you come like never before and then it will be my brother's turn. We made a deal to get you off before the evening show."

My lips tingled and felt swollen from the kiss, but after the initial wave of frustration, I felt oddly calm. These two didn't come across as amateurs and surely, they were going to take care of me.

That said, although Gregory seemed confident enough, he wasn't the first guy who'd assured me he could. I had been with several and each and every one had failed the test, so I wouldn't get my hopes up too high just yet.

I nodded, my boldness soaring as his hand trailed languorously up my arm. I leaned over to catch Emilio intently staring at us, lounging on the couch with his arm spread across the back. "So ... is it just two of you?" I let the question hang between us.

In the past year and a half, I'd been having these dark and twisted dreams on occasion, of me being fucked by three monsters on a four-poster bed. They were all deformed and ugly, but they had enormous cocks and in all my dreams, I always came out fully satisfied and more alive than ever.

Maybe I wouldn't have three monsters, but I *could* score a couple of guys, right?

"Our father should be here in a moment," Emilio stated with a wink. "He will be watching us." He was now standing behind his brother.

I blinked. "I'm sorry, did you just say your father is going to be here?" I stared at him with my mouth agape.

Emilio didn't have a chance to answer because a moment later, another man entered the room, shutting the door behind him.

He was the tallest of them all and had incredibly muscular arms encased in a black long-sleeved shirt. His dark hair was brushed away from his forehead, the sides dipped in a fetching silver that gave him a look of distinction. His fiery gaze sent an instant fire blazing through my core.

Holy shit fucking amazeballs jingle all the way with reindeers frolicking and bells ringing all around!

He had red pants on and a Santa hat, too.

Cocking his head to the side, I noticed his jaw twitch. Every movement he made called to me, creating a direct line of communication with my coochie, which was profusely thanking me for bringing this god of a man into its midst. His voice was deep and seasoned, like a good aged cognac.

"You can call me Daddy."

Chapter Two

JINGLE BELLS

Ivo

Today hadn't been the best of days, and above all of that, I rarely fucked the clients. That was something my sons liked to do on occasion when business was slow—such as it was around the holidays—and they were bored. I certainly didn't care about entertaining some young girl who'd never had an orgasm.

But tonight, I had to make an exception.

When I'd read Merry Frey's information on the online form, something didn't add up. Who paid that much money in cash? Even men cheating on their wives had a secret card they'd use to pay for the kind of entertainment we offered at Top D.

The girl was beautiful with rich brown hair, tinged with red. She had long legs and wide hips, a curvy body—exactly my type. But I'd had strings of pretty women before.

No, what intrigued me was her story. This hunch I had.

What was she hiding? And why hadn't she achieved an orgasm with a man before? Had something happened to her?

Too many questions begging for answers.

So I had Candy run checks on both her and her friend. I had all sorts of connections in this city. Yet, nothing was found on a Merry Frey that matched the woman who walked into the club tonight. What we did find was the info on her friend—Tasha Stewart. She was a student at UCLA, who roomed with a certain Meredith Camilleri.

Meredith ... Merry.

I saw the woman's picture—matched it with the flesh-and-blood version.

When I spotted her at the bar, live and in person, it felt like I'd been hit by an anvil, knocked out cold by her beauty. I knew I had to have her, despite what I'd found out about her. She looked young, but it turned out she hadn't lied about her years and she was legal. Still, my body didn't care that I was over twice her age, in my mid-forties. One look at those green peepers, that lush hair and ample curves, and my cock made the decision for me.

Getting hard for a woman wasn't as common a thing as it once was for me—not since Elena. First, that person would have to hold my interest, and most of the women who came to the club looking for thrills didn't pass muster for me.

We'd had people ask us to recreate all sorts of dark, depraved fantasies. Still, in the few years I'd owned this place, never had someone walked in asking purely for an orgasm.

The simplest of things, yet so important for this Merry girl. She wanted—*needed*—to have the best climax of her life, with a real man. Clearly not any of the unschooled bastards she'd been running with so far, who probably had to consult a map and a dictionary to figure out where and what a clitoris was.

My sons had already bet on who was going to make her come first. The Dobrev men always enjoyed a bit of friendly competition.

The worst part of this equation had to be that I wasn't sure how I felt about this. But it wasn't about me this time.

The client always mattered most.

"Daddy?" she echoed my request, staring at me with those incredible eyes, assessing and judging. "Are you really their father?"

"Yes, but you don't need to worry about him. He's only going to watch," Gregory interjected with a sardonic grin, "while we take turns. So, get on that bed and take off your panties, sweetheart."

She parted her lips like she wanted to say something, but then held back. A hint of apprehension and hesitation flashed across her face, which was understandable. This was completely unfamiliar territory for her.

I dragged my hand through my hair, weighing the situation, now that I'd been dragged into it. I should have mulled things a little more carefully, using the head on my shoulders rather than the other one, before showing up with my cock and balls primed and ready to go.

First off, I was still digesting the fact I had the daughter of Charles Camilleri right here in my club, about to get it on with me and my boys.

I walked over to the black leather sofa and made myself comfortable there, trying to figure out how to go about this. A moment later, Emilio joined me.

"She's fucking hot," he muttered in my ear. Even my son found her sexy. Although he had no idea who she truly was.

Charles Camilleri had been a highly influential man in LA, a respected leader in the mob circuit. He'd died in a car crash a few years ago, and his wife ran the business like a tight ship now. Bet she had no idea that one of her late husband's little angels was here now, in his den of iniquity.

I shifted on the sofa, running my hands over my chin. This had the potential of being both dangerous and tricky. What if word got to her family where she'd been? But that didn't mean anything—because I'd only fucked a client a time or two in all these years. Would my sons be in danger?

Nah. If she thought there'd be repercussions, she wouldn't even be here. She knew the stakes, and above all, she had grown in the mafia life. From what I'd read about her, she could handle herself well. And she was smart, too. Somebody worth getting to know...

All of a sudden, I wanted this girl for myself, and this wasn't a good thought. I never got territorial with the patrons.

Emilio and Gregory always competed over pussy, but I was too old for that shit—until I set my eyes on Meredith—*Merry*—Camilleri.

"Come on, sweetheart. What are you going to do? I bet you're all wet for me already," Gregory coaxed, approaching the bed and tapping the mattress with his palm, encouraging her to hop on.

"I changed my mind. I want him to leave us alone," she said, her unflinching gaze on me.

Emilio laughed, but Gregory looked annoyed. They both

glanced in my direction, expecting me to leave, but I didn't budge. I stayed put.

"Remember how to address me, princess. If you want me to do something, call me Daddy," I reiterated firmly.

Her face turned beet red, but she also licked her lips, which meant she secretly enjoyed what I was doing.

Kinky...

She sighed and then walked to the bed, giving me a glimpse of her sweet round ass encased in black lace panties as she climbed on it. My cock stiffened. The desire to mark my territory came on strong, making me feel like an inexperienced punk.

Holy fuck...

She shifted on the mattress, her gaze roving, assessing. All I needed was to have her alone ... get close to her, feel her, touch her ... and she would never forget this night.

"Daddy, will you leave us alone please?" she asked, putting on a sweet voice. I stood, but instead of leaving, I approached her, taking my time, savoring the sight. She looked like an angel with creamy skin, bejeweled eyes, and legs that wouldn't quit. What I wouldn't give to have those lips wrapped around my cock...

I'd spent a couple of hours scouring the web for information about her. It wasn't easy, but once I had Candy's leads, I could pull out a couple of interesting things.

Like how she religiously spent one full day a week at a legal defense non-profit, assisting the lawyers with pro bono work for underprivileged people.

How she always volunteered at the soup kitchen, and became a passionate advocate for domestic violence victims.

How she liked to visit the animals at a local SPCA and bring them treats.

How she lived simply at her college, always avoiding the limelight.

A young woman who had everything she could want, yet she enjoyed being a good human, walking the walk, without fanfare.

All things I hated to learn—because they made me want to discover her further.

But tonight, I had a goal. And that was to make her explode until she begged me to stop.

"Good girl. Now take off your panties for your Daddy. Gregory might be skilled, but he's not going to make you come like I would," I said with a smile. If I wanted her to myself, I'd have to play Emilio and Gregory's game. They always acted like eight-year-old children when they competed over something.

The caged look eased from Merry's face as she seemed to come to a decision. I wasn't sure she was comfortable yet, but she did obey me without saying anything, quickly taking her underwear off. I reached out for the prize and she gave them to me without hesitation. Bringing them to my nose, I smelled the sweet aroma, never taking my eyes off her. Her scent was already driving me insane and I hadn't even touched her yet.

"I'll be the one to make you climax, so don't listen to these fools over here, sweetheart," Gregory quipped, and Emilio snickered.

"Yeah, right," his brother mocked.

"Just get the fuck out of here, you two, because you're getting on my nerves. I'll get her screaming for me in no time." Gregory waved us away with an exaggerated gesture.

My younger son had no clue he wasn't skilled enough to give this girl what she wanted. This, I sensed deep in the pit of my stomach.

"But in the form I filled out, I asked for two men and another to watch us," Merry protested. "Can't you get me someone else as a third?" She didn't look too happy.

I inwardly sighed. I loved my sons but right now, all I wanted was for them to disappear. I doubted I could make this work without letting them have a go at her first, though. Controlling my desire to blast everyone but her out of the room, I caved.

"I understand, princess," I said, thinking ahead and telling myself that if we did it this way, one after the other, I'd eventually get some alone time with her. "So how about this? We try one at a time at first. The other two will be watching from my office." I pointed to the floor above. "If that doesn't work, we'll go with the original plan—no extra charge of course. How does that sound?"

She bit on her lower lip, making me so hard, I needed to adjust my crotch, but I stood still. Waiting. After a few moments of deliberation, she nodded.

Without a word, I put her panties in my pocket and then motioned to Emilio to follow me.

We left the room and headed to my office on the first floor, where I switched on the main screen that gave us a perfect view of the bed in the black and red room. I knew Gregory wouldn't hurt Merry, but I needed to take all the precautions. I needed to figure out why she couldn't orgasm. Maybe this was more psychological than physical.

It would have been better if she let us stay in the room, but this was the next best thing. It would have also been better if I didn't have to watch my sons touch her first—a ridiculous instinct to possess this girl I couldn't yet understand. She was young and ripe, and she put all my protective instincts on high alert. There was nothing I wanted more than for her to call me Daddy while I was fucking her from behind, but my sons would wonder what was wrong with me, and I had no time for that.

But Emilio's dangerous twinkle in his eyes concerned me...

"Wanna bet Gregory won't make her come?" he said once I sat down on the chair in front of the large monitor.

"He won't make her come and neither will you," I told him, noting she was already spreading her legs for Gregory. I focused on her behavior, her movements, the expressions on her face. Her reactions.

Gregory pulled her down to the edge of the bed. I quickly changed the song to another Christmas tune and adjusted my Santa hat. Even in her situation right now, getting ready to be pleasured by a man, her face had a sweetness to it. Purity—that was the word. The scariest part was that I had this insane urge to mark her so deeply, she'd never—*ever*, for as long as she lived—want to be free my touch. My scent. My hands...

I wanted to ruin her.

"You won't have a chance to get to that pussy, Dad. She only wants us to play with her," Emilio said with utter confidence, putting his hands behind his head and plastering his gaze on the screen in front of him.

"We shall see," I muttered, and left it at that. Why argue? All I could do was bide my time.

"Yeah, you're already wet for me, sweetheart," Gregory said, caressing her stomach and then running his hand over her wetness.

Over the years, I'd invested considerable funds into the club and the black and red room had great acoustics. Maybe the branding was a little over the top, but this establishment gave me another good source of income. Politicians, businessmen, and foreigners visited often, booking for private events, and I was the only one in the city trusted enough to guarantee their confidentiality.

I loved hearing her little whimpers in stereo. I guessed there was something to be said for being a voyeur, just sitting back and taking it all in.

Gregory lay on the bed next to her, hitched up her dress, and started rubbing on her clit. From the way she arched her head backwards, closing her eyes and breathing just a little bit faster, she was enjoying the ministrations.

"That feels good," she told him, so he kept the pace for a while. She moved her hips a little, but after a while, he changed position and kneeled in front of her. I had no idea why he kept ignoring those delicious breasts, that soft skin with graceful dips and curves. Sure, he was hitting the right spots but he should know—while a woman's largest erogenous zone was her brain, the rest of those delicious trigger points were scattered all over her body. Discovering each and every one of them was an exercise in patience, dedication, and detailed sensual exploration. Maybe he was still too young and mindless to understand.

Gregory wrapped his hands around her thighs and started to lick her neatly trimmed pussy, moving his tongue all the way from her ass to her clit. I couldn't deny, the sight made me squirm in my seat, my cock now painfully rock solid. The call of that sweet looking pussy was too strong to ignore. I slid my hand in my jeans pocket and wrapped my fingers around her lacey underwear, relishing the feel of it. I wanted to immerse myself in her, drown in her. Unload my cum in her.

Gregory was doing a decent job, working out what she enjoyed and what she didn't, asking her to guide him, which was considerate and sensible. Maybe he really would succeed tonight.

"I have to give it to him, he's trying hard but this girl is not a firecracker. She's like a volcano. She's going to explode just with the right amount of licking and teasing," I said.

Gregory was really going for it, licking and rubbing her clit like his life depended on it.

"What are you now, Dad? An expert in pussies?" Emilio asked, laughing.

"Expert in that one, for sure," I playfully countered.

Emilio was a few years older than his brother, but he was fucking around too much. Gregory, on the other hand, was looking a relationship but had been unlucky in love. When his last girlfriend left him, he'd taken it hard. On the outside looking in, one would think the tight-lipped, less extrovert and older Emilio would be the more mature one, but that wasn't the case. Gregory was still pretty young, but he knew what kind of women he liked spending time with.

As a dominant, Emilio was only interested in sexual kink. He liked bondage and giving pleasure through pain. He was never going to settle down and this wasn't good for the business, because he couldn't control his urges. I often found myself having to clean up his messes. One time, he had broken a girl so badly, she ended up on suicide watch.

"Gregory is having a go and you will have your chance, too, but I am warning you now, Emilio—be gentle with this girl or you'll have to answer to me. She has no fucking idea that you're a psycho," I ground out. And I meant every word.

"Why are you suddenly so protective of this girl? She's no one," Emilio spat, rubbing his hand over the bulge in his trousers. He had no boundaries. What he did have was a pair of cuffs sticking out of his pocket.

"She's a client, that's who she is. She's also not like one of your tough girls. She's a sensitive one, I can tell, so fucking watch out," I snapped back, seeing that my princess was moaning already.

"That's it. Let it out. Are you going to come for me like the good girl you are?" Gregory urged. He inserted two fingers inside her and she moaned some more, nodding vigorously.

Her body stiffened and she shut her eyes, straining, as he maintained his hard and fast rhythm, licking her clit at the same time. I loved the way she writhed on the bed, whimpering and palming her gorgeous breasts. He kept going for about ten more minutes, doing everything he could so she would finally come. For a moment, I thought she was there, for her moans got more intense and louder.

I had a feeling Gregory wanted to make sure she would come on her own, without the need for a toy or other accessories, but time was running out.

There was no doubt at this point that she wasn't going to get there and I could see that my son was getting tried.

His arms went a little slack and then he stopped, pulling away. He sat by the side of the bed, taking fast, shallow breaths.

When she quieted, she sat up on her forearms, her expression a mix of bemusement and frustration. Damn, I knew this was going to be a challenge, but I had no idea just how much, until then.

"Just give me a few minutes, sweetheart, all right?"

She muttered something under her breath, but I couldn't make out what it was. But when she let herself fall on the bed, beat and dejected, hair a lovely mess, hands covering her face, she looked so vulnerable. And so perfectly fuckable.

"I think maybe we should take a break..." she finally said.

Gregory's chest rose and fell as he took a deep inhale. His hands trailed to his jeans, hovering at the button. He would want to try again, fuck her and try to make her come that way—he didn't like to give up—but she wanted him to stop. Also, a vaginal orgasm might actually be harder to achieve in many cases, and he knew that. He had worked hard, stretched her well, but he needed to count his losses, walk out, and let somebody else handle it.

In the end, he made the sensible choice.

When he walked out, she sat back up and mumbled some words, talking to herself. She raked her hand through her hair and sighed, looking so lost, then started to reason out loud. "Statistically speaking, I'm less likely to achieve orgasm through penetration. There've been studies about this, so what am I going to do? Where did I read that study? Was it Scientific American?" She squinted her eyes, deep in thought. "Boy I should have stayed at the library and studied a little longer. I'm ready for the final, but I'd have been more productive... Oh, I need to ask Professor Gorman about the internship at the Mack & Taylor firm in the spring... Maybe I should get out of here... none of this is going to work," she kept on and on.

I chuckled. Damn, this girl loved to talk to herself. I wondered if this was a habit. But maybe I was on to something now. I'd already figured out she was a model student, excelling in everything. She was probably overthinking everything, which might as well be the culprit in this case.

Her left brain was in overdrive. I mean, the girl couldn't relax! What had she been thinking when Gregory was eating her out with all he had in him? A law exam paper? An appointment she had to set up for next week?

Gregory had left, so this meant Emilio was going to get his chance to play with her. After figuring out the issue, I had no doubt he wasn't going to succeed—and that worried me.

Emilio was into some dark and depraved shit and I wasn't comfortable with him being alone with her, even if I was watching from upstairs.

I looked up and realized he was already gone to claim his moment with Merry. I watched him enter the room and stand in front of her naked form. Her eyes widened when he put his hands on his hips and looked down at her.

A knot formed in my stomach, and I couldn't shake it loose. But it was too late—I had to let this shitshow play out.

"Are you ready for another round, pretty bitch?" Emilio said. "I'm not a gentleman like my brother, so buckle up, buttercup."

Chapter Three

IT'S NEARLY CHRISTMAS

Merry

Gregory was good. He brought me all the way to the edge, stroking and licking my clit, then sliding to my pussy. When he started fucking me with his tongue, my whole body ignited.

However, I lost that thrill when he added more fingers inside me. It felt like someone had flipped a switch, and I went from needy and throbbing to aggravated.

Now, his brother was here and he was looking at me like I wasn't even human. A tinge of fear crept up my spine, and I wondered if I was still safe. I had to be—this was a business and I'd purchased a service. They'd been around a while, so they knew how to treat a client.

Still, I had my reservations.

If I had to dig deep, deep down inside me, I'd admit their father was the one who lingered in my thoughts and got my juices flowing. The man was gorgeous, with a tall, powerful frame, and an intense dark gaze that seemed to drill right through to my soul. That knowing stare made all manner of sensual promises, and I believed him. Yes, I couldn't lie to myself—after all, I was a practical person. If anyone could get this feeling of completion out of me, it would be him.

For now though, I had Emilio, the fucker who couldn't smile without looking like a character out of a Stephen King book. That said, he was darkly sexy, and hot, and at this point I didn't want to be too picky. I'd get the one-guy-at-a-time deal. Not exactly the two-fer I'd requested, but in hindsight I believed this was best. Daddy had made a good call.

"I'm going to tear you apart, pussycat." Emilio gave me a dark smile, and I wasn't sure I liked it.

Okay, let me hold off on that good call comment for now...

I closed my eyes and braced myself, feeling like the one who always picked the fortune cookie with the shittiest predictions. Like, 'You will be constipated for a week' or 'Watch out for spiders in your pillowcase.' You know, shit like that, probably written by the disgruntled nephew of the fortune cookie company asshole boss person.

Well, my other cookie, on the other hand—the one between my legs, just to be clear—wasn't cooperating. *Bitch.* She gave me nada. Zilch. No 'find orgasm here' sign or some such. No clue anybody could make heads or tails of, including me.

This might turn out to be a bust. At least I could walk out of here any time I wanted. It's not like I was trapped in this place. I also had Tasha, and I could call her so we'd leave together.

Emilio gripped my leg in a punishing grip, so much I cried

out in pain. *What in the fuckety fuck?!* Showing no concern whatsoever, he raised it to one of the chains and cuffs dangling from the ceiling.

But before he could restrain me, the door burst open, and in came the very devil I'd been lusting for.

Daddy himself.

A knight in black and red armor.

The sight had me instantly squeeze my thighs together, for my cookie was indeed pleased to see him. More than when she accompanied me to a Daniel Craig movie, or when I sat with her to watch reruns of Lucifer or that Witcher hottie. Yes, my cookie, hoo-ha, coochie, punani, pussy, muff, whatever I felt like calling it at a given moment had strong opinions. And she was letting me know in no uncertain terms: this guy was THE SHIT.

If the huge bulge in his pants was any indication, he was happy to see me too. I felt like a freak for he was so much older than me, but his body was in so much better shape than that of some twenty-year-olds I knew.

The sickest part though was that calling him Daddy made me so fucking aroused.

There was no redemption for me, but did it matter? He was hot, this was a sex club, and kink was the name of the game. My pussy could weep whenever and for whoever she pleased.

I glanced at Emilio and he gave me a dark smile. Obviously, he had different plans for me than his brother. My mind started racing when Daddy made himself comfortable on the sofa in front of the bed, looking straight at said wet pussy.

This time, I didn't want him to leave and I had this feeling he just wanted to make sure his son wasn't going to do anything silly. Because Emilio came across as the crazy one and somehow my gut decided I felt decidedly less nervous with Daddy around. I did my best to forget the not so very minor detail that the guy about to touch my punani was his son, and also the fact that I was attracted to Daddy Santa more than both of his own offspring.

And on cue, my pussy wept some more. If I kept my eyes on Daddy, everything would be all right.

Emilio dropped my leg and produced a pair of Santa cuffs from his pants pocket. I wanted to laugh, thinking how no one had ever tried to turn me on with Christmas toys. The split image of his father but with shorter hair, he was also very handsome. In the right light, his dark brown eyes took on a rich whiskey tone. The tattoos gave him a dangerous air that likely made some women forget their own language at the sight of him.

"Go on all fours and spread your legs for me. I'm going to make you come. I'm not a wuss like my brother. I can take the challenge," he said.

I still had my black dress on and I was glad he didn't ask me to take it off. I couldn't explain why—but the fact his father was here, watching, assessing made me even more subconscious. And hot for him. Boy was it smoking in here.

The black sofa was close enough to the bed so he could see all my private bits at close range. My wet pussy. My ass. Every good trait and every flaw. Every wave of desire that washed over me. I'd be hard pressed to hide just how much I wanted to do that bone-jumping thing with him. Maybe I should tell them I changed my mind and I only wanted Daddy, but my pride reared its head and I would die before admitting that—not after I'd practically kicked the man out before.

"Get on your knees, bitch," Emilio ordered after cuffing my hands together.

I turned and got on all fours, my dress lifted to my waist to expose my ass. I didn't have time to wallow in my self-consciousness for Emilio slapped my ass hard, drawing a scream from me. And then again on the other cheek. My skin smarted, heat radiating off it, and pleasure-pain riffled to my lady bits.

Walking around the bed, Emilio grabbed me by the cuffs and yanked me up, raising my arms until he slid my restraints into a hook hanging from a chain above the bed. I was now on my knees, which were positioned far apart, arms raised up high.

He pushed my dress up a little further, exposing part of my back. I felt Daddy's gaze burning into it as Emilio trailed a hand down my spine and delivered another searing slap.

"Oh shit!" I cried out, shocked and suddenly filled with anticipation.

I felt him climb on the bed behind me and slip two fingers in my pussy, his arm pressing into my ass as he moved.

"Look at that cunt. It's dripping wet all because of a few slaps. I have no fucking idea how Gregory didn't make you come, but I think you need to be punished. You must be holding back." Retreating his fingers, he pinched my pussy hard.

"Ow!" Why did he do that? But oh, when the pain dulled, it kinda felt so good...

"You need to experience some pain before you get to the pleasure. Maybe then you'll appreciate it more," he said, then his ran his hand over my ass cheeks.

Mariah Carey was singing *All I Want for Christmas is You*, which was kind of fitting, but in that moment, I truly hoped Daddy would get to fuck me soon.

His finger grazed my ass and then moved once more down to my wetness. I moaned when he pushed through the folds and dipped a finger inside me once more, then the second one. His rhythm was a tad too rough but once I adjusted, it felt surprisingly good. I wondered if Daddy was watching—the very thought had me ride that hand, striving to catch a feeling that had been elusive for far too long. All I could think about was that beautiful man while his son penetrated me with his fingers—picturing him fucking me on the bed, against the wall, on the floor... Without ever having experienced it, I just ached for his touch, to feel his warm breath on my skin.

Emilio soon found my clit and started rubbing it gently. I closed my eyes. He might have been right. That slap had woken something inside me and I needed more.

More.

"I can't wait to fuck you until you beg me to stop but first, we need to make sure you're ready for it," he said. Then, I felt something moist spread over my ass cheeks.

"Is that lube?" I asked, my voice horse.

"Shhh, I want you to be quiet now and if you're going to be a bad girl, I will punish you," Emilio growled in my ear, and then slapped me again, harder, and I yelped, a stinging pain wracking me.

A vibrating sound reached my ears and he slid the toy inside me. The rhythm was slow, then faster ... slow, and faster.

"Shit," I gasped.

"What was that? Didn't I tell you not to speak?" he asked, so I quickly shut my mouth.

He kept thrusting that vibrator or whatever toy he was using in and out of my pussy for a little while. Then, he put more lube around my ass, and down towards my pubic area, coating it all with his hand. My hips were shaking with anticipation, because I had no idea what Emilio was planning to do next.

"This will make you squeal," he said, placing the vibrating toy on my clit while his finger caressed my anus. I bit on my lower lip, telling myself that he was only setting me up for failure until the intensity of all these sensations made me pant for air as my whole body shuddered. My pulse was drumming in my ears, Emilio then inserted a finger into my other hole and I shifted on the bed, unsure if I liked that, then at the same time he stuck the dildo inside me.

"So wet down there. Easy, little bitch. Your ass needs some training. You like this." Emilio pushed the dildo farther inside me, slowly, and kept penetrating my anus with his finger.

Holy mother of God...

It was a good place to be suspended in, indulging in the build of my thrumming pulse, the quiver in my thighs, the arousing harshness of the whispered words against the shell of my ear.

When he found a good rhythm, he paused for a moment and slapped me hard, never slowing the pace with the dildo. The pleasure-pain had me lose my breath. I thought I was finally going to come like never before.

Emilio pulled out the dildo and replaced it with his fingers.

"Fuck..." I mumbled, losing myself to a whirlwind of sensation, feeling slick heat on my inner thighs. My orgasm was right there waiting... I was on the edge, ready to explode...

But then, Emilio plunged the dildo into my ass. Deep. Rough, ruthless.

I shrieked in agony when intense pain shot through every nook in my body, radiating from that one violated spot.

Mindless to my predicament, he started rubbing on my clit at the same time. Never once did he pause to see if I was all right.

"Bitch, quit your whining," he growled—sounding aggravated.

I tried to pull away. "Fuck you! It hurts!" Strung up as I was, my wrists bruised, and considering the great discomfort I was in, it was hard to move.

Tears stung my eyes, and all I wanted was to crawl in a corner. I could barely muster a word.

Strong arms came around me, comforting, and slowly, gently the dildo was pulled out of me. A different scent awakened my senses, and just then, I knew—it was Daddy's embrace surrounding me.

"For fuck's sake, this one's is a fucking freak! Any other girl would have come five times already," Emilio snapped—heartless.

Daddy's body stiffened, and I could feel the anger roll off him as he uncuffed me. Meanwhile, my tears broke free and started to fall. How fucking dared he?

"You ... you're a monster. Stay ... away from me," I said breathlessly, my voice muffled as my face was buried in Daddy's black shirt. I hated how weak I sounded. A strong hand caressed my crown, and soft, soothing words reached my ears.

Emilio had never asked if I wanted anal penetration—which I didn't. He didn't care. How was this man allowed to work here?

But then I wondered as Emilio's father pulled away from me: Was I really that messed up? A freak?

Yes, it had been annoying to be like I was, but I'd never thought much about it until now.

My silver-haired knight laid me down on the bed and pulled the dress down, then kissed me on the temple.

"Hang in there. I'll be back," he said in a voice that broke through the sadness.

I didn't know what happened after that, but I figured Daddy must have punched his son, because Emilio stumbled and fell with a heavy thump on the floor. I tried to turn around, but that was almost impossible because I was still so sore and achy and humiliated.

Daddy's voice boomed through the room. "I don't care if you're my son—enough is enough! You crossed a line. Now get your shit and get out of my club, and don't come back until you've grown into a real man!"

"Fuck you, *Father*."

"Fuck you! Out of my face, before I tear you limb from limb. And learn some respect, will you?"

I couldn't believe he was kicking out his own son to protect me. Trembling and a little cold, I waited. Maybe coming here had been a bad idea. I needed to somehow muster the strength to get up, clean myself a little, and go back home.

There was nothing for me here.

"Yeah, get me out of the way, huh? That's what you want so you can fuck her yourself. You old fool." Emilio just wouldn't give up. But that was the last I heard of him for a big crash ensued—like the sound of something breaking—and then the door slammed shut.

I exhaled in relief when the room was bathed in silence for a moment.

After a while, I felt part of the mattress sink with the weight of a body sitting on it. Daddy's big arms came around me once again. "Are you okay?"

I nodded. He pulled my hair away from my face, then took my hands and checked my wrists. "Don't worry, Emilio is gone now and won't be back."

I sat up and started rubbing my wrists, leaning my head on his chest as though it was the most natural thing to do.

He was quiet then, seeming to know what I needed in that moment. I had to take some time to make sense of what had happened. I felt like Waldo—lost and never found.

"I'm sorry, I just didn't think I was ready for that," I said when his fingers found mine. He started to massage my wrists, and even through the surreal moment, something sparked between us when our skin touched.

"Don't you dare apologize. Emilio can't control himself. I had no idea what would have happened if I didn't stop him. I should have known…"

I looked into his brown eyes which were full of concern.

"What's your name?" I asked, shocked that I didn't even know it yet. He'd seen me at my worst—yet I didn't know his given name.

"Ivo," he replied. "And you're Merry."

"Yes," I said. "My full name is Meredith, but all my friends call me Merry." That wasn't a lie, at least. "I like Ivo." And I liked the way his name rolled over my tongue. "You know you look a little silly in that Santa hat."

Well, actually, he looked fucking hot in that hat and I wanted to rip his shirt off, so I could run my hands over his sculptured chest.

He smiled and his eyes twinkled at the corners.

"Thank you for saving me, Ivo, but I guess this is it. I have to get going. I need to see if my friend is okay. She might be wondering the same."

"And your orgasm?" he asked, sounding serious. "I know Emilio was a jerk, but I promise we're not all like that."

"I know. Gregory's nice."

He smiled with pride. "He's a keeper. Works hard, too. I'm proud of him."

"Thank you again for what you did. Takes a lot of guts to take some stranger's side against your son. I know a lot of powerful people who cover for their children's behavior and that's never a good thing."

He put his arm tighter around me and squeezed a little. "Don't get me wrong. I *have* covered for them on multiple occasions, but I guess there's always a breaking point." He sighed.

I picked at an imaginary piece of lint on his jeans, then his hand covered mine. Amazing how easy it was to let go and be myself with this stranger.

"Can you wait for me here? I will be back in a minute."

"Sure," I said. I guessed I could wait a while before heading out. Although I felt I had probably overstayed my welcome here.

I had a feeling these people were all part of the Bulgarian mafia and I didn't like Emilio one bit. Those guys had a knack for violence and revenge that trumped even the Italians sometimes. Ivo seemed like an exception, or maybe I was wrong.

I was attracted to him, but perhaps it wasn't meant to be. Plus, I wasn't sure I could go through with it tonight. Too much had happened. The worst part was, who could I tell about it? I could confide in Tasha, but I wasn't up to that. My sister was even more inexperienced than me, so she wouldn't understand. My stepmother—we just didn't have that kind of relationship. I had no one else to turn to.

Ivo made me feel comfortable for the first time in a long time and I knew if I was around him a bit longer, I could simply be myself and let go. I didn't have to prove anything to anyone.

But that was just a dream.

The sound of the door opening and closing cut through my thoughts. "Here you go. Hennessy on the rocks. Works wonders to soothe the nerves." He'd also brought a bowl of potato chips for me, as well as a small bag of sunflower seeds. My stomach rumbled and I realized I hadn't eaten in a while.

"Thank you. That's very kind of you," I said, taking a sip of the strong drink. The liquid burned its way down my esophagus—just what I needed. As I drank and munched on the snacks, our gazes hooked, and my world spun on its axis.

Age was just a number, because I certainly felt an affinity to this man. He was beautiful and as I had just found out, kind. I set the glass down and smiled.

"So," he said. "I bring news. Your friend is fucking a bouncer in one of the rooms of pain. From what I can gather, she's enjoying herself very much," he stated and I nearly choked on a chip.

"Excuse me? Tasha is fucking your bouncer?" I laughed,

remembering how I'd just thought about her worrying about me.

"Shouldn't be long though. They've been in there over an hour."

I nodded.

"I can see you're tired."

I nodded again. I should be going now but I didn't want to. I stared at the floor, so torn about what to do. I was so fucked up. A normal person would have run out of there STAT after what happened with Emilio.

"Listen, Merry." Leaning over to take my hand, he trailed his thumb over my knuckles. Again, his touch was electric. "I know you are thinking about staying here, with me, but Emilio's actions have ruined what was left of a perfectly good experience. I have a proposition," he said, then paused, likely to gauge my response.

"Yes?"

"Why don't you go home with your friend tonight… you need a familiar face to be around for a while. I can see you're much better, too."

My heart sank. Maybe after all the failed attempts at reaching a climax, he also thought me a weirdo.

"But I want you to come back tomorrow, at eight PM sharp."

I turned to face him, lips parted as a question dangled from my lips. He returned my gaze with a fervent one of his own. Firm. Determined. Serious.

He wants me.

"I need you to wear this dress again, and no panties, no bra, and this time, we will be completely alone. The club will be closed tomorrow. I'll send a car to whatever address you give me, and bring you here. Is that clear?"

"Yes, Sir."

"Sir?"

"Daddy. Yes, Daddy."

"That's my girl. Now go on and rest. You'll need it for your big day tomorrow."

Chapter Four

DECK THE HALLS

Ivo

She'd refused my offer of a car picking her up, and showed up here in an Uber. When she arrived, I thought it wise to take her to a different room, this one decorated in green and gold, with hints of red for the holidays. I had a table set up, and I'd brought in take out from the Chinese restaurant.

What mattered was that I had her all to myself. Emilio and Gregory both had their chance and blew it. Couldn't say I was sad about that.

The girl needed to be taken care of and I had to have a bit more time with her. She was so fucking beautiful, inside and out, and in just a short time, I was intrigued by her. I didn't want to let her go without her experiencing something that would change her outlook on life.

An orgasm with a man. *Me.*

A flash image of her sprawled on the bed with her gleaming pussy exposed, legs wide open, entered my mind. Last night, it was the last thing I saw in my mind's eye before stroking myself to a toe-curling orgasm, followed by a deep, long sleep with dreams of a dark-haired, green-eyed temptress.

Merry wanted to experience a first, but so did I. I'd never been into much younger women before, or even considered Daddy kink as a thing. But somehow, just finding out about Meredith Camilleri, I just couldn't help yearning for her. She was a paradox, not like other women in my brutal, unyielding world. The fact her family were rivals of mine, or that she still had no clue who I was, didn't stop me from craving her in the worst way.

I should know better.

Merry put her chopsticks down on her plate and rubbed on her belly. "Oooh, I'm full. Thank you for dinner. It was delicious."

"You're welcome," I said, loving how she'd enjoyed her meal with enthusiasm, digging in. She was an entirely different princess altogether...

"So tell me, how old are you, Ivo?" she asked. "I've been meaning to ask but we didn't have the time."

"Hmm, how old do you think I am, Merry?" I also loved how her name was so fitting for this time of year. Maybe she was my Christmas present, perfect for me to unwrap...

"I do have a good memory, but I'm not too good with the guessing game. Sixty?" Her eyes twinkled like gems.

"Fuck, no," I said, knowing she was pulling my leg. "I'm only forty-five."

"Are you married to Emilio and Gregory's mom? Someone else?" A delicate frown creased her face.

"No. We've been divorced a long time now."

"One more question. Why did you come to the room when Emilio was here? Were you trying to protect me?"

She seemed genuinely interested in the answer, so I'd give it to her straight.

"Well, my son's been known to be a little … impulsive and hot-headed."

"…And he's the true freak."

I laughed at that. "Can't argue with this reasoning."

She opened her mouth to say something, then seemed to think better of it.

"Tell me what you meant to say," I insisted. I wouldn't let her cower and retreat and fold into herself. I hoped she understood she didn't have to, with me.

"Well … I wanted to say although what Emilio did was … too much, I … I …"

"Yes? Go on…" I encouraged.

"I liked the tying up and the roughness and … dunno how to describe it. It's as if … as if I could let go and be overwhelmed but in a good way. If I feel safe I could … maybe, you know…"

"Come," was all I said in response.

Picking up both our drinks, I led us to the couch, where we sat comfortably next to each other. I handed her the glass and put my arm around hers. "Look at me."

"Hmmm?" She did as I asked.

Drowning in her eyes, I leaned down, down, down, until my lips found hers and captured them in a demanding kiss. She tasted even better than I imagined. Her lips parted and she didn't hesitate to kiss me back. I deepened the kiss, sliding my tongue into her mouth, and my cock went as hard as a rock. I didn't think it could get any harder. *Shit.* I grabbed a fistful of her hair and pulled her head back.

Her eyes were the color of emeralds, her mouth swollen and pink.

"I'm hungry again. Let your Daddy feast on you."

Before she could say a word, I stood, picked her up, and carried her to the bed. Time for us to play for a little while.

She kissed me again, nipping on my bottom lip and driving me absolutely crazy. I pressed her closer to me, kissing her deeply until our tongues collided. She moaned into my mouth that just about made me lose my self-control.

"Do you trust me, princess?" I asked, hovering above her.

She nodded.

"And from now on, you'll call me Daddy."

"Yes, Daddy," she replied, and I groaned at the sound of that rolling off her lips. I didn't think I could ever get bored of her calling me Daddy.

I pulled a scarf out of my pocket and quickly blindfolded her. Then, after making sure her wrists were healing nicely, and she nodded for me to continue, I put her hands in the cuffs that were built into the bed on each side. Her legs went into regular chains, with a Christmas garland I had weaved into them. She didn't make a sound, just let me restrain her without hesitation. The little festive details were hilarious. I put a lot of thought into pleasuring my princess.

"What are you going to do to me, Daddy?" she asked, trying to jiggle her arms. She was stuck, unable to move, at my mercy.

"What is the fun in me telling you, Merry?" I then

proceeded to rip her dress off her, tearing it apart. My heart hammered in my chest at the sight of such bounty. Full, deliciously round D-cups plopped out like a jack-in-the-box, the nipples stiff and alert. As I'd instructed, she wore no undergarments.

"Why did you do that?" she squeaked. "How am I going to get home now?"

I climbed on top of her and caressed her breasts, with feather-light strokes at first.

"Don't worry, princess. Daddy will take care of you," I assured her, and then took her perfectly round pink nipples into my mouth, stopping for a second when she jolted, inhaling sharply. Those little fools hadn't even touched her beautiful breasts, or paused long enough to appreciate her. They thought that if they licked her for a while, they would win the challenge, but a woman needed and deserved much more than that.

I started squeezing her breasts with both of my hands, their weight filling my palms, then licked her nipples until she was wriggling on the bed, begging me to stop.

"So you like this, huh? I now know one of your weaknesses, princess." I sucked hard on her nipples again, swirling my tongue over them and biting gently.

"Oh, God," she moaned.

"God won't help you now," I said, laughing, then bit her left nipple harder than I anticipated. She cried out, shaking her head, and I pinched the other one, rolling it around my fingers.

"Enough ... stop. Please..."

"Sorry love, I have no intention of doing that. I'm only just getting started."

I didn't require the aid of any toys this time. I just needed to use my imagination to make her lose her goddamn mind. Her hips tensed and she yanked on the chains.

"Are you wet for me? Do you want me to touch you down there, princess?" I asked, pressing my hand over my hard dick. I didn't even remember the last time I'd tied another woman up and fucked her hard. Never had I even had one in Merry's situation, and I had a fair bit of experience in the bedroom.

"Yes please, Daddy. I want to come so badly. Can you stick your cock in me?" she pleaded, falling so easily into the little girl role.

"Oh, darling, of course, but not yet. First you need to come for Daddy like a good little girl." Lowering myself down to her opening, I inhaled the sweet scent of her arousal.

She was already spread, ready, and so, so wet for me. I blew into the sensitive flesh there and she arched her body, ass off the bed, when the cool air hit her.

"Ivo ... fuck..." She pushed her hips downward, trying to get her sweet pussy in my face, searching for my touch. The anticipation of what was coming made me horny as fuck. Placing small kisses over her clit, I then licked it slightly, gently. Her pussy was so engorged and glistening with her juices, and I felt her throbbing for me, pulsating with the need for release.

"Daddy is pleasing you, my princess," I said, and then proceeded to lick her in earnest, because I just couldn't hold off any longer.

She moaned loud as I worked her up to a frenzy, her exquisite sounds echoing in the room. Her opening was wet and slick. I wanted to stick my dick in her, fuck her until she couldn't take it anymore, until I sprayed my cum all over her perfect, luxurious tits. Fuck her hard everywhere in this room... but I needed to be patient in savoring her.

"Oh, Daddy. Daddy, this feels so good," she said, squirming.

I licked, rubbed and caressed her clit. She tasted like a sweet wine, but I couldn't get enough.

I reached up and tweaked both her nipples. The more stimulation I gave them, the wetter she got for me. Now that I'd found what made her tick, I had to take full advantage. Yes, she loved rough handling, enjoyed the role play, but she also wanted a man who'd give attention to her body the way he was supposed to. Emilio had been too fast, too impulsive and inconsiderate. Merry might find herself gravitating to the world of bondage and submission, but what he'd done—pretty much bulldozed into her ass—just didn't cut it.

I let my tongue taste all of her, spreading her legs to get better access.

She whimpered with a tad more urgency now, but I wasn't planning on letting her come just yet. Rubbing her clit with my fingers, I spread her folds with my tongue, then fucked her with it, in and out.

"So wet, so soaked for your Daddy, but now I need you to stay very still for me," I commanded, pulling out for a moment.

She mumbled something incoherent and I reached out to squeeze her nipple while I continued to tongue-fuck her sweet, tight hole. At that point, she was panting, so I finally inserted my finger inside her, pushing to the back where her G spot was.

My little Merry ... she loved it all, going by her cries of ecstasy. And she was trying really hard not to move, listening to me obediently. She was so fucking wet, so fucking tight—

almost like a virgin. The thought that some other fucker had come between her legs before me, that my sons even might have done the same, made me so furious and mad.

I fingerfucked her and continued to lick the bundle of nerves that was the nub. Merry's pussy was so hot and trembling for me. I could feel it, so I added the second finger. It was a sweet, sweet torture which caused her to push her crotch harder in my face.

"Daddy ... oh, Ivo," she moaned, straining her whole body.

I knew she was close. I kept thrusting my finger in and out of that cunt, picking up my speed while my tongue kept doing all these wonderful things to her clit.

Then, when it was time, I sucked on it like it was a lollipop at the same time, never easing the rhythmic fucking with my fingers. She was coating me with her juices, shouting out her pleasure, and arching her back off the bed.

Yes, baby, yes...

"Fuck, omigod ... what—"

Her voice broke down, sweat covered her magnificent breasts, and then, just like that, her dam burst free, and she was coming for me.

And coming.

And coming.

She roared, screaming out my name, yelling intelligible words, cursing, spouting the most beautiful language I'd ever heard. And all the while, I kept thrusting my fingers into her wet cunt and intensifying the sucking on her clit, milking her. Her body finally spasmed with the last remnants of ecstasy, trembling and fully experiencing this release for the first time ever. It was the most beautiful thing I had ever seen.

Fuck, she didn't even realise how hot she looked right then, taking long, deep breaths, and staring at me with wide green eyes.

"Fuck, Ivo ... I think I finally..." Her body trembled violently, and she gasped for air, unable to speak further. Now that spot was so sensitive, but I didn't stop massaging it. I simply slowed down. Her nipples stood erect, and my cock was unbelievably hard. I think my boxers were smeared with pre-cum.

"You were such a good girl for your Daddy. I told you I could make you come, princess." I laughed, so fucking proud of myself.

When our eyes met, she looked pleased and most likely surprised with the intensity of her first ever orgasm. Reaching out to her hands, I quickly released her from the bondage. My blood boiled with excitement and anticipation, because now I'd earned the privilege of fucking her brains out.

She collapsed on the bed, running her hands over her breasts, then over that dripping cunt, exhaling sharply.

After that, I also released her legs.

"How was that, my princess?" I asked, drawing her in my arms. She leaned into my hold.

"Amazing." She shook her head. "I think I'm whole again and I have you, Daddy, to thank for it," she said, stretching out her endless legs on the green and gold sheets. I bought my fingers to my mouth and licked them, tasting her. Then, I put them in her mouth, running my hand over her red lips. She tasted like honey and vanilla.

"Suck on those fingers, princess," I ordered, and she did,

like the good girl she was. She sucked all around them, sensually, and my cock was ready to finally be taken care of.

After she licked it all clean, I undid my pants and took off my t-shirt. My boxers came next. When she glanced at my shaft, her jaw dropped and her eyes went wide.

"Good, but you have been a naughty girl, so now I have to punish you," I said, getting off the bed.

I was so horny for this girl, for her mouth and her hands....

She smiled, going on all fours, and then she started crawling on the bed towards me. Perfect—an open invitation to play.

"And how are you going to punish me, Daddy?"

"I'm going to fuck your mouth, kitten."

Chapter Five

ALL I WANT FOR CHRISTMAS IS YOU

Merry

I orgasmed. I *finally* fucking orgasmed. I kicked the beam, blew my lump, cracked the marble ... and it had been the most amazing experience of my life. A million times better than what I expected—and thank goodness I'd asked for three men, not one. If I had come here thinking to just have one, then I might never have met him. I was most likely finally fucking cured.

Ivo was twice my age, but he put a lot of effort into making this happen. He made me feel like I had gone to heaven and back. Plus, he had the stamina of a young man, and could more than keep up with his sons. Matter of fact, he was better.

I couldn't bloody believe it, but I did doubt him for a second when he put the blindfold on me and tied me up.

I was so restricted and somewhat uncomfortable, because I really wanted to see what he was going to do to me. In the end, it was all worth it and he had done many freaky, but wonderful things to me. I was in the literal sense dripping wet for him, for his cock that I hadn't seen yet—but there was nothing I wanted more than to have him inside me.

Now he was standing in front of me with his massive cock out, still wearing that silly Santa hat. His body was a work of art. He must work out a lot to keep that kind of physique. His stomach was ripped and each dip and curve was spectacular.

"I don't think I'm very good at this. I haven't given too many blowjobs before," I told him, feeling a tad embarrassed. His sons were hot; well, this entire thing was disturbing enough ... but Ivo? He was handsome, confident, and highly experienced. And most of all, he acted like he gave a damn.

His face brightened, then his eyes darkened as he stood in front of me with his erection pointed at my face. He was huge, thick, and veiny. I had been with a few boys in the past, but I had never seen such a large cock before. He was my Daddy, and they could not hold a dollar-store, fifty-cent candle to him.

"Oh princess, just start sucking it. Besides, this is not for your pleasure. This is your punishment, so don't look so excited," he said with a mad gleam in his eyes.

I sat on the bed, feeling myself getting wet again, and then wrapped my palm around his girth. Ivo shut his eyes as I licked the tip, unsure if that was what he wanted me to do. He tasted salty and wet as I licked what seemed to be his pre-cum. *Hmmmm* Then, before I couldn't protest, he put his hand around my head and shoved his cock in my mouth.

I struggled with that size, gagging right away, but Ivo didn't even flinch. He fisted his hand in my hair and growled when he forced my head to move.

"That's right, take it all like a good girl. The gagging will stop soon, princess. Relax and let me fuck your mouth," he instructed, staring down at me with fiery eyes. I placed my hands on his thighs as tears rushed to my eyes at the strain of it all, but at this point, I really didn't care how uncomfortable this was going to be. I just wanted to please him, because then he was going to ram his hard cock into me soon enough. My pussy jumped for joy at the thought of it.

He thrust his cock into my mouth, first slow, then hard and fast, pulling on my hair as he did. It seemed he was getting thicker and bigger as my tongue danced on the tip.

It was a punishment because he didn't give me any control. He was fucking my mouth, groaning out loud when I swirled my tongue around him. He didn't let me use my hands, which frustrated me a little.

Ivo was rough, pulling my hair so hard, I cried with pain. His hips were stiff and the tension around his groin almost visible. For a second, I thought I wasn't going to last as the intensity of his movements burned through my mouth. He sped up, then his cock bumped into the back of my throat.

At the same time, I was drenched with the naked desire and exhilaration of having him inside my mouth.

"Is that nice? Does your pussy like when I'm fucking your mouth so roughly?" he asked. Obviously, I couldn't respond for my mouth was stuffed fuller than a trussed turkey on Thanksgiving. Tears began streaming down my face. "I'm going to come and you'll swallow every drop, Merry. Are you ready to take your Daddy's cum? I know this is uncomfortable, but you have been a bad girl. You need to know your place, kitten."

Fuck, I couldn't take it anymore when he started to push

harder. Everything hurt—my jaw, my throat—but he kept going. I gagged, shaking my head, and a moment later, his whole body strained. The muscle in his jaw ticked, and his cock grew thicker as he slowed down his movements.

"Fuck, *fuck*!" he growled, spraying my mouth with a big load of semen.

This was all new to me. He tasted salty and warm, so I swallowed him quickly, trying to control my gag reflex.

When he finally pulled himself out of my mouth, I felt so used and abused—in a good way. I rolled on the bed, mulling what had just happened. Did I like this? Ivo had purposely made it rough, but maybe if there ever was going to be a next time, then I might be the one in control. I wanted to experience everything.

He wiped my tears away with his hand and then reached out for something.

"I think this could be your little reward," he said, holding his fist in front of me, palm up.

I scrambled off my feet and touched his fingers. He unfurled the fist and on his palm was a miniature Santa hat.

"What's that for?" I asked, my voice horse.

"A hat for my cock," he said, sounding amused.

I just couldn't help laughing. I quickly took the thing from his palm and kneeled in front of him. His cock was moist and still pretty much hard, so I slid the hat on the tip.

"Dear lord, it fits," I said.

Ivo glanced down at it and shook his head.

"Look at yourself. You took it all in your mouth and now you get to see me like this, all festive and ready to jingle your pussy," he said, grabbing my chin, and lifting it slightly. "Get back on the bed and spread your legs wide, my princess, because Daddy is ready to fuck you."

He didn't need to tell me twice. Grabbing my hand, he helped me stand up. I couldn't wait to have him inside me.

I lay on the bed, staring at his chest as I waited. I noticed he had some tattoos on his back, but none on the front. Amid some interesting symbols he had inked, I suspected some writing was probably in Bulgarian, or Russian.

"Are you going to fuck me hard?" I asked as he pulled the small Santa hat off his cock and strolled towards the bed, watching me.

My jaw still ached a bit, but that didn't matter in this moment.

"Yes, I am. Are you sure you want my cock messing up your perfect little pussy?" he challenged, getting on the bed and then straight away sucking on my nipples. No one had ever given so much attention to my breasts. Sure, my boyfriends had touched me, but no one had ever taken proper care of them. Ivo almost made me come again with the way he sucked on each of my nipples.

"Yes, please, Daddy," I begged. Every time I called him Daddy, Ivo upped the ante on his teasing, as though I'd won some super difficult battle in a video game and leveled up. He bit on my nipple, stuck his hand between my thighs, and rubbed all around with raw, animalistic fervor. I yelped with pain, for a second ready to slap him when suddenly, he flipped me around.

One minute I was on my back and the next I was lying on my stomach. He grabbed both my hands before lowering himself over me again.

"You need to know one thing, my princess. I don't make love, I fuck hard, so the question is: Are you ready to be fucked hard?"

I nodded enthusiastically. "Yes, Daddy, please fuck me hard. I need you," I said, struggling against him when he pinned me down.

Those three last words seemed to awaken some inner animal. He fisted a hand in my hair and then ran his other hand over my anus. This new sensation wasn't like before, for this time around I wasn't afraid, but full of anticipation.

"You have no idea how much I want to ruin that fine ass," he muttered. "Go up on all fours."

"No, Daddy, you need to fuck me. I'm so wet for you," I disagreed, whimpering that he was taking so long.

In response, he pulled my hair painfully hard, forcing me to lift myself up, and I whimpered with discomfort. Fuck, he hadn't been joking when he said he was rough. Still, I wasn't afraid.

"Are you fucking telling me what to do, Merry?"

My throat went dry.

"I'm sorry, Daddy," I mumbled, suddenly scared that he was never going to give me what I wanted most.

"Good. You should be sorry. I need to stretch all your holes and you're going to love it. Trust me," he said, with those last two words assuring me that I had nothing to worry about.

I had already reached an orgasm earlier on, so I was supposed to be fulfilled, but deep down I knew I wasn't. The man had just unraveled me, tore me up with pleasure, but he didn't fuck me yet and I needed to feel his cock pumping into me. He made me feel whole and right, so much I didn't think I could just walk away, and forget this ever happened.

He let go of my hair and then I arched my hips upward, so he'd have better access to my pussy and ass.

A mixture of trepidation and excitement warred within me as he gently grazed his fingers around my slit, then to my ass, and back all the way down to my clit. My knees shook when he spread my ass cheeks and licked me there with a skilled stroke.

So good...

He took his sweet time, making me wait for what felt like an eternity.

"Please..." I managed breathlessly.

"Shhh."

Realizing he wasn't going to give me what I wanted right then, I closed my eyes and submitted to the onslaught of pure pleasure.

He stopped licking for a moment, and I whined in protest. "Oh yes, you have no idea how much that turns me on," he said and then stuck two fingers into my anus. Slow and steady. Damn, that was different from yesterday. Exciting. Maddening. "Just relax and breathe."

He fucked me gently at first, rubbing my clit at the same time, with the same rhythm.

Oh God ... oh sweet fuck...

The pressure built so fast, I thought I was going to come from just that touch. I was so ready for him, my juices dripping on his hands.

"Tight ... you're so tight down there, but my cock will fit in," he murmured, shifting on the bed so his cock was nudging my pussy.

"Shit! Yes ... oh Daddy just fuck me. Do it! Please ... Daddy!" I thought I was going out of my mind, the fire in my body now too much to bear.

"Since you say it that way, your wish is my command," he said, and then he rammed into me, withdrawing his fingers from my backside. He filled me so utterly, so completely, more pressure built up in my core.

"Shit... Oh shit yeah..."

He emitted a deep, guttural groan as he started to move inside me, steady then faster, rougher, his fingers gripping my thighs

"Shit... You feel like heaven."

I coated him with my juices as he hammered his cock into me like he'd promised.

And I took him in—all of him. Every excruciating inch.

It felt unbelievable, amazing.

I gasped. "Harder, Daddy..."

He thrust with more force, satisfying my request.

Then he inserted a finger into my ass once again and I screamed because I really didn't know what was happening to me. My heart jackhammered inside my chest, heat bubbling on my cheeks and neck. His cock moved in my pussy simultaneously with his finger in my ass. I had no words for how this felt.

Better than fantasy.

Better than Carrie finally snagging Mr. Big in Sex and the City.

Better than the Arizona Cardinals winning the NFL championship after the longest drought in history.

Better than ... *chocolate*. There, I said it.

"How do you like it? Does this feel good?" he asked, keeping up the pace.

"Daddy ... oh, fuck. I can't take it anymore," I moaned.

He laughed, but ignored what I said with a, "Yes you can, and you will." The fucker.

My holes were getting a pounding, delivered by the sexiest man alive.

Wasn't I lucky?

He pulled his fingers out, slid his arm under me, and pressed up on my stomach, lifting me off the bed, so my back was flush against him.

"I need to come inside you. To feel you, raw, just like this." His voice strained, he poured those sensual words in my ear. "So tell me, princess, are you on birth control?"

I nodded, not really knowing my own name at this point or if I was even human.

"I'm clean, too. You knew this coming in—no one can fuck or suck if they're not clean."

"So am I, said it the form..." I bit out as he mercilessly massaged my breasts. He smelled like cinnamon and Scotch with a hint of smoke. I'd finally figured out his scent, and I loved it.

"Ivo, *pleeeeeease*," I begged, feeling a kinship with that meme of a skeleton waiting on a bench. My pussy waved the white flag of surrender, ready to be pillaged and turned inside out.

He thrust and thrust until at motherfucking last, I reached the promised land, floating under a blanket of stars.

I screamed for Daddy, seeing the fireworks as he let out a monstrous roar and released himself into me. Panting and moaning, we both came apart together. The orgasm ricocheted through me with a bang, taking with it everything that I was in that moment and dropping me dead in a pool of melting lava. I cried out his name, over and over, as the tidal wave of heat pulled me under.

Then, bit by bit, I rose back to the surface. My body felt raw and well-used. Ivo laid me down on the pillows, covering us both with the soft green sheets.

"That's my girl. Now let's sleep for a while. You did good, kitten. Daddy is proud of you," he whispered.

I just wanted to close my eyes for a second to relish this bliss, because he was so good to me and I felt so, so tired all of a sudden. I liked his warmth, and how well he fit around my body.

Soon enough I was drifting away, thinking that this was probably a dream. Only a pleasant dream.

Chapter Six

MERRY AND BRIGHT

Ivo

Merry erupted like a volcano—what a thing of beauty. She came so hard, so freely, so completely—witnessing that was a treat in itself. I was ready to curl up next to her and drift off, too, but that wouldn't be wise. After she fell in a deep slumber, I stayed by her side for a moment, listening to her breathe.

I checked the clock to see it was almost ten PM. It might seem silly but I was concerned how she could sleep so peacefully with a relative stranger, away from her familiar surroundings.

I couldn't leave her here in the green room. Tonight we were closed but Gregory and Emilio had keys and it wouldn't be the first time they showed up with some girl they were fucking or dating. Especially Emilio, since he was such a man-whore. The last thing I wanted was him coming over and finding Merry here, in bed, naked—alone. That wouldn't bode well for her, and I'd never allow her to be put in such a predicament.

After today, I had to give some serious thought to Emilio's future at the club. At this point, he had become something of a liability. But I'd think about that tomorrow. Today was for Merry. Only Merry. My princess. It had been a proper whirlwind since she first came to Top D last night—but from the start, the connection between us couldn't be denied.

Could it lead somewhere? *Dare I even entertain the notion?*

No. I could not.

I slowly got up and lifted her up in my arms. She gave a little moan, so I went still until I was sure she was still fast asleep. Then, I carried her out of the room, upstairs to my office.

Over the years I had refurbished the club, so now I had a stylish bathroom and a comfortable double bed in my private quarters.

When I had her settled in the sleeping area, I went to my desk and called Candy.

"Yeah, boss," she answered, sounding like she was working through a mouthful of food. Or maybe sucking on some candy cane, which she would never be caught without during her work hours.

Candy came across as a bit of an airhead, but nothing could be farther from the truth. She had been my loyal employee for many years, and we always looked out for each other.

"I want to talk to you about Merry." She knew about tonight. In fact, she'd ordered the takeout meal for us and had it delivered.

"You got it bad for this girl, Ivo. You need to be careful nobody finds out who she is. Good thing you had her in the red room out back all evening yesterday, and tonight nobody's there," she said in a whisper, even though I knew she lived alone with a black cat, and liked it that way.

"Once she wakes up, I'm going to send her home, so don't worry about it," I told her, because that was the plan. A plan I hated because I wanted more of my princess.

"Yeah, right."

He could practically see her smirking.

"Just make sure nobody saw or recognized her yesterday, okay?"

"Whatever you say, *Daddy*. Consider it done." Candy ended the call with a giggle.

I went to sit on the edge of the bed, staring at her, and wondered how on earth I hadn't met her before. Our paths must have crossed at some point in the past and yet, I had no recollection, which meant it likely didn't happen. With a loud sigh, I went to my wardrobe and grabbed some clean clothes to put on. I could still smell her all over me and I wished I would never shower again.

Merry had a hell of an evening today, reaching a milestone in her life, so she needed to get her energy back. I headed to the bathroom to take a quick shower. Once I was dressed and freshened up, I went downstairs to the club to see if everything was in order for tomorrow. I went behind the bar and filled up a glass with water, then downed the whole thing. I had a lot on my mind lately. After I'd broken my engagement with Anika, she wouldn't accept my decision. Her family was powerful enough to create some serious problems for me if I didn't backtrack and marry her like they intended.

Meeting Merry I already knew wasn't just a distraction—but

a complication. I just didn't have the headspace to deal with that right now, AND watch my hide at the same time. Turf wars always had a way of breaking out when one least expected them, and Anika's people were notorious for starting some pretty fucked-up shit. What had I been thinking to get involved with her anyway? It had seemed like a good idea at the time. Trouble free…

Now though, if I wanted to avoid an all-out carnage, I'd have to put the marriage proposal back on the table. That's what it would take to appease them, and that's what I would do. Mafia families were like royalty. Marriage was a convenient strategy for cementing alliances. My people depended on this. On me.

Hungry again, I grabbed a bag of peanuts from a bar shelf, and added to that a bag of chips and some Christmas chocolate to take to my princess. For sure, she'd be ravenous when she woke up.

My princess. I really had to stop thinking of her as mine. All we had was one night. One, and no more.

I needed to make sure Emilio and Gregory wouldn't start blabbing about her all over the place. First thing in the morning, I'd call them over and have a chat with them. I couldn't take any chances.

I went back upstairs to get some club admin work done. My lovely volcano girl slept on, during which time I'd finished all the tasks on my plate.

I watched her for a while, like a fucking stalker. I just couldn't help myself. She was additive and most likely the best lay I ever had—which was crazy and a bit ridiculous, too. Especially at my age, and everything I'd done.

If she ever got involved with another man, it was going to take him a while to satisfy her, and he most likely wouldn't unless he was dedicated to pleasuring her. In my experience, most men were selfish bastards.

I couldn't even imagine her with anyone else. The very thought repelled me and had me brooding.

After about two hours, she finally opened her eyes and stretched on the bed, looking around. When she saw me on the chair, her face instantly lit up.

"What are you doing?" she asked, sitting up on her elbow. The sheets fell to her waist, revealing to me her magnificent breasts with perky nipples. My cock rose to attention right away.

"Watching you and before that, I was doing some work," I said.

"Where am I?" she asked.

"My office, princess."

Batting her eyelashes, she pulled the sheets aside, showing me the rest of her naked, voluptuous bounty. "You said you're done with work, Daddy?"

Daddy.

Fuck—that pervy shit worked like magic for my cock. I was rock hard and I wanted to punish her again.

I stood and pulled down my jogging pants, making sure she could see my fully exposed erection as I'd gone commando. I grabbed her chin and made her look at me.

"You're a naughty little brat, you know that? Who the fuck falls asleep in a sex club, alone with a man they just met?" I growled, slipping my hand down to her throat. She had a very beautiful neck, long and graceful, and I bet her pussy was already dripping wet for me.

She swallowed hard, her gaze boring into mine.

"You just wore me out and I couldn't help it. What if I say I am sorry, Daddy?" she cooed, then reached out to caress my bulge.

"You can make it up to me..." Of course I wanted to fuck her again.

Her jaw looked a little red and it was probably because I'd been rough with her. I'd fucked her mouth until she cried, her tears smearing her beautiful face, but she was obedient enough to swallow me without a single word of complaint. That was impressive.

I shut my eyes and let go of her, feeling horny again.

"Let's get you all clean up and then you can go home," I told her, taking her hand and helping her to get off the bed. I stopped by the door and looked up, seeing that we were standing above the mistletoe. She was still naked, her nipples all perky and pink, ready to be sucked on.

"Oh," she said when she followed my gaze.

Bending down, I took what she offered, devouring her mouth and tasting her all over again. Deep and slow. Her breasts pressed into my chest. I set the pace of the kiss and shifted, making her tilt her head back. When I parted my lips, she followed suit. The feel of her tongue against mine sent a hot, sharp spark of electricity coursing through my veins. The kiss was hot and intense, yet wet and warm and all things nice. Her tongue tangled with mine in a dance as old as time.

Dipping my hand into her lush hair, I savored her. She fit

perfectly against my body, tall and curvy and soft. I bit on her lower lip and a moan escaped her mouth.

"Fuck, princess, why do you have to be so perfect?" I ran my hand over her tits, then I bent farther and planted a peck on her right one, followed by small kisses all over her chest. Then, I cupped her breast and sucked on her nipples.

"Ahh..." she sighed.

"Let's take that off, shall we?" she said, grabbing my t-shirt and quickly pulling it over my head.

I dragged her into the bathroom and turned on the shower, then she tugged on my pants. She couldn't undress me fast enough.

"How come you have a bathroom in your office?" she asked, regarding me with lust in her eyes when I was standing naked in front of her.

"Because I sleep in here sometimes when I have shit to do and I like to be fresh when I'm greeting important clients downstairs. Now get in that shower, princess," I ordered her, and before she walked in, I slapped her ass, leaving a red mark there. I could see myself marking her body all over, so she would know she belonged to me.

She went under the surge of water and started washing herself. Luckily, the cubicle was big enough for both of us. Not one to waste time, I dipped my fingers into her folds, quickly discovering she was ready for me.

"And you thought there was a problem with you? That you were frigid?" I said with a chuckle.

She responded by placing her palms against the tile and leaning into it, moaning and panting.

"That's right... That's how you do it," I urged.

"Ivo…"

Her moans fueled me further.

"Is my princess already wet for Daddy? Do you want a hard, stiff cock inside you?" I asked, working my fingers into her cunt.

Swiveling on her feet, she turned around and let her hands explore my chest, tilting her head backwards as I rubbed my cock against her thighs.

"Yes, Daddy," she breathed out as I started to massage her clit. When I strummed her like a violin, I slid my arms under her ass and hefted her up, so I could fuck her against the shower wall. Right away, I rammed my cock into her.

She cried out, eyes closed tight, her tits bouncing in my face as she adjusted her legs around my hips.

"Christ, you're going to give me a heart attack at some point," I grunted, burying my face in her neck. She felt so fucking good, so moist. I started to move in a slow and steady rhythm, while I kissed her everywhere.

"Just keep going and don't you fucking dare stop," she said in a tone that brooked no argument.

"Fucking brat," I muttered before picking up the pace, getting deeper into her core. I couldn't fucking go slow with her —this wasn't my style. Yet, I really wanted to prolong the pleasure. She took all of me in, the water pourin down on us intensifying the sensations.

I sucked on her nipples and fucked her hard, pumping into her until my heart thumped so loud, it rang in my ears.

"Daddy, *Daddy*! I think I'm going to come!" she cried, arching her body, head thrown back in sheer abandon.

"Good, but before you do, tell your Daddy who you belong

to. Tell me that you're mine." I needed to hear it. I needed to feel it. To believe it.

Her flushed face and pink lips swollen from my kisses gave me life. She opened her eyes as I slowed down and we stared at each other for a moment. Time stood still. I didn't know what had gotten into me, but I wanted her to tell me that I owned her. Lock, stock, and motherfucking barrel.

"I'm yours. Daddy, I'm all yours," she finally whispered, her tone laced with emotion.

Oh, I was in so much trouble. How did shit hit the fan so fast?

"That's right, because no one else will ever make you come like I do," I snapped, and I drilled into her harder, faster, deeper until she was screaming for me, pushing her back against the wall. "Yes … come for me nor. Over … and over … and over." She trembled uncontrollably and surrendered to the release.

My own release was near as she came apart over my cock.

It was the most satisfying thing to watch, her parted lips and her tongue sticking out, licking the corners.

Soon, I ejaculated inside her, catching her lips in a passionate kiss. It took me a moment to pull myself together and when I glanced at my princess, there was a lazy smile on her face.

I was the one who put it there.

"You learn fast," I said. "Let me wash you."

As we showered for real this time, dark thoughts snuck insidiously back to the forefront of my mind.

All of this couldn't have happened at a worse time. For I was either taken, a bargaining chip for Anika's family, or I was a dead man.

I'd be done for, and I wasn't about to go down for anyone.

Pushing the thought out of my head, I focused on the present. I reminded myself to put my Santa hat back on because the spirit of the season had certainly touched me—at least for tonight—jolly as can be. Merry was a helluva present. She'd made me forget all about my stone-cold reality for a while.

Jingle bells.

It was a real shame I had to let her go.

Chapter Seven

LET IT SNOW

Merry

This was fucked up. I hadn't wanted to fall asleep, but Ivo exhausted me so with his sexual energy and charisma, and then I just drifted off, forgetting for a time where I even was. The long nap had been just what I needed, and when I woke up, he was staring at me from the other side of the room.

I never thought I could experience this kind of sex with a man twice my age. It was wild, adventurous, filthy and so kinky. And now he was fucking washing my hair, cleaning my body like this was perfectly acceptable and normal. What was happening to me?

We both knew we weren't going to see each other again. I had commitments to honor. A duty to uphold. My stepmother would make sure of that. But for this one time, this one night, I was able to dream.

So I would be forever thankful to this man, Ivo, for that fantasy he made reality.

I just realized I didn't know his last name. Maybe I shouldn't ask him. It was better this way. Still, I couldn't get rid of the sadness that slowly ate at me.

Ivo was surprisingly gentle when he was washing my hair, massaging my scalp. After that, I returned the favor, squeezing shower gel into my palm, gliding my hands over his body, teasing his cock until he told me to get the fuck out of the stall.

Ivo dried me with a fluffy towel and then found some clothes I could wear. I had his t-shirt and a pair of jeans Candy had left lying around, which would do for my ride home. My dress was ruined, but he assured me he'd replace it.

It didn't matter, really. When we were ready, it was time to say goodbye. The fun was over and I, Merry, needed to face reality once again.

"You know we can't see each other again," I said when we headed downstairs. I let him know before he said it. Somehow, it felt easier to deal with coming from me. I didn't know what I'd do if the statement had come from him, so I had to preempt it. Ivo glanced at me, pinching his eyebrows together and working his jaw. His silver hair gleamed in the bright light. *Beautiful.*

"This was an amazing experience, but all good things must come to an end. I need to go back."

"Just like that, huh?" he said. A muscle twitched in his jaw. He seemed ... angry. High-strung.

"I'll be graduating next year, then maybe leave LA," I lied.

"Hmmm."

An uncomfortable silence ensued.

"Thank you for everything," I finally said, feeling awkward. "I need to call a cab."

"I'll handle that for you." Getting on the phone, he called somebody by the name of Pete and asked him to come over to pick me up.

"Is that—"

"The guy your friend was fucking last night. I trust him," he said.

I hoped my stepmother was still out of the house, because I really wasn't in the mood to explain myself to her. I normally liked to stay in my dorm room with Tasha, but my stepmother insisted I always stay at the villa on weekends and around the holidays.

Ivo walked me outside. He looked much scarier out in the open air, his dark t-shirt hugging his solid frame, and his jaw rigid. He also looked a little older. My heart was beating dangerously fast as we waited for the taxi.

"You were incredible, Mr. Santa," I said, although he wasn't wearing the hat anymore. I tried to keep my tone cheerful but failed dismally.

"So were you, my little volcano." We stared at each other for a long while. I shivered.

Taking off his jacket, he put it over my shoulders. "Here."

His expression was unreadable, but something flashed in his eyes for the briefest of moments, telling me he wasn't happy about letting me go.

I smiled at him, knowing that soon, he'd turn around and he'd become just another memory.

When a pair of headlights could be seen approaching in the distance, Ivo stepped toward me, up close and personal. The look in his eyes right then was one that rooted me to the spot. He seemed so different. Unapproachable.

A cold shiver ran up my spine. He was clearly wrestling with some demons, and there was nothing I could do to fix this.

"What—"

"Let me tell you something, princess. Sometimes, we get more than we bargained for." He caressed my cheek with the back of his hand, a fleeting touch. His expression softened. "So never say never."

And with that, he stepped back and waited until I was bundled up in the car, then walked away from me, back inside.

I told Pete to drop me off near my college dorm. I wouldn't disclose my home address so I'd take an Uber from there.

As he drove away from the curb in front of the club, remaining blessedly silent, tears started falling down and my heart broke for I knew that was the last I'd see of my Daddy.

Only then did I realize: I was still wearing his jacket, which smelled of cinnamon and Scotch with a hint of smoke.

** * ***

A few weeks later

"Oh, come on, we have to get back there. Pete was incredible," Tasha whined into the phone, and I couldn't help rolling my eyes.

"I told you, I don't want to. It was a one-time thing for me.

It was wonderful, and I don't regret any of it, but we are not going back there ever again. At least I'm not," I said in a firm tone. I opened my text book, trying to focus on studying for my exam. Not on orgasms with hot men with silver-streaked hair

"Gee, you're no fun," she said before hanging up.

She was right. I was no longer having fun. The last couple of weeks had been very stressful. Next year I would be graduating, so I had a lot on my plate. My visit to the sex club had definitely helped teach me about myself. I finally knew that I wasn't a freak of nature and was capable of having an orgasm.

Many orgasms.

But now I had to put my nose to the grindstone and think about my future. Also, I had to stop thinking about Ivo and how he'd made me feel. He was a guy with only a first name, and would always be such to me. An incredible, handsome, delightfully domineering and kinky man who'd given me sex that exceeded all my expectations.

The holiday season seemed strange this year, because every time I noticed certain decorations, I kept thinking about Ivo and the club and then of course about all the kinky stuff he did to me.

I'd also met his two sons, who'd failed to give me what I'd gone there for. The thought of what I'd done made me blush even now, weeks later. I couldn't wrap my mind around the fact I'd fucked a father and his two sons in one night. Wow, that was a mouthful—in more ways than one.

My stepmother must have noticed how distracted I'd been, because she kept asking what was wrong. I didn't know what to say to her, so I did my best to avoid her.

With a sigh, I forced my attention to my book.

Sometime later, I heard a doorbell ring and slammed the heavy tome on the desk, hoping I wouldn't have to get up and see who it was. *Always something or someone interrupting my concentration.* I had a crapload of stuff to do and I knew my sister was bored out of her mind, so she could deal with whoever was at the door.

Five minutes later, I heard Clara's footsteps and then she opened the door to my room. She looked flushed, as if she'd run all the way here.

"What is it?" I asked.

"There is someone downstairs asking for you," she said, and before I could ask her who it was, she vanished.

I shook my head in irritation and stormed out of my room. After my father's death, my stepmother made us all live in this mansion—until I went to college and insisted on experiencing how everybody else lived. However, she'd already told me that if I wanted to keep studying next year, I'd have to move out of the dorm and stay home. The whole house was just too big for us and it was no use if we didn't have at least a housekeeper who could answer the fucking door, like any other normal crime boss family.

I laughed at that thought. 'Normal' and 'crime boss' did not go together in a sentence. I sounded like a spoiled brat reasoning this way, but it was the truth.

I walked into the living room, where a man waited. He had his back to me and he was wearing a tailored suit. He looked quite distinguished.

A spark of awareness trilled through me.

"May I help you?" I asked, and when he turned around, my legs nearly gave out on me.

Ivo.

He was in my house, standing in my living room, looking absolutely breathtaking—exactly the same as I remembered. Tall, dark, with that glimmer in his eyes that slowly turned me into a pile of goo.

"Hello, princess. Daddy missed you."

Bonus Scene Ready to Jingle

Ivo

I was lucky tonight—so very lucky that my little princess was away from her stepmother, Elaine Camilleri, alone in her dorm room. Her best friend and roommate, Tasha, was visiting family, too.

Elaine, I'd learned, made her live in their mansion during all the holidays, so I was surprised Merry was defying her wishes and staying at the college. I found out there was a time a couple times a week when I'd be able to go in through a lesser-monitored side entrance, bypassing security—but *fuck,* the door was locked this time.

One of the guards did owe me a favor—that was my plan B which luckily, I didn't have to use. I decided to go another route. I walked around and looked up at her window on the second floor, which was partially open. The lights were off, which meant she was probably sleeping.

Tonight was my window of opportunity. My pulse sped up and I felt myself growing hard, thinking about our little date in my club.

Anika's people, the Russians, were putting pressure on me to honor my deal of marrying her, and I didn't want to think about this anymore. I didn't want to imagine a world where I didn't see or touch my princess anymore.

I also heard Elaine was in the process of finding her a husband.

The thought of her belonging to someone else drove me fucking bonkers, so I decided to remind her that I wished to stay in her life forever.

Tonight, I'd stake my claim once more.

Merry was mine and mine alone.

This campus was old. The dorms were on the south side, and I knew exactly which room Merry was in. I had Pete wait for me outside, in case anything went wrong—he knew about Merry, and could keep his mouth shut.

The fact I managed to sneak on campus so easily, with security never showing up, pissed me right off. What if a psycho decided to try his luck breaking in? Merry and the other girls would be in danger. No one stopped me to ask what I was doing there. No one could be seen in the corridors, up the stairs to the second floor. It was too easy to get in this place with ill intent. My princess's stepmother should have been taking better care of her.

I was sure I'd find her in her room. Merry wasn't a party girl. She was a little nerdy and always followed the rules—well, apart from that one time when she went to the club to experience her first ever orgasm.

That time, she'd gone all out ... to my eternal delight.

Finding the ridges in the stone, I climbed over them, stepping on the arches above the windows, and thanking years of strength and endurance workouts. Sure, still, I was too fucking old for these shenanigans, but it had been a few weeks since I'd seen her and I just couldn't stay away. She had left the club convinced we'd never meet again. But I knew better.

She needed a little reminder of who her Daddy was.

Several minutes later, breathing hard and sweating like a pig, I finally reached her window. I thanked the heavens that she hadn't thought to close it, as it was an uncharacteristically warm late December evening. I hopped over the sill and slipped inside her room to find her sleeping in her bed, ever so peacefully. A nightlight by her bedside bathed her in slight illumination.

My muscles were burning and once more, I felt the anger rise at the thought she was so vulnerable—just like that time in the club when she'd fallen asleep without hesitation in an unfamiliar location. I needed to do something about this, but first...

I pulled my black mask out of my pocket and quickly put it on. Adrenaline coursed through my system as I stepped closer to the bed and inhaled her incredible scent.

The scenes from the club began rolling in front of my mind and every muscle in my body tensed up. I needed to fucking break this cycle. I was supposed to be staying away from her, but instead I was here, playing a burglar.

I pulled the blanket down, revealing bare legs under a white tank top, and even then she didn't even stir.

Unable to help myself to ran my hand over her thigh. The skin was as soft as I remembered.

"Wake up, princess. Daddy's here," I said, and she stirred a little, turning over and showing me her amazing ass, clad in lacy panties that left nothing to my imagination. Mother of God, she was going to be the death of me.

And then, she turned back over and finally opened her eyes to noticed me in the darkness. She sat up and opened her mouth as if to scream but I quickly silenced her with my hand.

"Don't you fucking make a sound, princess, or I'll have to punish you," I growled, moving my face closer to hers.

Her eyes shone with fear in the darkness and her body stiffened under my hand, but then, a twitch of recognition flashed in them.

She'd recognized my voice, and I felt her relax a little.

"Princess, you should have closed your window. You know how easy it is for someone to climb to the second floor?" I ground out. "Daddy's not happy about that."

We stared at each other for a little while as her chest rose and fell with fast breathing. When her gaze traveled down my body, my dick turned hard as a rock.

I trailed my hand from her mouth to her throat as I lay next to her and pressed the proof of my desire against her lush backside.

"What are you going to do to me, Mr. Burglar?" she cooed, instantly falling into the role when she giggled a little. Merry was far from an airhead, but with me, she became a totally different person. Bold. Carefree. Uninhibited.

And sexy as fuck.

It seemed she was up for playing this game with me, but she didn't realise just what I had in mind. Her hard nipples were already poking out of her tank top, driving me crazy.

"I'm going to fuck you hard against your will, my little

princess, so you can remember who's your Daddy," I growled, squeezing my hand tighter around her neck and nestling my face into her soft, rich hair. "Ah, I've missed you."

A loud moan escaped her mouth as I slid my hand under her top, over her breast, squeezing and massaging the nipple. The very thought I was the first man who'd made her orgasm filled me with pride, and if I ever had a choice, I wanted to remain the only one. I doubted she'd let anybody play inside her tight hole since our night at the club. All these inexperienced boys around here couldn't satisfy my Merry. Not like I could.

If only I could…

Pushing my troubles out of my mind, I wrestled with the frustration of wanting something I might have to discard, for my family's sake.

Angry, I ripped off her tank and tossed it across the room, then landed my gaze on her full, round breasts before leaning down to bury my face between them.

I was too fucking hot with that mask on, even with the large holes around my mouth and eyes, but this was part of the act. Merry was probably already soaking wet for me and I wanted to get inside her sweet, sweet pussy. I felt the loud thumps of her heart in her chest.

"Oh, Ivo," she murmured, pulling me closer.

Overwhelmed by a wave of need, I bit on her nipple harder than I anticipated, so she cried out, digging her nails into my biceps.

"What the fuck did you just call me?" I asked, lifting my head and shoving my free hand between her legs. She was so wet, her panties damp with her sweet juices. She moaned as I began moving my fingers over that whole area, caressing the entrance and teasing her. "Here's a reminder—make sure you call me Daddy from now on or you'll pay for this. I have so many ways in which to punish you."

"Yes, Daddy," she sighed as I worked my fingers underneath her panties and dipped one into her folds.

"Shit, you're soaked for me, princess," I growled, wondering how long I was going to last.

But this wasn't like the last time. When she came to the club, she'd never experienced an orgasm until I serviced her the way she deserved. Now I just wanted to fuck her again because I couldn't seem to stay away.

She invaded my thoughts daily, her voluptuous body, emerald eyes, and full lips the stuff of my dreams. I was too old for her, my mind told me—but my heart and body had other ideas.

I quickly got off the bed and pulled out my belt from my trousers. She was breathing hard, spread on that bed and staring at me like she'd just won the fucking lottery. Merry, fucking Merry. She'd missed me too—her eyes wouldn't lie. I didn't think I'd ever been with a woman that exploded for me like a fucking volcano. With such abandonment—which was surprising since no man had ever made her reach that peak.

She was fast becoming my new addiction.

"Get on all fours and put your hands on the headboard," I ordered her. She obeyed me instantly, her white panties so pretty on her fine ass. I was going to fuck her so hard, I'd make sure she remembered who her Daddy was.

I quickly undid my trousers and took them off. She was already set up on the bed, so I walked around and tied my belt around her hands.

"I have missed you," she whispered when I tightened the belt and pulled on it to make sure she couldn't fucking move. "Been thinking about you…"

Her hands were secure. Merry wasn't going anywhere and I had all night to play with her before I had to make myself disappear from her life again. This time, probably forever. As I said before, if only I had a choice…

"Fucking shut it and spread these amazing legs," I ordered, knowing she liked when I spoke to her with authority. I situated myself behind her, on the bed.

Running my fingers over her ass cheeks, I slid them under her panties and caressed her beautiful ass. Her skin was so soft and she responded with low groans at my touch. Her whole body shuddered with excitement when I cupped her breast, gently caressing the left nipple at first, then the right. The nub puckered, getting hard … so sensitive.

A flash vision of her taking me in so well while I fucked her mouth came to the forefront of my mind. I remembered how I didn't hold back that night. I was rough with her, teaching her a little lesson—and she loved every moment.

"Oh, Ivo, please… touch me," she begged and I stopped touching her then, smiling to myself.

"Hmm, I think you've forgotten yourself, princess," I said. "You were supposed to call me Daddy."

I was so pleased she'd forgotten about our little agreement already. That meant I could do deliciously wicked things to her. Torture her…

"Fuck, I mean Daddy," she corrected herself, too late.

"You have been a very bad girl and you give me no choice but to punish you," I said, trying to keep my voice even, but I was too excited for this. She yelped when I moved to the bottom of the bed and pulled her knickers down her legs, off her feet, and tossed them aside. Now she was naked, tied up to the bed, and all mine to play with.

I bent down to leisurely kiss her backside, planting small pecks over her flesh, then trailing my tongue slowly from her butt to her clit. She tasted divine, just like I remembered, and I couldn't fucking wait to ram my hard cock into her tight hole. With my fingers I traced the contour of her ass, moving down to the wet folds, opening them, and then caressing the already swollen nub.

Merry threw her head back and arched her back, mumbling some curse word.

"You're dripping down my hand ... but I am not going to be nice. You have been bad and you're at my mercy. I can do whatever I fucking please with you," I said sternly, dipping two fingers inside her.

"Please, Daddy. Please, fuck me," she pleaded as I set a rhythm with my fingers, slow at first, teasing and stretching her.

"Don't you want to come like the good girl you are?" I asked her, slowly picking up the pace. She squirmed, her moans now getting louder, but I was only just getting started.

"Yes, Daddy, please. I have missed your dick so much," she shouted then.

I stretched down on the sheets and started licking her clit, pursuing a goal of driving her out of her mind with arousal. I swirled my tongue around the swollen nub, shoving my finger in and out of her at the same time. She was loving this, for her pussy was pulsating and throbbing with need.

After a while, I sucked hard on her clit, keeping on finger-fucking her until she screamed out.

"Aaaah! I'm coming! Daddy!"

She pushed her hips into my face, searching for paradise...

Her juices spilled everywhere then, and it was so fucking hot, to see her start to unravel like this.

"Oh, Daddy... Daddy, I'm so close, please don't—"

...And I withdrew both my fingers and my mouth, getting off the bed. She protested, frustration in her raised tone.

The sound of her voice, her begging, the way she violently shook her hands, making the bed rock as she tried to break free from her restraints, had my dick stand to attention. A few drops of pre-cum ran down my cock. Fuck, I was going to lose it with this girl... I chuckled and slapped her ass hard. She howled, turning her head around to meet my gaze. She looked so adorably confused ... and fuckable.

"Count for me, princess. Daddy has to punish you. We both know you have been bad," I ordered as I caressed her soaking folds.

"No, no, please, Daddy! I was going to come," she wailed.

"Shut your mouth and count. You're only going to come when I allow you to," I roared. She got under my fucking skin, filling me with desire, and my groin burned. I wanted to fuck her as much as she did—but it would be so much better if I waited.

"One," she finally said, giving in. Who would have thought this girl would be my gift—allowing me to be the only one to get her off? Not even my two young, virile sons had managed this feat. She only responded to me.

I slapped her ass again, then twice more, each time harder

than the last. Her flesh was probably on fire, but she was so ready, so fucking on the edge of her orgasm that I now controlled.

"Three!" she cried out in pain, her tone high-pitched.

This time, I didn't even wait to make her comfortable. I just pulled my boxers down, climbed on the bed, gripped her hips, and thrust my throbbing erection deep inside her. And it was fucking bliss.

Merry

I cried out as he entered me so unexpectedly, going so deep that I lost my breath for a moment. My whole body hurt. I felt humiliated and lost, my ass cheeks bruised. Ivo slapped me so damn hard.

I almost came by that alone.

I was immobile, the belt digging into the skin of my hands as he kept fucking me from behind, going hard and fast. I was loving it now, after the whole feeling of panic when I woke up all of a sudden and saw someone with a mask on in my dorm room. I was ready to scream, but he quickly silenced me with his hand. Then I recognised that voice and his unique scent—cinnamon and Scotch with a hint of smoke. How could I ever forget that?

In that moment, I knew I wasn't in any danger … but right now, he was acting like another person. Like he was showing me an entirely new side of him. Although he'd been rough when he took me the first time, there was a gentleness about him. Not now, though…

This Ivo was suddenly more demanding and aggressive. He

tied me up to the bed and spoke in terse words, almost making me come undone. He sensed what I needed right now—after my run-in with my stepmother when I told her I wouldn't be going home over the holidays. That happened a few weeks ago but I was still upset about it. She'd made threats I didn't want to think about. That she'd force me to go whether I wanted to or not. Force me to marry. Force me to stop studying... That I had too much freedom and I had to know my place.

I realized I'd made the right decision to get away from her. Maybe it was just me sticking my head in the sand, and I was sure shit would hit the fan soon, but for now, I could dream...

I could feel again, with this man I couldn't stop thinking about.

He brought me to the brink and then, when I was on the verge of a very big orgasm, he stopped. A few more strokes of his tongue and that would have been it. But it seemed he had other plans.

I missed him so much. I had been dreaming about him, wondering what he was doing, and now he was back as though he'd heard my deepest desires, ramming his huge cock into me. I screamed, not caring that there were other students behind that wall. This was common in the dorm anyway. Everyone liked to sneak their boyfriends in whenever they could, except me usually. So this was a nice change for once.

"Fuck, you're so tight and so perfect, princess. I'm going take you hard so anyone in this damn dorm will know who you belong to," he growled, and then thrust his cock into me, to the hilt. He moved in so fast a rhythm that I thought we might both be knocked off that bed.

I cried out, quickly forgetting about the pain around my ass cheeks, and ditched the humiliation and loneliness I had been experiencing in the past few weeks.

All my senses centered on this moment, when Ivo was plundering me with his huge cock, just as I wanted. As I *needed*. In and out, over and over, until my whole body trembled. At last, I jumped over the edge when he brought his hand to my clit and flicked it at the same time.

I screamed his name, spasming as he continued to move inside me and touch me with his skilled fingers.

My hands were numb, my body was ablaze, and my heart felt like it was going to explode in my chest as the orgasm rocked through me. I didn't know how long Ivo continued to fuck me after that, but I felt like he marked my body everywhere.

And he didn't stop until he roared out his release, so loud the sound bounced off the walls.

"Now you're such a good girl. You took my hard cock so well," he said soothingly when he was finished. He untied my hands, then flopped me around so I was lying on my back, attempting to come back to reality.

Then he leaned over me—through it all he'd never removed that damn black mask. I was so thoroughly fucked, numb, and exhausted. My wrists ached so, but I felt like a million dollars. Ivo had fucked me again and once more, I came. Only he could do this. He was always so damn intense. Perfect for me...

"This was amazing," I whispered, and then he captured my mouth in a searing kiss. I never wanted the kiss to end and when his tongue caressed mine, a soft moan escaped me. I wanted him to snuggle with me, to stay here and never leave me, but then, he pulled back.

"You need to sleep, my princess, and I must go now. I just

wanted you to remember this. What I can make you do ... how you feel when you're with me and no one else. Never forget it."

And just like that, he was gone. I was certain he just jumped out the window, but that couldn't be possible, could it?

With a sigh, I raised a hand to my lips and bit on my forefinger, feeling utterly, completely sated.

Not long after, I was drifting into the most comfortable sleep ever, wondering if this had only been a dream.

Consumed

Chapter Eight

Merry

"Elena might just kill us, Merry. She said we weren't supposed to be going out today, although frankly I don't give a shit," my sister shouted over the thumping music as we stepped inside Sputnik Dance Club in a semi-gentrified area in LA. What was it with these nightclubs in dodgy areas? Memories of Club Top D, Ivo Sergei's establishment, flashed through my mind. "You know, this place is owned by some Russian she knows, too. I heard her mention it."

She raised her eyebrow in a telling expression, as if I was supposed to know who our step-mother associated with. Ever since our father's death, I tried to stay as much out of the woman's way as possible. She wasn't horrible, but far from a maternal figure in our lives.

"Well, this is where Catherine wanted her bridal shower, so

what choice do we have? Guess we should make the most of it." I grabbed her hand and rolled my eyes, hoping she'd get bored quick and want to go home, which wasn't unheard of for Clara to do. She had a pretty short attention span, and sometimes turned into the biggest introvert.

Clara was right, though. If Elaine found out we were here, she'd give us a good tongue-lashing, but she could take that bullshit elsewhere. Catherine had been our friend for a long time. The daughter of a Russian don from San Francisco, she'd come all over here to celebrate her upcoming nuptials with her closest friends, who mostly lived in LA. How could we miss out on this?

Besides, I'd been legal a few years, and could take care of myself. Clara was younger but still twenty-one, therefore an adult. Elaine wasn't our mother, nor did she act like she wanted to be—although she loved control. After we lost Dad, who ran the Maltese mafia in California, she stepped in, thinking she'd easily fill his shoes.

But respect in this business was earned, not gifted. The same as with family. As far as I was concerned, she hadn't even started paying her dues yet. She *was* pretty good at making people fear her, I had to admit.

Now, the sooner my sister realized the kind of family she was born into, and what a big deal that was, the smoother her life would be. She was still so naïve and inexperienced in some ways, yet soon, she'd be forced to grow up and find her own strategy to work toward her life goals. With a background like ours, nothing was straightforward.

My whole family was always filled with secrets and darkness. We were the daughters of a mafioso, and that was one thing I couldn't erase or ever change, as much as I wanted to. I'd loved my father fully, but not the game he played.

I too wanted to live by my rules and not the family's. I'd found a way to pursue a law career and skirt the many pitfalls a young woman in my position would normally be subjected to. Such as being married off at a young age for the sake of an alliance.

I'd passed the bar in a number of states already and I was so close to finally starting over, ideally with a firm in New York I was now working with. At first, Elaine wasn't too happy with the fact I'd chosen criminal law as a specialty, then she figured I could become her new asset. She needed to have a trusted attorney in case trouble found her, and what better person than one who was such a close part of the family? Then again, she had no clue about my long-term plans to leave all this behind.

I didn't want Clara to live her life in denial of what she might be expected to do—completely unprepared. Only if she was aware of how things worked could she make plans to dodge the bullshit we were dealt.

At this point though, it was my job to protect her. An adult she may be, but she was still my little sister.

Her brows furrowed. "You think she'll be really mad at me?" She was somewhat afraid of our in-house Maleficent.

"Don't worry about Elaine. She will never know we were here," I shouted to her when we got inside and finally squeezed through a ridiculous crowd to the bar on the far end.

Truth be told, Clara was taking her college studies seriously —a fact which surprised me, if I had to be honest. Fashion design was her dream, and I'd insisted she get her wish, along with an opportunity to get out from under Elaine's suffocating presence. Although she started late and was a year or two older than her peers, she took to it like a duck to water.

She had been talking about this night out for ages, a sisterly bonding sort of thing, and it had to be tonight or never, for soon, she'd be neck deep in studying for her exams. I wanted to share good times with her.

The club was full to the gills and I noticed many men who looked like they weren't from around here. Of course, they had to be Russians.

"Better not, 'cause I've had enough of her sanctimonious lectures, Merry," Clara said, and then pointed at one of the main booths that wasn't too far from the bar. "Look, Tasha is here already. What do you want to drink?"

"Order some cocktails and tequila shots for everyone—you know what they like. That should start us off nicely. I'll go get us situated," I said, and left her at the bar. She was a big girl and pretty confident, so I was certain she was going to be fine. Clara was an introvert type—she hated crowds and liked her own company too much. And she was a little bit of a nerd, too. I pretty much had to drag her out tonight.

When a tall man with dark hair, greying on the sides, came to stand by the bar, my heart started racing and my mouth went dry.

From the back, he reminded me so much of the one who'd taken over my every waking thought for a long time—until I accepted that nothing could come out of our short fling. Well, it was more of an impassioned encounter that rocked my world and turned it upside down, but no matter what I called it, Ivo Sergei and I would not cross paths again. So much water had passed under that bridge and while I'd gone on with my life, the memory of him sometimes haunted me. A wave of sadness washed over me, but the familiar sounds of joy pulled me out of the doldrums.

Tasha and a few other girls from Catherine's bridal shower shrieked gleefully when they saw me. In moments, I was buried inside a cocoon of hugs and giggles. "Merry, Clara—we haven't seen you in forever! Tasha here has to let us know you're still alive or we wouldn't have a clue." Viv grinned when they let go of me, and she hit me playfully on the shoulder.

Catherine was getting married in a few weeks, so Tasha—being Tasha—had decided to throw her a wild bridal shower.

"All work and school make Merry and Clara very dull girls," I quipped. "Besides, Tasha is crazy enough to make up for all of us." I leaned back and winked at my BFF, who was now sporting a mock frown.

"Come on, let's get this party started," Tasha said with a shimmy of her hips. "I'm thirsty!"

"Drinks are coming in a sec," I said. "Clara's ordering."

We went a little farther in the VIP section and I realized how great it was to see everybody again. The girls looked great, and we were in for a great time.

"Where's Catherine?" I asked.

"She's on her way," Tasha replied.

I glanced back at the bar, which was still in my line of vision, and saw that my sister was still waiting there. Some guy was trying to chat her up.

I was ready to walk over there and get him off her back when Clara tossed her hair behind her and said something to him. Then, she turned around and walked away from him.

"What was that about?" I asked her when she walked up to

the booth. The barman followed her with a tray laden with drinks.

Tasha squeaked with excitement when he placed everything on the table in front of us.

"He wanted to buy me a drink and I said no," she stated with a shrug. My sister had olive skin like me and everyone always commented on our exotic look, but Clara was never really interested in having relationships in general. She'd had a boyfriend or two, but not anything serious or enduring.

"You should have stayed there a bit longer. The one with tattoos that's coming up to the bar looks super cute." I pointed in the direction she'd just come from.

She followed my gaze and then frowned when he said something to another guy he must have come in with.

My stomach twisted when he finally turned around in my direction and I recognised him as one of Ivo's men who worked at his club, and I'd only ever said 'hi' to him once. I didn't even know his name.

"No, he's too rough looking. Anyway, what are you doing?" Clara asked when I got up to get a better look and see if possibly Ivo was here, too, but the man quickly disappeared in the crowd.

"Nothing," I said, sitting back down and putting on an impassive face. "Just wanted to take a closer look."

Clara rolled her eyes and then I picked up my drink, situating myself by Tasha who was on her phone, probably trying to get through to Catherine. A few more girls started to arrive, but the star of the show was still running late.

I bit my bottom lip, thinking about my time in Club Top D

again. That night had changed my life, and I had the hardest time moving on.

A few months ago, Tasha and I had gone to this sex club on some shady side of town—at the time, it didn't feel like my brightest moment, but I needed something nobody could give me, and I didn't want to risk seeing anyone I knew. After my lack of success with men in the bedroom, I decided to take matters into my own hands. As hard as it would have been for anyone to believe, I had never experienced a real orgasm with a man before. I figured something may be wrong with me, but how could I be sure? Tasha's support meant a lot—she didn't think I was crazy for booking a session with not one but three men. Two to serve me and one to watch. I was desperate, figuring the traditional man-woman situation wouldn't work for me. I had one shot to figure it out...

I was led to a room where two brothers—Gregory and Emilio—were waiting for me, claiming they were experienced at pleasing women. The third wasn't who I expected it to be—the men's father. Also, the most handsome, charismatic guy I'd ever met.

The evening didn't turn out quite like I'd expected. When push came to shove, none of the brothers could deliver, but before I could give up, Ivo—*Daddy*—stepped in. And boy, was that the most mind-numbing, toe-curling experience of my life. I had to come back the next day for another taste from him. Dirty, sinful sex and orgasms wrenched from my very soul—dramatic and maybe too poetic a description, but the raw, unadulterated truth. Since then, I couldn't forget about the gorgeous man who was twice my age but ruined me for all other men.

Then, all too soon, it was over and we parted ways like nothing had ever happened.

I thought I'd never see him again, until one day he showed up my house for a meeting with my stepmother. One look at him, and the memories came rushing back. When he told me he missed me, I almost begged him to stay with me, hold me ... but I had other plans for my life. If only things weren't so complicated.

My resolve hung by a thread when one other time, he burst into my dorm room in the middle of the night, pretending to be a burglar, and fucked me senseless with all his kinky goodness, making me scream out his name. He wanted to make sure I'd know he owned me—lock, stock, and motherfucking barrel—and no other man would ever make me feel like he did.

He wasn't wrong.

To make matters even more twisted, I later learned he was spearheading the Bulgarian mafia operations in LA, working to expand their footprint and make strategic alliances. For this reason, my stepmother was interested in pursuing a connection between his family and ours. The fact he was half-Russian himself was bound make things more interesting.

Fuck me sideways and upside down.

Maybe we were from the same world, but this wasn't the life for me. I had dreams, ambitions to pursue in the legal field. I wanted to get away from the family business, as far as I could possibly get, not burrow deeper in the lifestyle.

Still, I missed Ivo. We'd shared a connection, and if I had to lay eyes on him right now, I'd be lost again, forgetting which way was up.

Before I could sink hopelessly into gloom, Tasha's squeal pierced my eardrums, rising above the pounding music.

"Finally! There's the woman of the hour!" She bounced happily to her feet when the young blonde approached, giggling with excitement. She was wearing a revealing bride-to-be outfit and a short veil, and was clearly ready to party.

I waited for my turn to hug her and then continued sipping my drink, still wondering why Ivo's men were here—or at least one of them.

"All right, let's toast our bride. Tequila shots first!" Tasha quickly started handing out the shots to all the girls gathered around.

I kept glancing back at the bar, inwardly chiding myself every time, but I couldn't help myself. I couldn't see those men anymore, so I kept searching.

"Damn, I feel a little tipsy already." I laughed, downing another shot of tequila. Maybe a couple of drinks could get me out of my head and help me relax. "I'm going to the bathroom."

"I'll be right after you. I have to powder my nose," Tasha called out once I got up and started heading to the restrooms. A group of burly-looking men stood by the bar, scoping the scene. The place certainly didn't lack security.

I headed through the throng, finally locating a more sparsely populated area where I could breathe. It took me a few seconds to realize I must have taken the wrong turn somewhere because there was no ladies' room in sight. An employee hurried past me before I had a chance to ask him directions.

"Maybe I should go back," I muttered to myself, feeling a little dizzy. The music was drumming in my ears. I hadn't eaten anything before I came here—bad idea.

Several moments later, I swayed, losing my balance. As I scrambled for purchase, I barged through a door that happened to be ajar. My gaze landed on two men who stood with their backs to me.

"Oh sorry, wrong door," I mumbled, holding back a hiccup.

I needed to get the hell out of here. I also should have waited for Tasha because I wasn't much of a heavyweight when it came to drinking.

As I turned to leave, a shiver of recognition crawled up my spine. I set my attention back on the men, who were now facing me, thanks to all the racket I'd made. How could I forget that face? Dark, brooding ... verging on cruel. The man in front of me was Emilio Sergei, Ivo's younger son.

"A fresh pussy ... well, unexpected, but I can't say no," someone else said—a third man, who now stood behind me. I swiveled around in the direction of the voice. The one I'd seen earlier by the bar. He was tall, blond, and bulky, with lots of strange and ugly tattoos on his face. He could have been handsome if it wasn't for all the ink.

He quickly shut the door, blocking my only way out.

I started to panic, and fought to gather my wits. How could I be so stupid?

"Holy shit, Craig. It's my father's pussy. One of the asses I was hired to tap in the old club." Emilio laughed, lecherously giving me the once over. I suddenly wished I'd worn a pantsuit, not a skimpy black dress that barely covered the critical parts.

"Really. Bet you were too high to get it up," the guy next to him joked.

"Merry, Merry, what a surprise. We have missed you,"

Emilio said, ignoring his friend. "Jack, she's off limits tonight. My father owns her."

"Your daddy isn't here now, isn't he," the guy behind me snarled, licking his lips. "I like her and she's going to get on her knees and suck my hard cock. I say *no one* is off limits tonight."

He grabbed my arm, and I yelped, frantically attempting to pull away. But he was too strong, at least twice my size.

"Get the fuck away from me, you disgusting piece of shit!" I snapped as he forced me down on my knees. I glanced at Emilio and the other guy, expecting them to react, but on the contrary, they seemed excited about this. I was in deep trouble.

Just then, I spotted the white powder on the desk, and the way Emilio's eyes glazed over. Damn it! Was he alone? Was his brother Gregory here? He had seemed kinder. Ivo?

I clutched at straws, trying to think of a way out.

I was alone. The girls wouldn't miss me any time soon, and even if they did, how could they find me here? The blond guy Emilio called Jack laughed and gripped my hair tight, pulling my head back, forcing me to look at him.

"Pretty mouth. Shame that I'm going have to mess it all up. Tell me, Emilio, will she suck me like a pro?" Jack asked.

"Hell yeah, I bet her mouth works better than her pussy. Last time, my father had to drag me out when I was just about to fuck her with a dildo," Emilio said, moving closer.

"Emilio, please. I didn't mean to interrupt you guys. I was just looking for the bathroom. I bet Ivo wouldn't be happy about this," I said, ready to scream as the fear settled deep in my bones. The music upstairs was loud and I didn't think anyone could hear me here. Also, what employee would dare walk into a private room? They were probably used to ignoring all kinds of shady goings-on.

Jack finally let go of my hair and started unbuckling his trousers, then pulled them and his boxers down. My stomach roiled, and every part of my body was taken over by a sense of uncontrollable dread. This wasn't happening for real. I was ready to rip his dick off before I touched it.

"You need to bow to Jack and his hard cock. We own you now, little Merry," Emilio growled pushing me down when I tried to stand up. I glanced up at them, silently pleading, but he had a cold, calculating look on his face that told me he wasn't going to have any mercy. I was on my own. "Damn right, because Dad told us to have fun tonight. He gave us permission to do anything we wanted."

Chapter Nine

Merry

I shut my eyes, willing this to be nothing but a terrible dream. But when I opened them again, nothing had changed. I hoped for someone to barge in the room and save me. My head spun, and I couldn't form a proper thought. I kept on fighting them but that gave the beast who held me fuel to hurt me more. Screams caught in my throat. I wanted to persuade them to let me go, but nothing I said would get me out of this. The dark looks in their eyes spoke volumes.

Emilio had to be lying. Ivo couldn't have told them to come out and do what they were about to do. *No.*

Tears stung my eyes and I whimpered when Jack shoved his huge, hard dick in front of my face. He was excited by this. Bile rose in my throat as I braced myself. The thought of sucking him off made me sick.

I hadn't been with anyone since Ivo. What was the point? The moment he made me his with his touch, I knew nobody else could do it for me.

But this was something else entirely. My body went rigid, and anger suddenly took over.

"You don't know who you're dealing with. I'm a Camilleri, and my family will make you pay if you don't let go of me right now," I snarled. I wasn't sure if Elaine would care about getting payback for me, but scaring them off was my only option at this point.

They all laughed as though I'd just told them the funniest joke. Then, Emilio leaned down, bringing his face close to mine.

"Princess, that's even better. Finally, we can screw up someone important. This is going to be great for my father and his status. Plus, your father is dead, Merry Camilleri, and your stepmother isn't worth shit, although I'd like a taste of those bomb tits. She doesn't even care if you live or die."

I swallowed.

"What? You think I didn't know about you? The Maltese mafia is done for in this city. Better get used to being someone's plaything, bitch." He reached out and trailed a finger down my cheek, and I tried my best not to flinch, to no avail.

"Enough talking now. I'm getting bored," Jack growled, pressing his cock against my mouth.

I struggled, trying to turn my head, but Emilio gripped my throat and squeezed, forcing me back toward them. He would have no qualms about killing me if I kept resisting, I was sure. At the very least, they'd hurt me more.

"Open your mouth and suck it or I'm going to drag you outside on the dance floor and just make you do it there," Jack snarled, staring at me like I was his next toy and not a human being. A tear threatened to slide down but I didn't want him to see me break like that. Emilio forced my mouth open and pushed my head forward to receive his cock. He thrust roughly inside, and I felt like I was going to choke. He was huge and I could barely take on his size. Humiliation and bitterness filled every cell in my body. I watched him as he shut his eyes, clearly enjoying it.

A whimper escaped me and this time, the tears poured forth for real. I couldn't believe this was happening to me. All traces of dizziness and the high from the alcohol were gone. The stark cruelty of this reality hit me like a ton of bricks, and I wanted to die.

"Such a good girl ... now suck him off, Princess of the Maltese fucking mafia. I bet my father is going to be proud that you're serving us so willingly. After all, he taught you, didn't he?" Emilio whispered, finally letting go of my neck.

I wished I had a knife to stick into his stomach, then twist it around, making him howl in pain.

"Just be quick, man. We have pressing matters to discuss and more fun to have with more experienced whores than this one," the man called Craig protested.

"Yes, baby doll, let me fuck that mouth of yours," Jack groaned, placing his hand over the back of my head and pushing his cock into my mouth. He gripped my hair so painfully, I was ready to scream. Panicking and gasping for air, I obeyed him, feeling like the worst trash in the whole wide world.

They were all vile but despite how much I didn't want to do this, Jack started moving his shaft in and out of my mouth. I could bite him, hurt him like he was hurting me, but I couldn't throw my life away like that. I had things to do, dreams to fulfill. I cried quietly as I took the abuse, going still when he fucked my mouth fast, growling and moaning and saying all the crude stuff that made me want to vomit all over him.

Then, I felt Emilio's hand moving under my dress, at my cleavage, and touch my left breast. Oh, if only I had never gone to his father's club with Tasha. If only things had happened differently and I'd never met Ivo... My jaw ached and my lips felt numb and I wondered when it was all going to be over.

I sank to the darkest depths of despair from which I wasn't sure I could ever emerge. Was I destined for this—to be used and tortured and then discarded like a piece of garbage?

"Hard nipples ... hmmm, what about your pussy? I bet you're soaking wet for us, princess. You want us to fuck you then?" he whispered, massaging my breast and breathing heavily over me.

I made a choking sound and the tears burned my eyes now.

A flicking sound and a flash of silver caught my eye, then, something sharp was pressed into my neck. God above, Emilio held a knife at my throat, while his other hand pinched my nipple hard. I released a muffled scream.

"Fuck yeah, use your tongue. I'm going to come and you're going to swallow me whole, bitch, or my man here will cut your pretty little face." Jack assaulted my mouth without mercy. Tears clouded my vision, now falling freely. I felt so hopeless, so betrayed and used. Filthy.

Emilio pinched my nipple again, then twisted it. His heavy, alcohol-laced breaths hit my face, and his excitement was palpable. He was getting off on seeing me abused, so there was no way this nightmare could end well for me. The third man,

Craig, had seemed hesitant at first, but he wasn't going to protect me or do anything to stop this. These men would get what they wanted and none of them would care.

I tried to get outside of myself—to take my mind to another place. Each time he violated my mouth, jarring me, I died a little inside. I gasped for air and braced myself with every thrust. My jaw ached, and at one point, I thought my face would snap in two. Emilio roughly searched under my dress, cupping a hand over my panties. He inhaled sharply and bit hard on my ear, making my flesh sting.

"You like Jack's cock in your mouth, don't you, bitch?" He dipped his finger inside me and then slid it painfully all over my sensitive skin. I stiffened as my stomach threatened to reject its contents and the drinks I'd just had, coupled with raw desperation, created a nauseating mix inside me. I shook my head while Jack forced me to gag on his cock, but that only seemed to please him more. A pitiful whine escaped me and the tears burned their way down now. I couldn't see through the fog, and maybe that was a good thing.

"Don't cry, slut. You're serving me like such a good little girl. I'm so fucking close," he growled as I felt him tensing. A punishing gloom filled me, followed by emptiness, because I saw no way out from this.

Emilio was massaging my clit with his fingers, telling me what he was going to do to me next, what his father wanted him to do, but these were lies. They had to be. So many lies, and I refused to believe.

"Your pussy is getting wet. Just admit you like this, that you're under our mercy."

No! I don't want this! Emilio's words drowned me in humiliation and helplessness. He shoved his fingers inside me, as if to make a point ... to show me my juices were coating his filthy fingers. But I loathed him, loathed these men ... loathed myself for not being strong enough to fight them.

Soon, Jack's balls and cock swelled, and I honestly thought he'd rip my face apart this time, and kill me.

Maybe that would be the only way to get out of this nightmare.

I fought hard, gave it as good as I got, but then his semen flooded my mouth. I tried not to swallow but that was impossible. The stuff was salty and thick and threatened to cut my air supply. His guttural groan as he came sounded like a strident scream to my ears. Emilio didn't stop touching me when Jack finally pulled away and let go of me, breathing hard. Letting loose a plaintive cry, I mustered the strength to tell him to stop.

Stop stroking my clit.

Stop hurting me.

Stop, stop, stop!

And then the blinding rage soared again from its simmering depths—above the pain, fear, and mortification.

"Get the fuck away from me or I swear to God I'm going to cut off your balls and flush them down the toilet!" I snarled, wiping my tears away and trying to spit out the bitterness in my mouth. Grabbing Emilio's arm, I did my damnedest to get him off me, but that only pissed him off more. Then, Jack slapped me hard and I saw stars as I slammed to the floor. The contact with the wood sent a searing pain up my left shoulder but at least, Emilio had stopped touching me. I tried to pull myself together, but my body was one big ball of agony.

"What the fuck, man? Haven't you had enough?" Craig

shouted in annoyance. "Or do you want to snuff out this piece of ass? We need to get a move on." He stepped up and shoved Jack, who retaliated by thrusting a fist in his face. Craig moved sideways to avoid the hit and then punched Jack right on the nose. The man swayed and crashed into some beer bottles they had on the desk, scattering the white powder all over the place.

"Motherfucker!"

The beat of the music in the club could be heard through the cacophony Jack was creating, but up above, I also heard some screams. Something was going on in the dance floor or bar area.

I lifted myself off the floor with difficulty, working through the pitch black that took residence in my very soul. I had no idea how, but Emilio and his two buddies would pay for what they did to me, if it was the last thing I did—I'd make sure of it.

Craig stared at me with hesitation in his eyes, as though he was sorry. Too fucking late—he could have made them stop. As far as I was concerned, he was an accomplice and just as guilty. Emilio was already heading toward the door.

"Come on guys, let's go. The others are here and already having their fun. We have more Russian pussy to enjoy," he ordered, clearly brimming with excitement.

Jack stumbled to his feet, bleeding and swearing loud when Craig took a step toward me. "If I didn't have shit to do, I'd kill you, you son of a bitch. And what's this pussy to you, when you know what we're here for? Get with it or go home. Ivo will deal with you later."

What the hell were they talking about? Through the haze of my whirling emotions, I almost didn't care ... yet something was very wrong, and I had a feeling that what happened to me wasn't the worst of it.

Slowly, I put one foot in front of the other. "Get the fuck away from me, you pig. You'll be sorry for this," I spat out, pushing Emilio away from me.

He laughed because I barely had the strength to stand up, let alone move a big man out of the way.

I was fully sober now, the buzz I had when I came downstairs completely dissipated. The tears hadn't stopped though, although I wished they had. Seeing the pain they caused me made them happier, and that tore me apart at least as much as the abuse itself.

A sense of dread ate at me as I ascended the stairs and the noise got louder.

Not the regular club noise of patrons having the time of their lives—but something else. Something sinister and *bad*.

What was that talk of the 'others' and Russian pussy about?

When I got to the top, people were screaming and running toward the exit. Shots were fired from somewhere up ahead, and everyone ducked, including me. Going against the crowd, I found my way back to the booth to see Catherine lying on the couch, unconscious. Tasha was sobbing as she tried to revive her. Blood was everywhere...

"What ... what is going on?" I asked, frantically scanning around me in search of Clara.

"She was trying to protect Vicky and these men beat her to a pulp. Oh God, Merry," Tasha cried. "They barged in and attacked us!"

"Ah, so this is where the bridal bitches' party is at."

We both turned around in the direction of the voice to see

Emilio holding Clara by his side, her eyes wide with terror. Three other men stood behind him looking like they'd just escaped from prison, their face covered in tattoos and what looked like hunting knives stuck in sheaths at their waist.

"Let go of my sister, you fucking pig, or I swear to God, I am going to kill you!" I started to lunge at him but he wrapped his hand around her neck and squeezed. I froze on the spot, horror tearing through my gut. I fixed my gaze on Clara, whose expression of pleading and alarm broke my heart.

"Uh-oh... Stay back, or I'll gut her like a fish, *princess*," he sneered, then smiled, his eyes cold and gleaming. "So ... this slut is your little sister then. Good to know."

An unholy fire burned inside me and I threw myself at him with all that I had. I'd die before letting him hurt Clara. I managed to scratch his face before he pulled back, tightening his hold on my sister. She cried out in pain.

"Bitch!" he shouted, and then I saw the flash of a blade. Before I could move away, he moved his arm out in a slashing motion and I felt a slicing pain on my left cheek. I lost my balance and crashed to the floor, narrowly avoiding hitting my head against a table. When I raised a hand to my face, my fingers were tainted with blood.

He turned to the men behind him as Clara and Tasha screamed at the top of their lungs. "CJ, Tank, hold her and her other friend while I have some fun over here. Seems like I caught two birds with one stone today."

The bastard laughed as one of the beasts pulled me off the floor by my hair like a caveman. Pain radiated from my scalp, forcing me to grind my teeth.

"If she makes any trouble, you can get rid of her—but have

some fun first," Emilio told him before turning his lecherous gaze on Clara.

Gunshots and screams rang in my ears. People scattered and nobody paid us any mind or even got near our private booth. Emilio raised the knife to my sister's throat and made a small, paper-thin cut on her flesh. Then, he ripped her dress, exposing her underwear.

God, no. Please!

Agony like I'd never felt before formed a ball in the depths of my gut, and I could barely swallow past the lump in my throat. This couldn't be happening ... no, this was just my imagination. I tried to wrench myself free but each time I did, he pressed that blade more against her flesh, reminding me he held the upper hand.

"Now your sister is going to pay for that little stunt," Emilio said, his eyes sparking with rage.

I sobbed, begging and pleading with him not to do this. Pushing Clara down, he started undoing his pants. My head was buzzing, my vision was blurry, and I let myself slide to the floor, becoming a dead weight to the beast, who held my arms in a bruising grip. I had to save Clara, but how?

"Get the fuck away from her, you sick fuck!" I screamed. Blood from the cut trickled to my mouth, and the taste of copper made me sick.

Clara's heart-wrenching sobs as the bastard got on top of her would be forever etched in my mind. Tearing off her panties, he moved the ripped shreds of her dress out of his way and rammed himself inside her. She screamed for dear life, but when she tried to fight him, he slapped her hard, then pressed the knife into her neck and nicked her. Grabbing her hands in one of his, he restrained her while he thrust inside her. After a while, she stopped moving altogether. Her neck and lip were bleeding and she looked numb.

I was worthless because I couldn't protect her.

"Let her go!" I shouted, desperate, but my voice was hoarse and weak. "Clara! Look at me ... look at me please." She turned her head slightly toward me. Her eyes were dead—as if her soul had been sucked out of her and nothing was left.

I held her gaze for as long as I could, doing my utmost to show strength, and hope ... even though I was falling apart inside.

The men laughed while Emilio raped my little sister, as though she wasn't human, a flesh and blood person. Anguish tore me asunder, and moments turned to minutes, and then what felt like eternity as he kept driving and driving and driving himself inside Clara. For a while there, I thought she was dead because she went completely limp. I sobbed quietly because I couldn't bear for them to see me like this—a bigger victory for them. When I started to think it was never going to end, his face contorted and his body stiffened. The filthy creep came inside her, and I let loose a barrage of insults, calling him everything but a child of God.

Getting off her, he stood, zipped up his pants, and nodded to the man who held Tasha. "Your turn to fuck her, amigo."

Clara lay still as a statue, a lone tear sliding down her face.

"No!" I cried, the sobs rising to the surface and pouring out of me.

Emilio and the nasty-looking dark-haired man swapped places. The guy grinned, showing a chipped tooth, as he pulled out his cock from his jeans.

Tasha was visibly shaking, and she kept whimpering.

All I could do was watch as the other guy raped my sister, too, dying a little more inside with each passing second.

This was a nightmare from which I'd never wake up. The scent of blood, sweat, and evil assailed my nostrils. Emilio said something to me when the man finally finished with Clara, but I wasn't acknowledging him anymore. I had to block him off and pray that they wouldn't kill us, too. Then, the beast holding me captive suddenly let me go.

I looked around to see a few bodies lying prostrate, blood pooling around them. Furniture was trashed, broken glass everywhere. Those who could make an escape were gone by now, and whoever created the chaos and killed these people had also disappeared. Emilio's cronies. *Ivo's cronies.*

Emilio practically threw Tasha on the floor, like trash, and stepped close to me—too close. His breath singed my neck, and I closed my eyes, hoping I wouldn't throw up all over him.

Where did we go from here?

How would we pick up the pieces?

I had to be strong for Clara ... to survive.

"It wasn't personal, princess, but this had to be done. My father wanted to send a message, and I believe everybody got it, loud and clear." I bit my bottom lip until I drew blood and wasted no time rushing to my sister. "So long now."

With that, they left us drowning in a quicksand of despair, revulsion, and humiliation.

*　*　*

2 years later...

. . .

"Girls, I have something important to share with you," Elaine stated, flashing me and my sister a dazzling smile.

I really didn't want to come for dinner today but my stepmother insisted that I had to be there. She said it was imperative for me and Clara to hear what she had to say.

"I have a conference call in an hour and I need to get home," I said, sighing. This wasn't exactly true, but Elaine didn't need to know that. Since I was here, I wanted to spend some time with my sister.

Elaine was a beautiful woman. Slender, blond, with large natural breasts and a becoming tan. Many had underestimated her for a long time, but I had to admit, my stepmother wasn't the airhead I'd first thought her to be. It seemed she was born to run the family business.

"Well, I have decided to remarry. I think it's time and I finally found the perfect candidate," she announced, and my jaw dropped. This wasn't what I expected to hear tonight.

I knew for a fact she'd had an affair with one of her old security guards for a long time, but I believed she'd called it quits. She was too ambitious to get stuck with someone who couldn't offer her much. Elaine was like a sexual butterfly, and she only deigned to flutter more often to those blooms worthy of her interest.

"Who is he and why now?" Clara asked.

Elaine was pushing me to get engaged to Robert, a junior partner with a firm I worked with in New York.

"To be honest, it's a strategic alliance we need. You will meet him tomorrow night at the engagement party. Trust me, this all will be good for us," she explained.

It seemed she already had made up her mind and we both knew that if Elaine wanted something, there was no stopping her in getting it.

"I hope he is not some old git who can even move," Clara muttered.

Although, to be fair, our father was quite a bit older than her when they got married.

"Oh no, darling. He's handsome, a bit older than me, and smart. He has a unique position and prospects in our world. You will both love him. Trust me on this."

I nodded. "Fine then. I can't wait to meet him."

After a bit of small chat, Elaine excused herself to take care of some paperwork.

Clara glanced at me, looking washed out. She had black circles under her eyes and likely, she hadn't had a good night's sleep in a while. She was taking care of the family's 'above board' finances, and although it wasn't her calling, it kept her occupied, aside from school. Being a detail-oriented person, she was good at it, too.

I wish she'd talk to me more, the way we always did before. I wondered if she blamed me for what happened that night in the club. Maybe I shouldn't have let Emilio know she was my sister, and then, he wouldn't have touched her.

I smiled at her, and at the pins stuck to her shirt. She'd been working on her garments—something that always gave her peace. I was glad she was back in school. She'd started slowly after these years, and still, she couldn't bear to sleep alone in a dorm anymore. She came home daily. The nightmares had subsided, but the darkness still reared its head at times. She'd never stepped foot inside a nightclub since that fateful night, and I worried for her. I did more and more work from home, remotely for my firm, so I could spend more time in Cali.

I went to the kitchen to make us both some ginger tea. Clara's favorite. Returning with two cups, I sat across from her and sipped on my warm drink while she read from a fashion magazine. I let her be, loath to disturb her, and happy to just be here, watching her.

After the raid in the club, Clara had to go to therapy. Catherine had barely survived that night and even though there were lots of witnesses, no one wanted to talk. The girls were scared, and all begged me to keep silent for everyone's safety. It was an unspoken rule in the family that you minimized any association with the police, for obvious reasons. Even though there were those on Elaine's payroll, I had no doubt they'd be kicking tires and not take this seriously. After all, the mob families all had their allies to call on. Elaine seemed to believe what we'd done was enough and Clara was fine by now, as if time healed everything.

So, we were at an impasse.

But I would get my revenge, one way or the other.

It had taken me months to come to terms with the fact that Ivo Sergei had ordered the attack at the club. Even worse, the police had chalked it down to a turf war among Russians, with the attackers vying for a takeover bid. Nothing could be further from the truth, and nobody really cared about a bunch of mobsters fighting each other.

Meanwhile, although I had to tell Elaine about the harrowing experience we'd had, I kept Emilio's words about Ivo ordering the attack to myself. Before I threw the man to the dogs, I wanted to look him in the eyes and see for myself if Emilio had been telling the truth. Deep down, I just couldn't believe it. Although I didn't know him all that well, I thought I understood him. I'd seen his kindness, his caring, his passion. Was he really such a monster?

I'd made some discreet inquiries and found out Gregory, Emilio's brother, had been severely beaten by a group of Russians in a deal gone wrong, and fallen into a long coma. Such a shame, for I'd met the man and he was more like his father than Emilio, who seemed out of place to me. A number of Ivo's men had also been murdered that night.

Ivo must have wanted those Russian heads on a silver platter. Somehow, I doubted he knew we were going to be at Sputnik that night—it was usually patronized exclusively by Russians. I also doubted he'd ordered his men to rape women and use gratuitous violence.

But, to be sure, I'd sought Ivo out.

I went to the club where—surprise, surprise—he'd beefed up security. I felt emboldened because, since the attack, Emilio and his henchmen had been MIA. I didn't think I could face him ever again.

It took me a moment to drum up the courage to go inside and face the darkness. See, this was why I wanted out of this life. It wasn't truly living—it was just existing, each day marred by blood and the twisted honor of the mob. I thought Ivo was above it all, but maybe losing a son so horribly would do that to a person.

Because of this, and because of Clara, I stepped inside the mostly empty coffee shop where I'd arranged to meet him and sat across from the man who made my heart beat faster than a speeding bullet. I spoke past the rage, the regret, all the feelings he awoke in me and I didn't want to acknowledge anymore.

I quietly told him what Emilio and his crew had done to me, to my sister, to my friends. He saw my scar, which today I decided not to hide behind makeup.

It was hard, but I got through it. Ivo was devastated, and his body language screamed authenticity. The man wasn't lying. So many emotions passed through his face, but when he looked at me with an expression of sheer torture, as though his heart was being rent in two, I could not possibly think he'd hurt me on purpose.

Yet, he *had* wanted chaos. He wanted his men to ruin the Sputnik business and drive people away. For Gregory.

We were simply collateral damage.

He shouldn't have sent Emilio to do his bidding—the man was unhinged, and he should have known. For this, I considered him responsible.

That day, I understood without equivocation that I was one hundred percent done with Ivo Sergei, Bulgarian-Russian don on the rise, who lived in a world I did not want to be a part of. His territory was small, but his unique heritage granted him some degree of immunity on both sides.

I wanted none of that.

I had to think of Clara, and how to get her back to what she once was. Sometimes, I could barely get her to speak half a sentence, when she used to be so bubbly and exuberant. She was but a shadow of her former self, and my soul cried every day for her. For us.

When we exited the establishment, Ivo tried to get close and reached out to touch me, but I slapped him hard, then stepped back, attracting some attention from passersby. If his skin connected with mine, I'd be done for. Right now, I just wanted to be mad. Anger saved me, helped me move on.

"I never want to see you again, you son of a bitch. You might not have intended to do this," I pointed at the scar on my face, "but actions have consequences. Stay out of my life."

My mind was made up. For the last time, I said goodbye, turned around, and walked away, putting him behind me, vowing to bury him deep in my memory, so deep it would be as if he'd never existed for me.

As if I'd never, ever surrendered my being to the man called Ivo Sergei. The man who broke my heart.

Chapter Ten

Ivo

It had been two years. Two long fucking years of anguish, pain, and bleakness. My family was torn apart, and I was being pulled in all directions.

Not everything was bad. Up to two months ago, my son was still lost in the ether, and I thought maybe he'd never recover. In all that time, I refused to pull the plug. I refused to give up hope. At last, he was awake, and the doctors informed me he was doing well, better every day. I visited him daily, made sure he had everything he needed. He would require therapy, both physical and mental, but he was on the mend.

He was working in the club with me now, although this was his day off and I put our trusted manager in charge for the night. At least, one of my children was normal.

The other son though, the prodigal—I still couldn't say his

name without being hit by a powerful rage. If I ever saw him again, I'd kill him with my bare hands. We had a huge fallout after the incident, and I kicked him out of the business, out of my life—and he had to go crawl into some hole, on the run. Too many people wanted his head on a gold platter. The police were after him, but the way we settled things in our world, he belonged six feet under.

Then, there was Merry. He'd hurt her.

My Merry.

I hadn't seen her in so long, but I'd asked my men to keep tabs on her in LA. She didn't have another man here, but I had no idea what she did when she went to New York. During this time, I drowned my sorrows in other women, but somehow, none compared to her. I just couldn't forget her. I wanted only her.

She'd made it clear I couldn't have her.

Since that terrible night at Sputnik, one of Victor's clubs, everything changed.

And now, today, was going to be tough.

Today, the shit would hit the fan. Why was I doing this?

"The car is waiting, boss," Ryga said, walking in my quarters in the office. I'd left the door open.

I took a deep breath, telling myself to keep calm.

"I'll be there now," I snapped at him, staring at my face in the mirror. I cleaned up well in a suit, and I supposed I was dressed the part, trying to stay on top of my game.

"Get your shit together, for fuck's sake," I growled at my reflection, then hurried outside.

The silence in the car echoed in my ears. The drive to the Camilleri residence wasn't long and before I knew it, I was through the gate and out the car, walking toward the large white house. Two guards gave me the once over and frisked me, then opened the door to the mansion. My presence was expected but one couldn't be too careful.

I smirked, nodding at them yet sending a silent message that they better show respect, for things were about to change. Inside, however, I was a wreck.

"Ivo, how good to see you here. Gregory has already arrived. He is such a sweetheart," Elaine said, welcoming me by the door in a white dress that clung to her slim curves. She placed a soft kiss on my lips before I'd fully processed what she'd said.

"Dammit. What is he doing here? I haven't even said anything to him yet," I snapped.

I liked to keep my business to myself. Gregory was trying to start something on his own, but he wasn't a coward like Emilio. He blamed me for initiating a war with Russians, so I understood we needed to cement some alliances for the sake of protection. We were both surprised when Victor didn't retaliate straight away, despite the fact his own niece had nearly died in that club ambush. Two years had passed and it was almost as if he was biding his time. A long silence before the storm. Or maybe with me having my foot in both, competing worlds, I had an edge. Elaine had somehow kept things on an even keel, too, with backroom deals—which made this alliance even more crucial. I needed her and she needed me.

I let it all happen because I deserved to pay some price.

Because what else could I do?

"He's having a good time, so chill out, darling, and have a drink before I introduce you to the rest of the family," she purred, handing me a glass of champagne. I didn't like the stuff much but maybe it would help settle the tension inside.

"All right. We can talk about business later."

Elaine said something in response, but I stopped listening when I spotted a familiar face in the distance. The whole world suddenly froze when my gaze landed on the woman who'd managed to cause such turmoil inside my heart. I swallowed thickly as heat poured around my groin, causing my cock to stir. She looked absolutely stunning in a strapless red dress that showed off her amazing figure, her olive skin smooth and glistening.

Elaine was still talking when Merry finally turned around and our eyes locked for a moment. Shock and disbelief flashed on her face.

And then came the suckerpunch to the gut when my gaze landed on the faint scar that marred her cheek. Even from here, even with the makeup, I could see it. My son did that to her. He'd marked her for life.

Elaine proceeded to introduce me to some people, so I shook hands and made small talk, but I was too enraged to pay anybody any mind. I wanted to punch the walls, rile at the world, shoot down half of these self-serving, sniveling guests. I had to calm myself down, talk myself off the ledge.

Merry was as exquisite as ever—the scar did nothing to mar her beauty. All I had eyes for was her, and the expression she made when she saw me with her stepmother.

I had to remind myself why I was doing this. Why, when Elaine proposed it to me, considering the circumstances, it had almost sounded like a good idea.

Only one big wrench in the game: my traitorous emotions.

Because I still wanted her, and right now, as I stood there, I thought myself a fool for even putting myself in this situation. Perhaps, subconsciously, I just wanted to be close to her ... but like this? I was completely fucked up.

"Oh, and there is Merry. Come on, Ivo. I believe you all are acquainted but I want to officially introduce you to my step-daughter," Elaine's voice pulled me back to reality as we approached the woman of both my purest and filthiest dreams.

She glanced at a smiling Elaine, raising her left eyebrow, then looked back at me. I had tried to keep this whole arrangement under wraps, prolonging the inevitable as much as I could. But as I saw it, this marriage was the only way forward.

I gave her a bright smile, pretending that seeing her here didn't fucking faze me.

"We already met once... How do you know him, Elaine?" she asked in a sharp tone.

Last time we'd met, she told me she never wanted to see me again. This close, the scar was more visible yet smoother and not as prominent. She didn't like using a lot of makeup, but the small imperfection made her even more alluring, if that was possible.

It would also be a constant reminder of how I'd always carry this burden inside me—the fact that my own actions had caused her harm.

"Oh, honey, where are your manners? This is my surprise, Ivo—my new fiancé that I told you about. We are getting married, connecting our two families," Elaine explained, and I wished she would shut up.

Merry looked like she'd just seen a ghost. I wished I could have spoken to her in private first, and prepared her for this. I owed it to her, no matter the fact we never really had a relationship.

Elaine laughed and gave me a peck on the cheek. Merry's eyes darkened, and antagonism sparked from them. My blood pounded in my veins.

"Are you fucking kidding me?" Merry whispered, then pursed her lips.

Elaine paled and then laughed nervously, smoothing her blonde tresses.

"Merry, calm down. Someone could hear you…"

"I'm *whispering*. How can anyone hear me?" she hissed under her breath.

"I think it's better if I talk to your stepdaughter in private, Elaine, so we can iron things out," I said, reaching out for her, but she jumped away from me as though I had the plague.

"Don't you dare touch me. I have nothing to talk to you about and you should reconsider this alliance, Elaine," Merry spat, her voice low and her eyes burning with barely contained rage.

"Merry, please. We need to talk," I insisted, my voice rough and gentle at the same time. If we kept this up, people would soon start noticing we weren't simply chit-chatting.

In the back of the room by the patio doors, I spotted Gregory. He lifted his glass as though toasting me, a smirk on his face. Elaine lobbed her baffled gaze from Merry to me. But she had no clue how my psychotic son had raped her sister, and how I couldn't blame Merry for her attitude right now. She was never going to forgive me, and maybe I deserved it. After all, I should have said more … done more to fix the unfixable.

I should have killed Emilio, torn him limb from limb and

cut him into little pieces for what he did. I'd gladly spend all my life in jail if it brought back the light in Merry's eyes. If I banished the shadows that now held a permanent home on her face.

"Merry, this is unacceptable behaviour. I'm not going to reconsider this marriage. This family needs an alliance with the Bulgarians so we can compete in the current climate, and you know it. Besides, Ivo has an unusual connection with the Russians. This way, they won't touch us..." Elaine rambled on, firmly taking a step toward her. "But I'm not discussing this right now. Get a grip."

Merry opened her mouth as if to protest further, then must have realized the futility of it all. I saw her gaze shift to something behind me and her expression changed from anger to ... concern. And heartbreak? I turned around and spotted her sister Clara, staring at me, frozen.

Damn it. Being here during an event, with people around, was not the brightest or most sensitive idea. I should have known better.

"Fine," Merry snapped. "Let's go talk, Ivo." She probably wanted to get me away from her sister, who seemed to be shell-shocked right now. My presence triggered a memory she should never have had, and I hated myself for it. I hesitated, feeling like the biggest scum on this planet, but eventually followed her. In that moment, my own feelings didn't matter at all.

We headed past the guests to the office downstairs. Once inside, Merry went to stand by the bookcase with her arms folded over her chest, her back to me. So beautiful, stunning ... and I longed to reach out and comfort her. I quickly shut the door and exhaled, telling myself that I was in control, that I had to find a way to get through to her.

My heart reminded me that this wasn't the plan. She was going to be my stepdaughter and whatever attraction there was between us couldn't be relevant anymore. The very thought of what I was about to do horrified me.

Yet, Emilio had ruined so many lives, and it was all my fault because of my rage at the time. The Russians had hurt Gregory and I'd had no idea if he'd ever wake up from his coma. I thought I'd lost him forever, and couldn't see straight.

Revenge is a motherfucker. No such act goes unpunished. I should have known Emilio would go overboard. Even in our business, the unnecessary destruction of life is a tragedy. Now look where that brought us. *What* it brought us. Hate, pain, loss...

So now, it was up to me to make sense of this. To do damage control, in the only way I knew how. To avoid bloodshed, I had to bring all the families toward some sort of truce.

I didn't see myself married to Elaine, but what other choice did I have? Merry hated me with a passion.

I could possibly find another way but eschewed that because I had to pay the cost. Every single cent of it.

"Why did you do this? Have I not made myself clear when I said that I never want to see you again? Now you're engaged to my stepmother? You twisted son of a bitch." Her shoulders moved as she took hard breaths, as though struggling to keep it together.

"The Russians are out for blood yet they hesitate to touch me because I'm useful to them. I'm a half-breed, Merry. Half-Russian, half-Bulgarian. But for how long could I buy my own safety? When will there finally be a bounty on my life? An alliance with the Maltese buys me time ... and resources. It will save lives and keep balance."

"Bullshit. You just want to hurt me, like Emilio did. His bastard friends... But *why*?" She turned around, her eyes ablaze. "Why do you hate us? What did we ever do to you? What did *I* ever do to you?"

The pain in her glistening eyes, the acute desire to comprehend the warped reason for my actions in their depths ... it all damn near broke me. How could I tell her the rage had taken over my common sense, my worry for Gregory ... and in those moments, I didn't care who else I'd hurt to satisfy my thirst for retribution. The dark emotions made me blind. Consumed me. Forced me to ignore the havoc I'd bring to so many lives. Either way, no matter the reason for what happened, I'd never be anything other than a monster in Merry's eyes.

The consequences were there for me to see.

There was no discount, no sale on my dues. No stopping this shipwreck.

I had to pay. Period.

"I have to do this," I said gruffly. "For us."

She laughed then, the sound harsh and sarcastic. "Really. Why is that?"

Where did I start?

"Gregory, he ... he almost died. I had to—"

"Had to what?" she cut me off. "Fuck us all up?" Her brows furrowed, and she looked about ready to scratch my eyes out. Better suffer her ire than seeing her weakened, broken. Maybe that's what I needed to do to stop her tears. Make her hate me.

"I had to do what I had to do," I said blandly. "I have interests to protect."

"I see," she said, letting her hands fall to her sides, as if tired. "So you'll marry Elaine to get ahead." She looked around the room, purposely avoiding my gaze.

"Well, yes. Unless you want Victor to shoot us all up. He owned that club, and I hit him in the pocket. Somehow, I've managed to keep a delicate balance, but it's becoming increasingly difficult. I know why he keeps me alive ... but when will I outlive my usefulness? It's a slippery slope," I said truthfully.

"Victor only had a beef with *you*. Now you want to involve us in your messes, too, as if you haven't done enough."

"I—" I stopped myself because as much as I'd mulled things, figuring out ways to keep hell from breaking loose and trying to keep everyone safe, I realized she had a point.

The deathly silence that followed was tough to bear. I wanted to yell at her, make her talk to me, but what would that change?

Marrying Elaine would bring me closer to her—the woman of my daily dreams since that time she'd first set foot in my club. It would be a constant torture. Hell on earth.

To want her, yet never touch her.

I couldn't...

The air felt heavy, suffocating. I took a few steps toward her against my better judgment, closing the distance between us.

"I will be close to you..."

She vehemently shook her head and stepped back. "Close to me? You heartless son of a bitch! Whatever plan you have in that head of yours in regards to me is not going to happen. We are done, Ivo. Besides, we were never a thing anyway. I'll never forgive you for what you did," she stated, backing farther away from me toward the bookcase.

The heat from her body was driving me crazy and the scent of her muddled my brain. I knew this was wrong, but I wanted her more than ever. It stunk that she thought me heartless, and more so because it was the truth. Yet, I'd never been like that with her.

"I can't stop thinking about you, Merry. Never did. I never stopped thinking about the way you screamed my name and moaned when you fell apart in my arms. The way your soft body fit against mine... I think about you when I'm awake, and when I sleep, you haunt my dreams. My life has spanned over four decades, going on five ... yet here I am, lost in you. Always in you."

I hooked her gaze and refused to let go. I leaned over and gripped the book case with both hands, trapping her between my arms. Inhaling her sweet perfume. Wounded, wide-eyed and guileless, she almost brought me to my knees. My body was primed, ready to sink itself into her softness ... against the wall ... right on that desk behind us ... hot and heavy ... but there was no way. Especially when she pursed her lips and straightened up. She had come to a decision, and it wasn't in my favor.

She drove me out of my damn mind.

"I'm trying to mend things," I insisted, my lips now an inch from her temple. "And I know, what happened will always haunt me. I had no idea you and your sister were at Sputnik that night. I swear I didn't." I moved my hand to caressed her cheek with the back of my hand, tracing her scar, and she flinched, then pushed me away.

"I fucking hate you," she said, gritting her teeth. She got in my face, her body almost flush with mine. My cock begged and pleaded and screamed out her name... Oh, God. "Don't you dare touch me. Just so you know, Elaine doesn't like sharing anyway. I'm done."

And with that, she bent down and exited the physical cage I'd put her in, just when I was about to bury my fingers in her hair and taste her mouth. There was only so much a man could take.

She could say she hated me, that she didn't care about me, that she didn't want me, but the eyes didn't lie, and I didn't miss the flash of desire in hers.

"Just keep telling yourself that, princess, but I know how you were when we were together. I could read you like an open book. Still can... the connection is still there. Can't you feel it?" I said.

If looks could kill, I'd have been struck dead.

"So maybe Elaine doesn't like sharing," he continued, "but ours is a business arrangement anyway, and I cannot renege on my promises." She looked away, biting her lip. This was eating at her—and that was how I knew she still felt something for me. Still craved me, like I craved her. "Tell me what to do," I added.

"There is nothing you can do. I pulled myself together after what your son did to me, but I will not forgive you for what he did to Clara. You all ruined her," she spat, turning toward the door.

"So this is it?" She stopped in her tracks. "Elaine has no fucking clue how you know me, only that we met once. Certainly not that I was the first man to make you come until you couldn't any more. We have history. Do you remember how you called me Daddy? How you responded to my touch? Are we going to throw it all away, just like that?"

She turned to me and shook her head, her gaze haunting and sad.

"Am *I* throwing it away? Think well about what you're saying. Yeah, I cannot feel sorry for you. I cannot ignore my principles for a man who would do the things you've done. Even if I hadn't been there that night, Emilio and his friends would have hurt someone else's daughter, someone else's sister. Are you so callous that this doesn't even cross your mind?"

"Trust me, it has. And I never—"

"Shut the fuck up. You destroyed our lives. Damn near killed my sister ... and she might as well be dead sometimes. When I look into her eyes ... I see only a shell of what she once was. She may have overcome in some ways, but then again, she's not truly living. She's existing. Thanks to you, she'll be damaged for the rest of her life! As far as I'm concerned, you can go to hell, Ivo Sergei!"

And with that, she walked out the door.

Chapter Eleven

Merry

My thoughts abuzz, my heart pounding, I went in search of Clara. She had met Ivo before but thankfully, she had no idea that he was responsible for sending his son to Sputnik that fateful evening. I never shared any details with her because that would have broken her more. The last thing I wanted was to cause her more pain.

Still, his presence upset her because it reminded her of what she couldn't forget.

As for me, I needed a minute to process the fact that Ivo was getting married to Elaine. It felt like I was in some nightmarish, alternate universe. When I saw him with her and she introduced him as her fiancé, I thought I had finally lost the plot.

I needed a cold shower to scrub Ivo's delicious scent from my senses. Why did he have to barge back into my life like this?

A marriage? What angered me most was how he made me feel when he was near. No matter how hard I tried, if he pushed enough, I'd become like putty in his arms.

I couldn't do that—not when Emilio was still out there, a free man. Not when Ivo had ordered the attack on the club.

And now this man—this ruthless thug—was going to be a part of our family.

Besides, I now had a caring and sweet man in my life, while making strides in my career as a defense attorney. I'd move to New York City, where the partners of a major law firm were waiting for me to make a decision to join their team. I'd gotten what I wanted without making use of my family connections, without the drama—only hard work and dedication.

Once my new life took root, I'd never have to lay eyes on Ivo again.

"Merry, what the hell was all that about?" Elaine asked, cornering me by the fireplace. She was pissed and normally I would have tried to smooth things over, but not today. I was just not in the mood for playing games.

"Why did you have to get engaged to Ivo Sergei?" Rage filled me, making me lose control, and I didn't care anymore. This would end now. "You know who that is, Elaine? I'll tell you who it is. It's the man who sent his son to that club where Clara and I got raped," I snarled. "That's who he is."

Elaine frowned. "What are you talking about? Emilio wasn't there because of Ivo."

"Because Ivo said so? Emilio told me that night that Ivo had given him the go ahead to do anything necessary, in retaliation for what happened to Gregory and his men. If you care about me and Clara, you will break this engagement," I said firmly.

She parted her lips and released a breath. Normally, nothing fazed this woman, but she was clearly figuring things out. The business implications especially, knowing her. Not for a moment did I believe she was attracted to Ivo, or in love with him. Elaine had been in love with her bodyguard Stephan for years. It was a known fact, but she would never act on it. She wouldn't marry anyone who didn't bring something to the table. And that something would be money and connections.

Clara had been isolating herself, pretending and acting that everything was fine. She had gone through a lot, but after all the therapy, it seemed as though she was giving up. She was refusing more help. I still suffered nightmares, but at least I could throw myself into my work and I had Robert. The man who cared about me.

Clara, on the other hand, was different. An introvert, she clammed up and withdrew into herself. I did what I could, but I was running out of options. I felt guilty each time I had to go to New York and leave her behind.

Elaine put her hand on my shoulder. "Darling, obviously you're hurt and you're worried about your sister, but this is not your business. I really don't believe Ivo is involved in anything his nitwit son does. On the other hand, this union will make us one of the most powerful families in the region and you have no idea how much effort it took me to convince Victor we could work together. To backtrack now could potentially ruin all my efforts. What Emilio did was unforgivable, but it's been two years and it's time you moved on. Ivo and I are getting married," she explained, her voice both soft and stern.

I couldn't fucking believe it—although I shouldn't have been surprised. Elaine always wanted power and she was determined to carve out a bigger niche for herself. She had no idea what it meant to sacrifice for one's family.

"You cannot be serious. His son is a psychopath and he's no better," I snapped, feeling so livid, I wanted to smash something. I wanted to get Clara out of the house.

Elaine smiled and wet her lips.

"I'm done discussing this. You will be civil to him or you will regret it," she warned, and I'd known her long enough to realise she wasn't joking.

"Fine, whatever. Just don't come running to me when things go to shit. I'm leaving," I said, walking away from her.

Clara was probably hiding in her room upstairs and I had to go back past the guests to get there.

I spotted Ivo with Gregory, engaged in what seemed to be a heated discussion about something. "You better behave," I managed to make out before Gregory noticed me and smiled.

"Hey, Princess Merry. I hope everything is okay with you?" he called out, ignoring his father. Ivo turned too and his eyes burned into mine, moving over my body as if he owned me. As if I was supposed to fall into a puddle at his feet—and I almost did.

Almost.

Refraining from responding to Gregory, I ran upstairs searching for Clara. I didn't want her to be alone for too long.

In the past two years, I did everything I could to separate myself from the "family" and concentrate on my blossoming carrier. There was an arrest warrant out for Emilio but he was in hiding. Right after the incident in the club, Elaine had set out to find him and make him pay, and that was likely when she met

Ivo. She said spoke to Emilio and asked him to turn himself in, but shortly after that, he's gone on the run.

I passed a window and saw the reflection of my face. That scar was there to stay, a reminder of the worst night of my life. I did not even bother with surgeries any longer.

I knocked softly on Clara's bedroom door and walked inside, shutting the door behind me. She was lying on the bed, listening to Linkin Park.

"Hey, are you okay?" I asked, touching her leg.

"I got bored at the party," she replied, and frowned at me. "What's wrong with you? You look like you saw a ghost. Is this about Ivo?"

I exhaled sharply, trying to ease the tension in my body and forget our exchange in the office.

"Sort of. I just wasn't expecting to see him here with Elaine. Never in a million years would I have thought she'd choose him to reinforce the family ties," I scoffed, staring at Clara and wondering what was happening inside her mind. "Are *you* okay though? I told her that his son was responsible for what happened to us at that club two years ago and she shouldn't seek to unite our families." I hesitated. "But there's something else..."

"What is it?" she asked softly.

I sat on the bed next to her and played with her tresses, channeling some comfort in that simple act.

Clara shifted on the bed and looked up at me. "What's wrong?"

"Nothing ... I ... it's just that I think Ivo had sent Emilio to Sputnik that night. Emilio said it, and I let Elaine know."

Clara sat up, panic on her face. "I was so out of it, I didn't hear anything he said…" Her voice sounded so far away.

But she had a right to know. I wanted to avoid any secrets between us, even though I just wanted to protect her.

She bit on her bottom lip. "Why do you think that?" She let her head fall on the sheets, as if exhausted. I hated the fact that Clara kept the pain and grief squashed inside her and refused to let it loose. She should be crying, screaming, protesting.

"Elaine had no idea, and I'm not sure she's convinced. She won't break the engagement, either. Maybe it's not all about business." I couldn't help a pang of resentment and jealousy as I spoke.

This was silly. I shouldn't be feeling this way because Ivo was never mine.

"You like him, don't you? I remember when he came to the house and the way he was looking at you, then you told me about that day in the club with him," Clara said.

"Yeah, but that's water under the bridge. And what matters is your well-being while I'm in New York for work. I've been meaning to ask, maybe you should come and stay with me for a while," I suggested.

She got off the bed and opened the computer.

"I'm fine, sis. You don't have to worry about me. I can handle this," she insisted, but I knew she wasn't being honest with me. "You're the one with a problem. You like Ivo—he'd given you the best sex of your life and this must not be easy for you. Ivo is not his son. Will you let Elaine do this?"

"This is not fair," I said, aware that she was stripping me bare to the bone. Clara was very preceptive and she tended to put other people first. But I knew, what I'd just told her had to affect her. Yet, she acted as though I'd revealed nothing of import. "He's engaged to Elaine and this is the first time I've seen him since the confrontation in the club. I will never forgive him for what he did. Granted, he didn't know about us being there, but he told his crazy son and his man to have their fun. As far as I'm concerned, he's guilty."

Clara wasn't saying anything and I was so done talking about this. If she didn't let me in, what could I do? A wave of powerlessness washed through me—a familiar emotion in the last two years. I needed to get some fresh air but couldn't go back to that party while Ivo was downstairs. I had done my damnedest to hunt Emilio down using my resources, but it seemed as if he'd vanished from the face of the Earth. Someone had helped him to become a ghost.

"I think you're an idiot," Clara insisted. "He's obviously still into you, and again, I just don't buy it that he's the one who did this. From what you told me, you figured out Emilio is a piece of work from the first time you saw him. He's a manipulator. I have no idea why Ivo's marrying Elaine, but you could convince him it's a bad idea." She smiled. "Stay out of my head. I'm going to be fine, and I don't need you fawning over me. Just do something, for goodness' sake, before you blow this."

She sounded like Tasha. I didn't want to listen to this anymore. It shocked me that she managed to divert all the attention to me. Shaking my head, I asked her if she wanted a drink, but she declined, so I left her room and went back downstairs to get me one—I needed something strong, even if I risked coming face-to-face with Ivo. Clara looked like she couldn't wait to get me out of her sight.

When I went downstairs, I did my best to avoid Elaine and

Ivo. Asking the bartender to pour me a glass of wine, I headed to the garden. Just when I was wondering why Tasha hadn't shown up yet, and how I wished I could just fly away from here, a voice pulled me from my deliberations.

"What's the matter with you, princess?"

I turned to see Gregory approaching. He didn't look great—his face and hands were riddled with scars, and his eyes didn't have the usual spark. On top of that, he was using a cane to move around.

"Nothing worth talking about. What are you even doing here? It seems your dad isn't too pleased with your presence."

Gregory smiled. I truly liked him. He was not at all like his brother.

"He wanted me to look after club. He likes keeping me in the dark." He laughed. "But it looked like that you were surprised, too. You stepmother didn't tell you about this?"

"No. She let us know she got engaged but didn't say to whom," I explained. "She likes drama, I suppose."

"Well, I guess we're both seeing some changes in our lives," he said, sounding a little sad. Those Russians had really done a number on him. It wasn't fair that good guys had to suffer but the bad guys got away.

"I guess we do," I said with a sigh, then downed my entire glass of wine at once. In that moment, I needed it more than air.

Chapter Twelve

Ivo

Everything went badly, but as I expected. I watched from a distance how Gregory was interacting with my Merry. I shouldn't have been jealous because there was nothing between them, but I couldn't help myself. I wished she'd be so comfortable with me.

Emilio knew I'd kill him as soon as he came out of hiding. He was my son, and I'd loved his mother once upon a time, but she'd abandoned him at an early age and went back to Bulgaria. Maybe that was why he had so many issues.

"So, was it you who'd sent Emilio and his men to the club where the girls were raped?" Elaine asked me point blank when she approached me a moment later.

"Yes, but I had no idea that Merry and Clara were in that club. I made a huge mistake trusting my psychotic son," I told her, taking a sip of whiskey. We were done with introductions and despite the little hiccup in the beginning with Merry, Elaine seemed pleased with this party.

I had never been leery of any woman before but there was something about Elaine had me on edge. Her bossiness and general attitude irked me. The sex was fine—she knew exactly what expect from me in the bedroom—but she'd never be Merry. If I'd harbored any hope Merry would stop hating me after what Emilio did, I would have done things differently. I'd have claimed her for myself, and Elaine would have never been a possibility.

But now, it was up to me to clean up the mess. I wasn't covering for Emilio. I was handling the chaos he left behind, stopping the shit from hitting the fan.

Tonight, when I saw Merry, I wasn't so sure she didn't feel anything for me anymore.

When I got close to her, let my breath caress her face, felt her body so close ... I knew.

I knew that what we once had wasn't lost.

But hate was a powerful thing...

"Merry is worried about Clara and Emilio is still nowhere to be found," she said.

"So, what do you want me to do, Elaine? Merry is thirsty. She wants vengeance and I am not surprised, nor do I blame her," I said, fury and guilt having a field day inside me. Emilio had touched what was mine because he wanted to have a swing at me. He hated that I took her for myself in that club, because he came out of that experience looking like a fool.

When Emilio had given me the low down on the Sputnik

incident, enjoying every moment as he described the horrors he'd caused, I had to think hard about how to proceed.

Sometime later, I had a few trusted men round up CJ, Jack, and Tank, and I executed them myself. Emilio disappeared then. No matter what I did, though, it wouldn't erase the past, or my part in it. Merry was still furious and disappointed with me, and she had a permanent mark on her face to show for it.

Elaine sighed. "Nothing. I'll deal with it, darling. You just keep your men in line. We need to discuss the wedding plans right now," she said. She grabbed my tie and started dragging me upstairs just when Merry glanced up and saw us. Fuck, I felt like a trapped animal and suddenly wanted to get out of there.

With Merry.

* * *

Two weeks had passed since my engagement party at Elaine's, and we had a few promising meetings with the Russians, who approved of the union. My mother was born in Bucharest to both Russian parents. She had never called herself anything else. She brought me up speaking the language that later on save my life. That was the only reason why Victor hadn't killed me yet, because Russian blood ran in my veins.

After our conflict started, the place I owned, Club Top D—where I'd met Merry and gave her the first orgasm she'd ever experienced with a man—was burned to the ground. They didn't like that I'd broken off my engagement to their most precious princess, Anika. Her family was furious and felt betrayed, and then this whole war between us started. With

Anika, I was trying to act like a decent man, letting her be with a man she loved.

It seemed as though women would be the death of me yet, or at least leave me to deal with a catastrophe. Broken engagements, unrequited desire, drama ... it was all too much.

The Russians wouldn't kill me then, but they did get a few of my men and injured Gregory, who ended up in a coma. Furious and desperate, I ordered the retaliation, thinking that Victor would back off from trying anything else. But it only made the situation worse because there was no closure to be had.

I finally managed to acquire a new club that had been opened now for a few months, but I hadn't seen Merry since the engagement party. Elaine mentioned that she'd gone back to New York and had no intention of coming back, which surprised me since Clara was still here and she wouldn't leave her sister permanently.

Nonetheless, Merry intended to relocate, perhaps because she was running away from me. The truth was that I didn't see myself being married to her stepmother. Not now that Merry and I had locked gazes and I could look deep into her soul to see the truth she'd buried deep inside. She *cared* ... and loathed herself for it.

No matter what I did, what I made her do, she'd lose a part of herself in the process.

At this point, I had a responsibility to minimize risks for everyone. An all-out war or even extended hostilities were not in my books, and I wanted to bring peace among the families because Emilio's actions taught me I didn't want to live this life forever.

Elaine had ruled the roost for a few years now and she was a proud woman in search of more power and influence. A marriage with me, now the head of the Bulgarian mafia in this territory, however small a group, would be a show of strength, for both of us. In our world, a truce was often triggered by fear of another person's reach. This was something I couldn't get away from at this time.

As I drove to my club, I took a call from Elaine who wanted to talk to me about flower arrangements. At least, she didn't mention my moving into her home, which she brought up more often lately. I just wasn't ready for that.

Then, the discussion somehow shifted to Merry—her doing, because I tried my best not to discuss her with her stepmother. Elaine could never hold a candle to her, and I never wanted my bias to show.

"I think soon enough, Merry won't be a problem. She'll probably have her wedding with Robert to plan anyway—a lawyer who works in the same firm she's with—if things keep going the way they're going. He's a junior partner, you know. He's going places. This will keep her occupied for a while," she said dismissively.

Elaine couldn't be serious. Merry couldn't be ready to tie the knot, too. I breathed in, ignoring the sudden, stabbing sensation in my stomach.

Elaine was ambitious and in charge, and I bet she was pushing Merry to get married—this man, Robert, must have something she wanted. Was he connected? What did he have that she could use? With me, she had access to Victor, a ruthless don who was usually hard to deal with, and this could open many doors for her. Elaine wasn't playing.

"And is that lawyer connected to the family in any way?" I questioned, trying to keep my voice even.

She laughed.

"No, he's not, but Merry had been looking for a way out for a while now. I was planning to set her up with one of my cousins, but she flat-out refused. So, even if she's pulling away, I'd have access to good legal representation as this is one of the top criminal and civil law firms in the United States. She owes me that, at least. On the other hand, Clara is still not ready, but she's too much like her father. I'll do well with her. She understands the family values and will do exactly as I ask when the time comes," Elaine said, and I gripped the phone tighter.

This wasn't going to happen. Over my dead fucking body… Merry wasn't going to marry some fancy lawyer from New York. She was fucking mine.

"Are you spending the night with me, Ivo? I miss your cock," she added with a sigh.

The proposition made me ill right now.

"Not tonight. I have a busy night in the club. I'll talk to you later because I just made it here." I got off the call and parked the car, spotting a bunch of people gathered outside, along with at least three police cars.

"There are cops everywhere, boss. Do you want me to turn around?" Ryga asked, seeming to materialize out of thin air. "I was about to call you."

I noticed five cops hanging around talking to a few of my staff. A sense of dread filled me. *What now?*

"No, I need to see what's going on. Stay here," I told him, then got out of the car.

I spotted the woman in the distance—Detective Lucinda

Morales. I knew she was here because of Emilio. I'd met her before. The bane of my existence, she showed up periodically, still thinking I had information about his whereabouts.

"Detective Morales, it's a pleasure to see you again," I lied as I approached her, giving her a dashing smile.

She narrowed her eyes on me and said something to the cop standing by the door.

"Mr. Sergei, it's great for you to join us. I believe you're the owner of this establishment?" she asked with a sneer.

My pulse sped up because Morales wouldn't just show up here without a reason.

"You know I am, Detective. What's this about?" I asked.

"Mr. Sergei, my men found a large amount of cocaine in your club. This doesn't look good for you," she said, pulling out a set of handcuffs and dangling them from her fingers. Oh, she was enjoying this.

I'd been so careful, always making sure the club was clean, including last night. Gregory was in charge of distribution, but he rarely met people in the establishment. Someone had framed me, no doubt about it.

"I don't know how you'd think that because I don't deal in drugs," I assured her. I looked around at the gathering crowd and my heart sank.

"Well, the evidence shows different. Ivo Sergei, you are under arrest for drug possession. Anything you say or do may be used against you in a court of law..."

As she read me my rights and put me in the back of one of the police cars, my blood pounded in my veins. They must have gotten there on a tip, and Morales for sure couldn't contain her excitement because she'd like nothing more than to lock me up and throw away the key. For a while, she'd suspected my involvement in certain activities and catching me red-handed would be a big notch in her belt.

Once I found out who did this, I was going to tear them limb from limb.

Throughout the drive, I wondered if I had landed in a nightmare without end.

Once at the station, I was thrown in a holding cell. I leaned my head against the chipped wall, and released a silent curse.

Guess the shit *was* hitting the fan now.

* * *

Merry

"Just let it go to voicemail. We haven't spent any time together in the past week," Robert complained when I reached out for my phone. I noticed Elaine's number flashing on the screen. We'd just made it to bed after a long day, and he was being frisky tonight. I wasn't in the mood.

"I'm sorry, hon, but this is my stepmother. I have a feeling this might be important," I said, giving him a peck on the lips and getting up. He growled in disapproval and I gave him an apologetic look. I spoke to Elaine briefly, then ended the call. "I need to book a flight to California. It's my sister." Apparently, Clara was in trouble, and my stepmother couldn't—or wouldn't—deal with it. She wouldn't give me any details, either.

Robert released a breath. "Okay, how long are you staying away?"

"Can't say." I sat down on the bed and grabbed his hand. "I'm guessing just a few days. I'll make it up to you, okay?"

"You better." He grinned. "I'll hold the fort at work, even though you're the better attorney."

I swatted him on the arm. "Stop it! *You* are the junior partner, not me."

"What? That's because I've been there longer. But what I say is true. You haven't lost a case since you started working for the firm."

"But you're kickass, too. Business law is a minefield."

"Yeah, yeah. Go on now," he said, playfully waving me off.

Robert was a nice guy and he treated me well. He cared for me and showed it—I couldn't do any better than him, I kept telling myself. Besides, it was time to move on, to make a life for myself, and Robert wanted to have a family. So, as I sat here, looking down at him, why did I not feel anything? I was missing the thrill, the spark of energy I'd experienced with Ivo.

Maybe love wasn't supposed to be a tidal wave under stormy skies—just calm waters on a summer day.

I leaned down and kissed him, slow and easy, taking my time. The sex with him was good, and he was a skilled, giving lover. If only I could feel the butterflies—just the butterflies... and if only I could surrender to the pleasure and climax when I was with him. Just like before Ivo, the same problem plagued me. I couldn't reach orgasm with any man, and that included Robert. I was the queen of faking it.

Only Ivo had ever breached that wall. Could I live with the fact I'd likely never meet anyone to make me feel the same way? I had to move on, and Robert was here for the taking. Either that, or keep searching. Good things come to those who don't give up.

"Go before I make you stay in bed for a couple more hours," he urged with a laugh and a light spank on my ass.

"Fine." I giggled.

Going to my laptop, I booked my flight back to California for later that day. I packed a carry-on and soon, I was heading out.

It was late afternoon when I arrived home, filled with worry. Luckily, the firm in New York allowed me to work remotely. Besides, Elaine was a client, so I had to be available to her for advice on gray-area activities when needed. I hated doing business with the family, but when I joined the firm, the arrangement was set up for me to gain experience while bringing a new client in. As much as I wanted to cut ties to a point, Elaine wouldn't trust many people with her affairs.

I left my carry-on by the door and found Elaine. "Is Clara okay? Where is she?" I asked, ready to go up to her room. I needed a shower but that was just going to have to wait.

"Oh, I'm glad you're here. I've been so anxious. I didn't want to call anyone else," my stepmother greeted me, nervously wringing her hands.

"What happened? Where is Clara?" I asked again, my heart pounding inside my chest.

The house was so quiet, and that unnerved me all the more. Elaine was dressed in a business suit, well put together as always, her face impeccably made up as though she was about to step into a soap opera ... but that didn't calm me any.

"Don't be angry with me, but this isn't exactly about Clara.

She's all right. She's in the office working as usual," she explained.

"What the hell, Elaine? What do you mean? So I flew over here for nothing?" I was about to lose my shit, what with all the worry I'd felt coming all the way here, and all the various doomsday scenarios playing out in my head. I imagined the worst had happened to Clara and by the time I got here, I'd reduced myself to an emotional mess.

"Well, I knew you wouldn't have come if I said the truth. I need your help. Ivo's been arrested and you must get him out."

Chapter Thirteen

Merry

Elaine had dragged me all the way back to Los Angeles because of Ivo. I was shaking, and had a hell of a time trying to stop myself from slapping the shit out of her. She had me drop everything for the man who was responsible for my sister's misery.

"I can't believe this," I snapped, turning around and starting to head back out. I would not be treated like a pawn, a puppet to do with as she pleased.

"Wait, Merry. Please." Something in her tone made me stop and face her. "We both know I can't call anyone else. Your father's attorney passed away, and I don't have anyone else I trust," she said desperately.

I'd never seen Elaine so wound up. In the mafia world, she was a ruthless queen with ambition to sell. Although I barely tolerated her at times, and she'd never been a warm, motherly figure in our lives, the truth was that she always treated me and my sister well—as long as we didn't cross her. When my father died with no siblings or close kin, she fought tooth and nail to gain respect and take over his responsibilities, but her games were so tiresome—especially when she played them at my expense.

I sighed. Elaine was justified in not wanting to involve outsiders she didn't trust. Now the clincher was: how could I do this without getting close to Ivo? That would prove impossible.

"I can recommend a great, trustworthy attorney who could handle this case. I already said I'd prefer that you start searching for another lawyer to work with you. You assured me you would," I said.

She looked away, folding her arms around her chest, and sighed.

"I know ... and I will. I've been so distracted," she explained, and I rolled my eyes. I knew she was just stalling. She wanted to keep me tied to the family. A slave of the business, forever. That was the way I saw it, anyway. "And it would be good for you to stay for a few days. Clara would love to see you. She has been a little absent lately and needs a little cheering up."

Elaine knew just what to say to make me do what she wanted, and in this case, it meant having me stay by using my love for my sister to her advantage.

"Of course she feels that way. She refuses more therapy and now, you're bringing one of the people who caused her trauma in this house. Even though she acts like it's fine, Ivo will always remind her of Emilio and what he did to her!" I shouted, dangerously approaching the point of no return. I hated being manipulated.

"All right, calm down," she said impatiently, and that only riled me up more. Yet, I bit my tongue and kept my mouth shut lest I burst a vein somewhere in my body. "Just please, see what you can find out to get him out on bail or something. He told me that his club was raided and they found drugs. Apparently, the detective in charge is under pressure to put someone behind bars, so she is making an example of Ivo," Elaine explained.

"This sort of case isn't a wham-bam kind of deal, Elaine. It takes time I don't have. I have to go back to New York," I stated, grabbing my suitcase and practically racing outside. I walked around to the garage and got in my car to call a cab, so flustered I couldn't think straight.

I knew that I should do something to help, and maybe in the process, I could find Emilio and finally bring him to justice. In my past research, I'd discovered that the other men who abused us—Jack, who forced me to blow him, and the other two—had been found dead. Emilio though was as elusive as ever.

If only I could set aside my pain and disgust … even my treacherous attraction to Ivo, it might bring us some closure.

Then again, if Ivo remained locked up, Elaine would be forced to put her wedding plans on hold…

A moment later, I got a text message from Elaine.

Clara will have to bear the consequences of your actions if you won't help. Sort it out. Ivo's being held at the West LA police dept

. . .

I hid my face in my palms, trying to breathe. Elaine might be amenable but once you denied her something, she'd turn into a raving bitch. She could make Clara's life a living hell if she wanted to, and if I left today, whatever happened would be squarely on my shoulders. Texting her an 'ok, talk later,' I drove to my apartment five miles away to shower and change, as well as steel myself to deal with the Ivo situation.

I was glad I'd kept my place that I'd bought a year ago, as well as a well-stocked wardrobe, here in LA. I needed a private spot where I didn't have to be constantly bombarded by family-related issues. I smiled because if Dad had still been alive, he'd never have wanted me to live outside the family home. He'd been such a traditionalist. In a sense, I had more freedom now, but I missed him, still.

Then, when I found the job in NYC, I met Robert, and it looked like my new life would take me thousands of miles away from the Camilleri stronghold. I'd have been happy with that, were it not for my sister.

I wondered if Ivo was going to accept my help. He probably had his own lawyer, unless Elaine had already told him about me, which I doubted.

I stood in front of the bathroom mirror, brooding. "You can do this. Just treat him like a client and there won't be an issue." I'd put on one of my favorite classic outfits—a fine black pencil skirt with matching blazer and white blouse. Simple and elegant, clothes like this always made me feel in charge, especially when I had to deal with crap in the courtroom.

This was the new me—confident, no nonsense yet emphatic. I was proud of how far I'd come, and I had to remember that. With what happened, the odds had been against me. Underneath these layers, I was still the nerdy, self-conscious girl who worried too much, but each day I made a conscious effort to be great. To grow tougher skin. And when I was out there, fighting for my clients, it worked. I was good at my job.

Through traffic, it took me a minute to get to the police station. If he didn't make bail, Ivo would likely be transferred to a prison, awaiting his case to go to trial. First, I had to go through his file, which I'd already requested, and have a chat with him—the last thing I wanted to do. I had already scanned through some information that was emailed to me.

"I'm Ivo's Sergei's attorney, and I'm here to speak with him," I said to the officer who greeted me at the desk.

After a short wait, another cop led me downstairs to where I assumed Ivo would be waiting. When we reached a door, he whispered, "I know Ivo's innocent. I know him. Take all the time you need ... in privacy." With a wink, he disappeared down the hallway, leaving me stumped. I shouldn't be surprised though. People like Ivo would have allies within police ranks, favors to cash in on—that was essential for survival.

I entered the interview room, which was pretty small and dimly lit. Cameras were hooked on a couple of walls, but I'd hazard a guess there'd be no one checking out our interaction. The officer I'd just met had likely taken care of that.

My stomach was in knots, and I couldn't deny now that I'd wanted to see Ivo so much. That I'd missed him so much. But there was the other matter of me hating him. And of him being with my stepmother.

I was slowly losing my mind. Just me being here was proof of that.

Ivo was sitting on one of the chairs and when he saw me, his eyes widened in surprise. I tamped down the yearning that suddenly took hold of me. *No.* This was not the time, place, or lifetime...

He stood. "Merry? What the hell are you doing here? I was expecting my lawyer."

I walked towards him, my high heels clicking on the floor.

"It seems I'm representing you now, Ivo. Elaine sent me here, so let's get on with this," I told him, placing my briefcase on the table. His gaze pinned me down, stripping every layer of resolve I'd built, but I put up a hell of a fight. I forced myself to smile. Ivo needed to understand that he was just a client now. What happened between us in the past didn't matter.

Reaching out, he pulled a chair out for me to sit on. His tall, ripped body towered over me, and with him so near, he almost stole my breath away.

"Thanks," I muttered, folding my fingers together. "Elaine explained what happened, and I am privy to a few details about the case, but tell me, have they questioned you yet?"

He didn't answer. Instead, he stared at me, looking a little lost and also a tad ... amused. I had a problem trying to concentrate on the matter at hand, and not on him. I pulled out a pen and pad from my briefcase and put them on the table, busying myself as the tension mounted. Meanwhile, he just kept staring at me as though counting every freckle on my face.

Focus, Merry. Focus.

"Why are you looking at me like that?" I finally asked in annoyance. Did he not care that he was in trouble?

"What are you doing here, Merry?" he asked again. "I thought you were back in New York, trying to create a new life with your man, Robert," he asked, and I didn't miss the mockery in his tone as he mentioned my boyfriend's name.

"Trust me, I'd rather be there but Elaine had me come here under false pretenses ... and let's just say she asked me to help you," I said, tapping my heel. Surely, he'd figure out that 'asked' was not the word to describe what she said.

He tilted his head to the side and glanced at my lips. And just like that, he struck a fire within me, flickering, spreading...

"Does he make you come like I did?"

A simple question I couldn't answer because he blindsided me. We weren't supposed to discuss this—*ever*.

As much as I made a living from words, there was not a one that made it to my lips in that moment, and for a short while, I couldn't even find my brain.

No, I haven't had an orgasm since you...

Of course, I'd never admit this out loud.

"So, Ivo, do you want to get out on bail or not?" I asked, attempting to sound firm, but my voice was shaky.

He could read me so well, so he smirked.

"I thought so, and I bet you're fucking wet now, just longing for my tongue to work you up into a frenzy," he rasped, leaning closer.

I flinched and lifted my eyes to his. Holy shit. I was in trouble. But he always knew how to flick on that switch inside me. It was like he was built for me.

I stood quickly and hooked a stray strand of hair behind my ear. "You're unbelievable. Do you realize your life is at stake here? You can go to prison for a long time," I snapped, feeling flushed, angry, and so damn frustrated.

He still didn't give me an answer, but got to his feet and put his hands on my waist, then pushed me against the table.

"And you smell absolutely unbelievable, princess. Daddy really missed you," he whispered in my ear the very word that sent a tremor through my core. I hadn't heard it in years—he was the only lover I'd called Daddy, and it had come so naturally then.

All the memories from my short time with him flashed through my mind and I became increasingly conscious of his hands on me, his body so close to mine.

I remembered how he made me feel, and how that would never change. I knew that now. I could say I hated him, I could say this was forbidden ... but none of that changed the truth of my desire for him. There never was anyone like him, and there never would be.

He gave my ear a little nip. "Call me Daddy again," he ordered in a low, deep tone.

"Ivo..."

"Princess, do it."

"No."

He trailed his hands up my torso, bringing them to just under my breasts, teasing. His breath warmed my face, and the scent of his cologne drove me wild. Something broke inside me. Years of restraint, resentment, and fear. Years without *him*, the man who'd unlocked my heart.

I'd pursued my life as I thought I wanted, yet, I never could have imagined that being without him would bring so much emptiness.

Why did he have to come back?

Why Elaine?

But right this moment, there was just me and him. We were in a bubble, and this was my world. Back to that time at Club Top D, skin to skin, bodies ablaze.

I weakly attempted to push him away but my heart wasn't in it. A tiny sob made it past my lips, and my eyes stung. "Why?" I mustered, my voice breaking.

"Because I can't fucking forget you," he said. With that, he brought his lips to mine and kissed me hard, taking all that I could give.

He coaxed my legs apart with his and set me on fire, devouring me like a starved man.

That was it. I was lost all self-control because my senses were overwhelmed. My mind was screaming at me to push him away, but my heart launched itself against my ribs, beating so fast and urging me to cling to him.

His deft fingers worked to push my skirt up my thighs.

"Ivo," I gasped against his mouth.

"Daddy," he corrected, now kissing my neck and grabbing my ass as though he couldn't get enough. His nails dug into my skin, and his passion wrapped itself around me, leaving me no room for escape.

Not that I wanted to.

"No, I won't say it," I insisted. At least I still had two lucid cells to rub together.

"You will," he grunted. "I missed you so fucking much..." Sticking his head in my cleavage, he started licking the sensitive skin over my breasts. His thumb brushed over my lace panties, over the pulsating center. I sucked in another desperate breath, for God help me, I *needed* him to touch me there, and I needed him to do it now. To make me come again, to make me fall apart like only he knew how.

I throbbed for him, drenched, wanting as he grazed my most intimate spots, knowing damn well what he was doing.

I had to have more. Thirsted for more.

I told myself that I had to stop him, that anyone could walk in on us anytime, but it was too fucking late.

I was grasping for purchase, past the point of no return, and the most horrifying thing was ... this man who flipped my world upside down belonged to my stepmother.

Chapter Fourteen

Ivo

This had to be a dream. It couldn't possibly be happening for real. Merry was here and I was touching her silky skin, licking her hardened nipples like the world's most addictive gelato. This was risky and fucking wrong but I couldn't stop myself when she was standing so close, driving me crazy with her incredible scent ... and just being Merry.

Always my Merry.

Mine.

I knew she was wet the moment she started asking me questions and when I ran my finger over her pussy, I had my confirmation. She was fucking soaking wet for her daddy already. My cock was hard as a rock, but I was a little nervous thinking that anyone could interrupt us *in flagrante delicto*.

I just couldn't fucking keep my hands off her.

Couldn't stay away.

Seeing her had triggered my inner beast. I wasn't expecting to see Merry here today for I thought Elaine had made other arrangements with my people. But one look at her and all of a sudden, all the restraint we were supposed to have around each other didn't matter one bit. Not just that: it was futile.

And now, I was planning to make her explode in my arms like her supposed fiancé never had. She didn't need to admit to anything. I knew he couldn't make her come because her body only responded to me, and me alone.

Again, she was mine.

No one else knew how to push her buttons, what she felt deep within. We had a direct line of communication—heart to heart. This was meant to be, and in that moment, I felt like a jerk for ever agreeing to this union with her own stepmother. Subconsciously, I wanted to be close to her. But at what cost? What was I thinking? No matter how I looked at it, I lost something I couldn't put a price on.

I had to ask myself, was I prepared to lose Merry?

Right now, I had her in my arms again and wouldn't let her go. Claiming her lips again, I lowered her body on the table. She fought with me, pretending that seeing me didn't faze her, but I knew fucking better. Then, I released her lips and took her hardened nipple into my mouth, biting on it until she cried out, so I put a hand over her mouth to muffle the noise.

"Ivo, please, you have to—" she mumbled through the muzzle of my palm.

A muted moan escaped her mouth as I slipped two fingers into her sweet pussy, while continuing to suck on her nipples. I wanted to feast on her, but we didn't have much time. Soon, someone would come to let us know our time was up.

Her sweet scent was driving me insane.

I finger-fucked her for a little while until she was gasping for breath. The sounds of her muffled moans were like the most beautiful music. A moment later, I pulled out my fingers, and went down on my knees, also freeing her mouth.

"Be quiet now," I instructed, and she nodded, her cheeks flushed and her pupils dilated, her chest rising and falling with her fast, choppy breaths. She was putty in my hands.

Holding on tight, I dragged her sexy skirt up over her hips and pushed her panties aside, then dove my face right between her thighs.

Twisted as I was, I'd always wanted to fuck someone in prison, or role-play as a prison guard or inmate. This wasn't exactly that, but close enough.

I was going to devour Merry's pussy—and the thrill of it just made me so fucking hard, my dick hurt.

"What are you doing?" she asked breathlessly. I lifted my gaze to find her staring down at me with her lips slightly parted. Her shirt was open, her bra pulled down to reveal her perky, hard nipples. What a gorgeous picture she made.

"Daddy is pleasing his princess," I said. I didn't care that I was pleasing a woman who claimed she hated me more than my worst enemy. Our jaded past brought us closer, but also created a wall between us. Somehow, we had to move past that, because no matter what, Merry was always going to belong to me.

I quickly gripped her lacy white underwear and slid them off her. I had to eat her before she came fully to her senses, to make her come here and now. "And again, I want you to be fucking quiet. Otherwise, we'll be in big trouble. Well, I might be in trouble more than you."

She opened her mouth to probably tell me to get off her, so before she could speak, I pushed her in a more comfortable position on the table and went to work on her pussy. I was hungry, and so turned on by the scent of her arousal, I got light-headed.

I was going to regret this later, but right now, all I wanted was to please her. Getting a firm hold on her thighs, I started licking her, opening her legs wider for me. She moaned, dragging her hands to my hair and pulling hard.

My cock went impossibly harder.

I licked her all the way from her ass to her clit, then slid my tongue inside her. She was soaking wet, moaning faintly and begging me to stop. Merry wasn't easy to please but after the night in the club, I knew exactly what to do in order to make her explode. I pushed my tongue in and out of her until her hips started to tremble. Then, I brought a hand to her pussy and inserted two fingers, while I kept my mouth and tongue on her clit.

She smelled like vanilla and roses, twisting her ass on the table as she tried to keep from screaming for me. Her juices coated my hand. I imagined her sinking into my cock, riding me and coming apart like she had never before.

"Ivo! Shit, I think I'm going to—" she murmured.

"Come?" I asked, pulling away from her for just a second so I could look at her.

Her face was red and tense, her eyes gleaming with desire and need. She wanted this and I didn't care how much she was going to deny it later. She wanted me to fuck her any way I wanted, so I kept on going.

I pumped my fingers in and out of her, picking up the pace and hitting that G-spot. She shut her eyes, and her breasts bounced as I thrust hard and fast until the pressure rose to breaking point inside her core.

I sucked on her clit as though we only had seconds left and the world was about to end. She gave a keening moan, and I could tell she was trying hard not to make a ruckus. She begged me not to stop, to go on sucking, fucking, loving her … until her body convulsed in pure ecstasy.

She gripped my hair so tight, for a second I lost my balance. She climaxed, drawing long, shuddering breaths. Her body shook uncontrollably and she bit hard on her bottom lip, pained grunts escaping her lips as she tried not to scream. I loved the way she looked, deliciously unraveled, just for me.

I finally stopped licking her, feeling like a kid at Christmas to have watched her orgasm so intensely once more.

She dragged her hand over her now messy hair, finally opening her eyes and staring at me with appreciation and acceptance—in that special, fleeting moment, we shared something. We understood each other, back where it all started, back in my club.

"You still taste and feel unbelievable, Merry," I said, licking my fingers and relishing her taste.

A shadow of annoyance passed through her eyes and then, she started tidying herself up, stuffing her breasts back in her lacy bra and buttoning her shirt. I craved her, ready to explode in my pants.

"This doesn't change anything, you jerk," she snapped

jumping off the table and quickly picking her panties off the floor.

And just like that, the magic was gone. I laughed out loud, attempting to stand up, but it took a minute for my knees were numb.

The problem with any challenge, physical or otherwise, was to never give up.

We had issues that we both needed to solve, but I would not stop pursuing her. I knew this now with a clarity I somehow didn't possess before. She was my brightest light. I just couldn't let her go.

This wasn't a simple problem, but a clusterfuck times a hundred.

"I'm sorry, Merry. I apologized countless times, but no matter what I do, I can't change the past. Emilio is going to pay. I'll hunt him down myself—"

"And then what?" she asked, pushing her skirt in place. All of a sudden, she was presentable again and she had that hard look on her face that told me she was done being the Merry I once knew. "You're going to kill him? Your own son? Don't be fucking stupid."

"We don't have to talk about it. You came here to help me, so let's focus on that. You caught me off guard. I wasn't expecting to see you here, but admit it, there's still something between us. Or what we had was never gone..." I said, raking my fingers through my hair while sitting down on my chair.

She shook her head and did the same, now fully composed.

"Just don't touch me again. You're *engaged* to my stepmother and I'm your *attorney*," she said, stressing those words in a manner that brooked no argument. She looked down at her papers, probably to gather her wits.

I really did just rock her world if I said so myself. Smirking, I put my hands behind my head and caught her glance at me through her thick eyelashes.

"Yes, Ms. Camilleri. Want to talk about my case? Here we go. Someone planted those drugs at my club—Club P—and then set me up. I bet Victor is behind this. He acts like there's a truce between us and all, especially with me marrying Elaine and her smoothing things out … but they're still trying to teach me a lesson. They've bided their time, but now here I am," I said, opening my arms wide. "In the slammer. Second best to six feet under, I suppose."

We stared at each other. I wondered how I was going to wriggle out of this fucked-up situation, while she was likely sizing me up, figuring out if I was telling the truth. Her gaze pierced mine, and I gave her the space she needed. In the end, she gave a small nod and jotted down something in her pad.

I let out a ragged breath. I had faith in her professional abilities, but this was not merely about skill. If they didn't get me in one way, they'd get me in another. That was how these things worked. They might not kill me, but they'd try to ruin me. Emilio's actions affected all of us.

My only way out was to find him and deal with him.

"You need to write down the names of the people you believe might be working against you. The police have the CCTV footage, but I'm not sure how good it is. We need solid evidence and, in the meantime, I'm going to try to get you out on bail," she explained, then started putting all the paperwork back in her bag.

She was the picture of professional competence. So hot, also because it was genuine.

Merry was a badass in the courtroom, from what I'd heard. Maybe one day I'd get to fuck her in one...

"That's great, princess, but where do you think you're going?" I asked, staring at her lips.

She detested me for good reason, and I had to perform miracles to win her back.

"I just needed to make sure you're okay and get more insight. Now, I can dive into this case with an open mind," she said, giving me a small smile. "But what happened earlier is not going to happen again. I'm not the shy, insecure Merry anymore. I'm in a committed relationship now."

I smirked at her as heat crawled over my raging hard on. I was going to have to take care of this in my cell later. Damn it.

"Keep telling yourself that if you want, but what I'm about to say will sink in someday, princess," I growled. I leaned in, placing my elbows on the table and bringing my face close to hers. "He can't make you come like I can and I don't believe you want stay miserable for the rest of your life."

Anger clouded her features, taking centerstage. I must have hit a nerve because she glared at me.

"Once I get you out on bail, you can find yourself another attorney," she snapped, then got up and left the room without a backward glance, her heels clicking with each step.

I pressed my hand over my dick, trying to still the throbbing. I needed a cold shower now, or I'd go out of my mind.

Carl, the cop who'd brought Merry over, walked in a moment later and took me back to my cell. As I thanked him, he glanced at my hard on and smirked, then took me back to my cell.

The anger I'd felt that morning had been washed away and suddenly, the day from hell had turned into one of the best in my life, just because of her.

* * *

Merry

I woke up with a headache several hours later and it was still dark outside. Yesterday, my emotions took over and I let Ivo take control of the situation. That was a mistake. Now, the milk was already spilled and I didn't know what to do with myself.

I called a few of Ivo's most trusted men and I would be meeting Ryga at Club P later on in the day because he said he had some information that could help his boss. It was going to be closed to the public for a while because of the ongoing investigation. I was confident that I could get him out on bail. He had no previous criminal record for drug possession. He'd been careful to keep his nose clean, although his involvement with the mafia wasn't exactly top secret. Besides, he had allies on the force. I simply had to know which path to tread.

Elaine texted me to thank me for taking on the case. She was full of bullshit because she'd given me no choice. Of course, I regretted caving in. He'd played my body like a violin, a feat Robert hadn't been able to achieve in the time we'd been together. All right, Ivo knew what I liked in the bedroom, bringing me the stars and the moon and then some, but I wasn't ready to give up on my boyfriend just yet.

Just thinking about it sent pleasure ripping through me. When I came, my legs felt like jelly and I could barely make myself walk out of that room. Ivo could read me so well and I should have stopped him, but I couldn't. I hated him for having such a hold on my feelings, for this was so wrong in every respect.

I sighed loudly and went back to sleep for a few more hours. Then, in the morning, I took a quick shower. I had an hour before my meeting with Ryga, which I hoped would be fruitful. Once Ivo was out on bail, and I made sure Clara was okay for now, I'd get on the first plane back to New York. Ivo would have enough time to find himself a new attorney—maybe his friend, Killian, who I'd heard Elaine mention once. Officially, this would no longer be my problem.

Half an hour later, I was pulling outside the club and still thinking about that asshole. He made my heart beat faster and confused the hell out of me, causing me to question everything, but apart from any other problem, he was engaged to my stepmother. Elaine had him in her clutches, and there was no way out of there.

No way for us to go.

Chapter Fifteen

Merry

I was let into the club by a young woman and checked out the place as I waited. Since the police had taken the evidence, it had been cleaned up. The interior looked well put together, and it was clear Ivo had done well after the loss of his previous business. It looked even better than his old club.

I was still a bit apprehensive about this whole thing, especially after going through all the evidence described in the file last night. I still had to sift through much of the CCTV footage, but from the description on the file, there was nothing to see, and there were no witnesses. Whoever had done this had hidden their tracks well.

To make things worse, that Detective Morales seemed out to get Ivo, and I still hadn't spoken to her in person yet, only on the phone. This could bring more wrenches in the game. I remembered my father saying how it was easier to buy off politicians than cops, and I had no doubt there was truth in that statement. Besides, I wanted to get Ivo freed not through bribes, but a solid case.

There was also a warrant out for Emilio's arrest. Maybe Morales believed Ivo was protecting him. What if he had something to do with this?

The woman returned and asked me to follow her through a door that led to another section of the club, with a bar and a stage. A few of Ivo's men, including Gregory, sat at the bar. I waved to him and he acknowledged me as I walked past them, up the stairs. At this point, I felt like I'd been transported back in time. This area, and even some parts of the club itself, looked a lot like of Club Top D. Images flooded back to the forefront of my mind of all the deliciously dirty, filthy moments I'd spent with Ivo there, and all the things he'd done to me.

I ended up in a small room at the end of the corridor on the first floor. Ryga, a bulky Bulgarian guy with a bald head and beady grey eyes, was squeezed on the small chair inside something the size of a storage closet. He smiled when I entered.

"Ms. Camilleri, I'm so glad you're here," he said when we were alone. This room was suffocating and cramped—not the best place to have a meeting, but I wasn't going to complain.

"Hey, Ryga, I take it you wanted to show me something," I asked, sitting down on a small folding chair set against the wall.

"I installed another camera downstairs a few months ago. Even Boss doesn't know about it," Ryga explained, grinning at me, and I wondered why he didn't tell Ivo about it. I stood and went around the desk, negotiating my way past a pile of boxes, to stand near him, facing the computer screen.

"So, presumably, the police don't have what you're just about to show me," I said, and he nodded.

"No, Molares was snooping here all afternoon yesterday but no one tried to get inside this room. I made it look like a storage space, and the police had already searched it anyway. I had the laptop safe at home," he replied, moving the mouse. The monitor he had the laptop connected to was dusty and several more boxes were piled up around us. "I don't trust that bitch, Morales, and I wouldn't put it past her to destroy good evidence to keep Ivo locked up. You can get it in the right hands."

Soon enough, the video started playing on the screen but when I checked the date, it was taken a day before the police raid. The club looked busy as usual. Music was blasting, and people were having fun. Then, in the melee, I noticed a number of women hiding the drugs. Not all at the same time, but throughout the night. None of them looked suspicious. They were all dressed like they'd come out for a good time, but I could clearly see them hiding small packages around the club. I counted at least five, pretending to pick something off the floor and then innocently dropping the package under or behind a piece of furniture—a couch, or a decorative pot or stand. My stomach made a funny jolt. This had been a clever way to go about it, because obviously, security wouldn't check these women other than asking for IDs. There were hundreds of people in there, and fake IDs weren't that hard to get these days.

"This is good, very good. We could use it to get him out on bail at least, even exonerated. Although the DA could argue these women had been working for Ivo. We have a hearing this afternoon, so this should help and I can present it as evidence," I said, feeling a little queasy.

That short video had me remember the last time I'd been in a club. The years of therapy had helped, but some things always triggered the trauma, and I needed a moment to gather my wits.

I concentrated on my breathing, hoping Ryga didn't notice anything, but my heart was jackhammering inside my chest.

"Are you okay, Ms. Camilleri?" Ryga's voice finally reached me and I wanted to slap myself.

Ivo was going to get out and this whole case was going to be put to bed. After that, I'd be able to start my new life in New York, keep family connections to a minimum with the exception of Clara, and do my utmost to forget I was the daughter of a mobster. Elaine kept saying that I would never be free of this world, but she had no idea how determined I was to prove to her wrong.

"Yes, I am fine," I lied. "Here is my card. Please email me this video as soon as possible and I promise you, Ivo will be back here this afternoon. They might still try to pin it on him, but I know the angle I need to go for to make sure he walks free."

Ryga looked pleased. He accompanied me to the door and I texted Clara when I got back to my car. I needed to see her before I left California. She texted back almost instantly, saying that she was going out to a party with some of her friends tonight.

Me: *What friends? I thought you hated parties and loud music? Do you think this is a good idea? It will be busy today in town*

. . .

Clara: *Yes, but I'm trying to get out of my comfort zone and have fun. Stop mothering me. I'm fine*

My sister knew she wasn't fine. After I began spending a lot more time in New York, Clara had decided to move out. She still had her room at home, which she used whenever Elaine held events at the mansion, such as on engagement night. But for the most part, she lived away. I was worried about her because she was still fragile. She insisted that living alone was good for her, but there had been a few instances when she had panic episodes in public and Elaine had to intervene.

I wanted to ask her again who her friends were, but I had to get to court. I arrived inside the courtroom at two in the afternoon. When I entered, Ivo had already been brought in. I sat beside him to set everything up and pretended not to notice his smug look, or the way his gaze roved greedily over my body. I also tried to ignore my racing heart and the blazing heat that flared over my cheeks and in my belly.

"Did you think about me last night?" he whispered, leaning close.

I quickly inhaled a deep breath.

"No, I was dreaming about Robert," I replied with confidence.

Luckily, a moment later, we were interrupted by the judge coming in to commence the hearing. I noticed a woman sitting on one of the benches, who fit the description of Detective Morales. She kept her gaze pinned on Ivo, and I couldn't decide if he was being defiant by staring back in an insolent way, or trying to make me jealous by undressing her with his eyes. He was probably doing it on purpose, to get a rise out of me because I'd mentioned Robert.

It was really tough to keep in mind he was supposed to marry Elaine. She had no clue about our history, and I wanted to keep it that way. To say she wouldn't be pleased was an understatement. It wasn't about love, but nobody took what she deemed hers. It was a marriage of convenience, but for her it was more than that. Elaine was a proud woman and she couldn't stand betrayal. No telling would she'd do if she found out.

After the initial opening ritual, I requested that I and the DA approach the bench. I knew the drill. Everything would be put on hold while the judge took us to his chambers and I presented the new evidence. I'd clearly state I'd just received it and therefore wasn't able to come forth earlier.

The process would be respected, we'd watch the footage, and after due analysis and deliberation, the DA would drop the charges as there wasn't enough evidence to hold on to Ivo. It wasn't even a question of bail.

This might not be the end of the road in the long run, but it would be for now. They would have to keep an eye on that detective, and stay away from shady business. More importantly, whoever was responsible for the frame-up was still out there, and they likely were not done with Ivo.

We returned to the courtroom and everything went like clockwork. Ivo took advantage of the opportunity to drag me into an embrace. "You're amazing and fucking hot in your no-nonsense getup."

I cleared my throat and felt myself blush when he stared at me with need and lust. I was so stupid.

"Great, so now that you're in the clear for the moment, I can finally go back to New York," I announced, then quickly added, "Try to stay out of trouble. I did this purely and simply as a favor to Elaine."

I started to pack up my briefcase, along with my heart. This was it.

It pained me to leave Clara on her own, but at the same time, I couldn't bear to stay here and watch as my life fell to pieces. I'd never get over Ivo, and seeing Elaine with him would crush me in ways I'd never recover from. I'd try once more to get Clara to move away with me, but I already knew she'd say no.

People started to move, but Ivo remained seated, staring at me while I continued to quietly put my paperwork in my case. Tension filled the air, sucking oxygen out of my lungs. Trying to empty my mind was an exercise in futility.

"Don't do this, princess. We both know this Robert won't give you what you want," he said, quietly enough for only me to hear.

All I wanted was to end this moment and disappear, but Ivo wasn't letting me. Why was he making it so difficult?

"And what is it that I want, Ivo? Since you know me so well?" I asked. "You think it's just about sex? I have desires, yes, but I want way more than you can give me."

I felt sick. Everything was crumbling around me and I was scrambling for a reprieve.

"You still want me, so stop denying it. That's a start," he said, his face so pale, as if this was taking a toll on him.

I averted my gaze for a moment, then faced him head on, crossing my arms. "Ivo, do you want me to spell it out for you? You and Elaine are set to marry in months. It's a done deal. To add insult to injury, this mess with the Russians is not over, and there's Emilio to worry about," I ground out. "Say what you will, I won't get involved. I have other shit to worry about."

Speaking of which, I had to track down Clara before I left tonight. Something about her message felt off and this sudden night out on the town was not in character for her. Although she had set up a wall between us, we were sisters. I wished we could be close again and that I could be the one who put Emilio behind bars, so he could never hurt her.

With Ivo, we both knew the odds were against us. Not to mention, he was almost twice my age, although that didn't matter when it came to intimacy. A tiny voice in my head reminded me that he was hot as fuck, great in bed, but logistically we couldn't be together because he and Elaine had what could be called a binding contract—what a promise was called in our world. At least, she'd consider it so.

"Ivo, I just heard the great news! Thank God for Merry!" Speaking of the Devil, Elaine's sharp voice rang in my ears.

She was walking through the door and only then did I notice that everyone else must have cleared out when we were talking because we were the only ones left. Elaine looked immaculate as always, strolling through the hearing room with her super high heels, wavy blond hair, and radiant complexion. I'd never looked so good, even if I spent half the day at the salon.

She threw herself all over me and hugged me, thanking me that I got Ivo out of his predicament, at least temporarily. I returned the embrace. Ivo's passive expression didn't fool me. He had to know I wasn't the kind of person who'd sneak around and take someone else's man. Yes, to say Elaine was difficult at times was an understatement, but she was the only family we had.

I left them to discuss the events of the day and headed outside, hoping they'd watch their backs going forward. Those women had planted the drugs to frame Ivo, but exactly who sent them? Ivo was certain Victor held the biggest grudge against him at the moment, but there was no certainty. There were other possibilities.

My mind was racing when I made it to my apartment. I thought about the plane I was supposed to catch later in the day. The truth was that I wasn't sure if I was ready to leave this life behind me so soon.

* * *

After freshening up, I started to pack my things, quelling the urge to sob. Against my will, my heart was bleeding. I hated Ivo, but I also wanted him. Yet, no matter what, there was no hope for us.

"Get a grip," I chided myself as I zipped up my luggage.

Robert had been calling me all day, wanting to know if everything was all right and if I planned to go back by evening. I finally answered to let him know I'd be likely catching a redeye after being tied up with family business all day.

It was just after five when I finally drove to Clara's. I kept getting this feeling I should be with her, that she shouldn't be alone.

I stopped the car in front of her apartment building and looked up. There was a light in her window, which meant she was still there. I knew the code to her place so I let myself in. My stomach was filled with unease and a sudden urgency. I wished I'd been able to get here earlier.

I headed upstairs to the third floor, then knocked her door. There was no answer and I bit on my bottom lip, wondering if I should just go inside. Clara had never given me the key but when I turned the knob, the door opened right up. I needed to remind her that she had to be more careful and lock up, especially after everything she'd been through.

I cautiously stepped inside the open plan kitchen/dining/living area. "Clara, you there?" I called out.

My question was met by silence.

I walked to the kitchen and looked behind the counter.

My breaths ceased. For a terrible moment, I thought I was dreaming and this wasn't happening for real.

For my sister lay unconscious on the floor, an open box of pills tipped on its side next to her. I rushed to her, crying out her name. I touched her still form and called her name, over and over. Yet, she gave me no response.

So I cried out to the universe.

Railed against the world, pleaded with God. Dug myself a sliver of hope in the all-consuming darkness and pain.

On my knees, I prayed to the sky I couldn't see through the fog of tears—because this couldn't be.

No.

Clara couldn't be dead.

Chapter Sixteen

Ivo

I thought about Merry all afternoon while Elaine rattled on about random things. Then, she started talking about expanding her 'empire,' dropping a bomb about the possibility of marrying Clara off to Victor's second cousin.

Elaine was power-hungry, but I had to find a way to put her foot on the brakes. If Merry knew what her stepmother was planning, she'd blow her top off. I told Elaine just what I thought of her idea, and of course, she wasn't pleased.

Each day that passed, my decision to marry her started to become more and more of a yoke around my neck. There seemed to be too big a price tied to this charade. But now, too much was invested in it, too, especially since Elaine was wooing the Russians so aggressively, promising them a beneficial alliance. Friends with benefits on a pretty large scale.

In the end, I told her I had stuff to do and managed to leave. Merry was right. I had to see what to do going forward, as well as face the consequences of what happened. To find who had it out for me. I'd made my bed, and now I had to lie in it.

I got into my car and drove. I knew where Merry lived because I'd made it my business to know everything about her. I wasn't sure why I was doing this because I knew what she'd say, but I couldn't help it. The streets were empty. Soon, I found myself parked outside her apartment building. I didn't see her car, and when I rang the bell, nobody answered. Where was she?

I called her number. No response, either.

A terrible thought hit me. Had she already gone to the airport? I didn't think so. I thought I'd heard her mention in passing she'd be visiting her sister.

Clara...

I knew where the young woman lived because I'd seen Elaine get the driver to deliver things to her. Acting on pure intuition, I plugged the address into my GPS and headed there.

Seeing Merry's car there had me park in the nearest spot and rush to the building. I pressed the buzzer. Nothing. Then again. I tried to call Merry once more, but got no response. And I didn't have the code.

Should I leave? Wait?

Why was I even here? It would only make Merry angrier at me, and possibly traumatize Clara. I just ... had to do something. I'd never been helpless in my life. I knew how to cope, get by and get even. But my mistakes were becoming bigger and bigger, out of hand. This might backfire, but I was done hurting people, even indirectly. Especially the ones I cared for.

I started to panic when a third call yielded also zero results.

Just when I was about to give up, someone walked out the door and I grabbed it before it closed shut. I bypassed the elevator and flew up the steps, three at a time.

At Clara's floor, I noticed her door was ajar and dread took root inside me. I paused to think, knowing I didn't have a weapon on me. I was getting sloppy—a man like me should always be prepared for the worst, especially after what I'd been through.

I looked around for something I could use, but the place was spotless and bare. Inching closer, I pushed the door gently, and the sound of sobbing had me startle. I walked in to see a large bag I recognized as Merry's on the floor by the kitchen area.

"Merry?" I called out.

A scrambling sound and her head appeared from behind a counter. Hair all over the place, face a mess of tears.

I rushed to her to see Clara sprawled on the floor, still as a piece of wood.

"Fuck," I breathed out. "What happened?"

"My sister took some pills and she's unconscious," Merry said in a trembling voice. Shock marked her features.

"Have you called an ambulance?" I asked, crouching beside her.

"Yes, they should be here soon … oh God, I hope she won't die! She's still warm, and has a pulse, but was I too late?" she asked.

I gently gripped Clara's head, then placed my fingers under her jaw by the carotid artery to feel for a pulse. Then, I picked up the pill bottle that was still beside her.

"You're right. She's alive. We'll give this to the doctor. It will be okay, princess. Let's just wait for the ambulance. I'm here now," I soothed her, taking her hand and trying to calm her down.

The paramedics didn't take long to arrive, although each second felt like an hour. Merry broke down when they loaded Clara inside the ambulance. She insisted on riding with her sister, so she did. I followed in my car, wondering if I was supposed to call Elaine, but I thought better of it. This was Merry's decision to make.

It took me another half hour to get there and another few minutes to find Merry in the ER. She looked a wreck as she paced back and forth in the waiting room.

"Do you know anything? Have you spoken to the doctor?" I asked, taking her in my arms. I hated seeing her like this, and old guilt reared its head, bringing me to my knees.

"No, they asked me to wait while they look after her," she replied, and I handed her a tissue. She gave me a weak smile, tinged with bottomless grief. "Why are you here? Why were you even at Clara's? You know where she lives…"

I brushed my hand over her hair then rubbed it soothingly over her back. I sighed. She wasn't going to believe me, but I was done with bending the truth. Done with walking on eggshells. Tired with the lies. We needed to be honest with each other.

"I just wanted to talk to you. Thank you … be honest about everything. When I didn't find you at home, I remembered you mentioning you were going to visit your sister. Also, I don't know … just a feeling," I explained. I had to tell her about Elaine's plans for Clara but now was not the time.

"I'm glad you were there," she admitted.

She was supposed to leave tonight. Although I'd wanted her to stay, never at this cost.

"I can call Elaine if you want me to," I offered, although she was the last person I wanted to see right now. She was too intense and would bulldoze her way over everyone.

"No, not until we have answers about how Clara is doing. My stepmother can be..."

"Challenging?" I laughed a little and she nodded because she understood. It was strange, talking to her about this.

"I have told her countless times that Clara wasn't all right. She always dismissed it, so maybe now she'll finally get it."

We sat down and I put my arm around her. When she leaned into me, warmth filled my being, and I felt at peace with myself. Merry had always had this effect on me. Her presence made me forget my troubles, eased the tension I couldn't shake loose. Although we'd only interacted a few times, she always brought the sun with her, and our unbelievable chemistry couldn't be denied. How could this be wrong?

"Let's just wait for the doctor. We don't have to discuss this now," I said, but Merry gave me that hard and intense look which told me she wasn't planning to let this go. She was so protective of her sister, and wouldn't let Elaine run roughshod all over her when it came to Clara's well-being.

There weren't many people around—just two other women and a man with a teenager.

I came to a decision. Since I'd decided to be honest, I had to share what I'd learned. Turn a new leaf. "Merry, I have something to tell you. Today, Elaine told me she wants to arrange a marriage for Clara. She thinks this could urge her to move past her trauma," I said.

Merry cursed under her breath. "What the fuck is wrong with that woman? First, she wanted to set me up with one of her uncles," she stated, and I clenched my fists as jealousy punched me in the gut. Elaine didn't care about her stepdaughters' future. It was all business to her. The thought of Merry belonging to somebody else was wrong not just because she'd have to settle for the sake of the family, but because it didn't sit well with me.

The doctor finally showed up, a middle-aged man with kind eyes and square-shaped glasses. "Ms. Camilleri, I'm Dr. Borken. I understand Clara is your sister and you found her in her apartment?" he asked.

"Yes. She was unconscious when I found her. She took all those pills?"

The doctor nodded.

"Yes, it was some strong sedatives. That's out of her system now, but I don't think she took that many because otherwise she'd have caused way more damage," he explained, staring at his clipboard. "She still hasn't woken up yet, but we have to keep her under observation overnight."

"So she's going to be all right?" Merry asked.

"I believe so, but we need to run a few more tests and refer her for a psych evaluation. Your sister attempted suicide, Ms. Camilleri. It was a cry for help."

I nodded. "I understand."

Merry told the doctor she'd stay until Clara had woken up. The doctor let her know it might take all night, and he couldn't give her a timeframe. But I knew, she wasn't going to leave Clara alone.

"You can go if you want, Ivo. I appreciate everything you've done, but I'll be fine. If Clara wakes up, I want her to know she's not here on her own," she said with a sigh.

I stretched my arms, working out a kink.

"No, princess, I'm not going anywhere," I said, taking in her tired features and expression etched with worry. My cock stirred in my pants and my heart slammed itself against my ribcage. Nowhere else I wanted to be but with her—not just for sex but for all the right reasons.

"Why are you doing this?" she finally asked, sounding surprised.

"You need me here," I said simply. "That is all."

Her gaze bore into mine for a good long while. "You know, I've been so busy hating you, putting the blame on you, I forgot how considerate you can be. You've been good to me, really. Despite everything." She looked like a puppy dog with sad eyes.

"Come on, princess, we both know I have never been good. I'm a killer and a gangster. No one has ever called me good before," I growled, rubbing my face.

When I glanced at her, she was still watching me.

"I haven't truly seen that side of you," she said. "Which was why I couldn't believe you were responsible for what had happened at the club that night." She hesitated for a moment. "So tell me, why did you ask Emilio to raid that place?" she asked, biting on her lower lip.

This wasn't an easy question to ask. After all, she had been trying to forget about that horrible night, but she had a right to know. My mistake was never reaching out. I thought I'd tried to do so, but I really hadn't. I'd stuck my head in the sand.

"The Russians wanted an alliance with us for a long time but I always refused to get involved in their dealings. My mother was Russian and I was brought up in Moscow, so they thought they could use me for their gain. I was more of a means to an end, to be honest. Finally, after months of negotiations, I agreed to marry the sister of the head of the Russian brotherhood. She'd lost her husband to cancer several years back and her brother, Victor, was willing to make a deal with me. I agreed because she genuinely was a beautiful girl, inside and out, and we got on pretty well," I said.

"Anika was a bit younger than me and both of my sons liked her. Things were going well and I truly believed this was going to work out until I discovered she was in love with a man who worked as an accountant for a big corporation. A regular guy. Anika begged me not to say anything to her brother. She knew he would have killed her if he found out. And in the end, I agreed it would be best for me to break the engagement. She'd have her freedom and I didn't mind taking the fall."

"I don't understand these marriages of convenience," she muttered, giving me a disbelieving look.

What could I say? My position was complicated. Merry wanted to cut ties with the mafia world, especially after her father was no longer here to control her.

"I know you don't, but at the time, I did want to get married. I thought I could start over with a woman who sort of understood me. Then we broke the engagement because I found out that she was in love with an accountant. I wanted her to be happy, but her family turned out to be a big problem, as I should have anticipated," I explained. "Of course, I couldn't say anything to her brother because then, Anika's lover would be dead, so I made some sort of excuse that pissed them off. Anika had a big heart. She was a hopeless romantic, but she was trapped in that world without a way out.

"Anika had been so scared, but I'd promised to help her disappear. The problem got bigger, of course. Emilio told me I was a fool to cave in and let her put us in a bind like that, but I didn't want to see her miserable. Because even when I ended the engagement, she still couldn't be with the man she loved..." I shook my head.

"So I gave them money to start over somewhere else. Victor told me flat out that I was going to regret this, that Anika's leaving her home was on me. She was upset because I broke things off, according to him, things escalated pretty quickly afterwards. He blamed me for everything. That same night, his men killed two of my associates. They cut one guy open and left his guts on display, the other was burned alive. They also burned the club down and put Gregory into a coma."

Chapter Seventeen

Merry

Ivo's story was not what I expected to hear. Deep down, I felt bad that I made him responsible for everything that happened. He'd been through a lot, losing his men and going through hell with both of his children, in different ways.

Emilio was a psychopath who felt no remorse. Although Ivo should have been more careful giving him such power, they were two different people. Gregory had been in the hospital for an extended time, in danger of losing his life.

"I just wanted them to fear me," he said. "Not for Emilio and his cohorts to do what they did. I should have known…" He hung his head, regret forming a black cloud over him.

"This is terrible, Ivo, and I am sorry. I had no idea," I said, but I wasn't ready to just forgive him. He broke the deal with the Russians because he wanted to protect Anika, then everything went to Hell in a handbasket, and they retaliated. I didn't know what I would have done if I had been in his position, but everything snowballed from that situation he'd created.

Ivo looked lost, staring away in the distance. My father had always told me I was destined to take over the business from him, to lead our family. He always thought I would marry a man he had chosen for me from our world.

I understood that Ivo was still craving revenge. This was how we did things—my family was no different.

"I made a hasty decision, and didn't think it through. Emilio mentioned Victor's niece was going to be in that club that night, and I just wanted him to send a warning, scare her a little bit. Of course, he would disregard my directions and go overboard."

"Because you told him you'd let him do whatever was necessary. You gave him the go ahead," I pointed out.

"No, I said I wanted him to do whatever was necessary to deliver a warning message. Maybe do away with a couple of the bodyguards at best. I'm not a saint, but I don't hurt women and children, Merry."

The look in his eyes showed me he wasn't lying, but I shook my head, lost for words. I picked at an invisible piece of lint on my jacket.

"I was filled with grief. If I didn't let my anger blind me, things wouldn't have escalated. You and your sister wouldn't have been in harm's way," he said, the words pouring out of him. His eyes glistened, and I knew he was all torn up inside. "You may forgive me one day, but I don't know if I'll ever forgive myself, and that's the goddamn truth. Won't change a thing, I know, but I'm truly sorry."

I wanted to scream at the top of my lungs. His words broke me but the fact of the matter was, his actions had led to so much destruction. Why couldn't I just forgive him?

"After what he did, Emilio came back and started bragging about giving everyone a taste of their own medicine. Then he mentioned you, how he and his men had finally gotten a piece, and at first, I didn't believe him. I thought he was fucking with me," Ivo continued, and I wished he would just stop talking. All of this was difficult for both of us, but what I truly wanted to know was what he had done to Emilio. "Well, I almost killed him that evening. I beat the shit out of him after I saw a recording of what had happened—not a very good one, but it was enough for me to figure out everything. Emilio had asked someone to film him. If someone hadn't stopped me and got me off him, he'd be dead."

I stared at him horrified, trying to remember if anyone was pointing a phone at me that night, but the memories were hazy. I swallowed thickly, getting some satisfaction from the fact that Emilio had experienced some pain, but it would never be enough. He'd used me and my sister to show his father that he could do what he wanted, that he could own us and take us any way he wanted.

Soon after, Emilio disappeared. All I wanted was for him to pay for everything he'd done to me and Clara.

"I do believe in justice. I admit I'd like to see him dead, but that's my emotions talking. Maybe I should have listened to you when you tried to explain, but I was so livid," I said, feeling a little ashamed of all the things I'd said in the past, right after I left the hospital and headed over to see him. He was heartbroken and so guilt-ridden. I didn't even see it then. I was blinded by rage and I raved and raved.

"I banned him from ever setting foot in any of my properties, and he's shunned by the family. If my men ever come across him, they have orders to detain him. He didn't think I'd ever turn on him like this but when he realized what he was dealing with, he ghosted everyone. I suspect Victor is helping him. But there is something truly evil about my son—his soul is tainted and he tried to hurt me because we've always had a difficult relationship, so that's why he went after you and your sister that night," Ivo said, getting up to pace around.

The emotions were running high but I was glad we had this talk, and we were able to be honest with each other. Yet, some things between us were most likely going to remain unresolved, so although I understood him, I was having a hard time forgetting his role in our troubles.

"It was good that we talked about this, Ivo. Maybe if I had known, I would have reacted differently then," I told him. "Please at least tell me Anika is all right and she's happy with that accountant? I need a happy ending."

"I have no idea what happened to her. Hopefully, her brother didn't find out the real reason why we broke up, but Russians are ruthless," he said.

He was right. The Russian mob was riddled with next level savages. My father had dealt with them in the past and he always warned me about them.

As we sat in companionable silence for a bit, the doctor arrived to tell me that Clara had started to come around, so I flew from my chair and raced to her room.

Just outside her room, I swallowed my tears, took several

deep breaths, and a nice nurse gestured for me to go inside. Clara was hooked up to a number of machines, but she had her eyes open. She looked pale and weak, but I was so glad she was finally awake. Sudden relief washed over me like the rain on a scorching summer day.

"Clara, thank goodness you're awake. How are you feeling?" I asked, approaching the bed and taking her hand. She was warm but drained of strength.

"I'm sorry," she said, swallowing. "It was ... too much. The voices..." Her voice was rough and tired. I kept telling myself I wouldn't cry, that I couldn't break down in front of her. I was her big sister, supposed to protect her from all the nastiness in this world.

"Stop it now. You don't need to apologize to me. You should have talked to me about this, told me how you felt..." I said, now unable to stop the tears from streaming down my face.

"I met this guy, Mark. I thought he liked me and we were supposed to go out with some of his friends, but then he texted me to say it was better if I didn't come," she said, and I quickly wiped my tears and frowned.

"What do you mean? How did you meet this guy?" I asked, worried that Clara was always doing everything too fast.

"It's the guy I've been sort of seeing. Please don't be angry with me. I was upset because I just wanted to be normal. To know someone cared ... to not mess up every relationship that comes my way. Maybe I'll never be able to have someone to love me. But when they touch me, I ... I can't take it," she said, breaking my heart. "So I figured, why not end it all?"

"Fuck him, Clara. You just met a jerk who doesn't deserve you. Please promise me you won't do this again?"

"Promise," she replied, but I wasn't sure if I should believe her. I wish I knew what was going on in that mind of hers.

We talked a bit more, but I left shortly after because I could see she was still exhausted.

Things were complicated but I was determined to make sure Clara found herself again.

Ivo was waiting for me outside. I hated him, hated that he was still here and standing by me, but at the same time, I couldn't stop thinking about him. And the way he was staring at me told me that he cared for me, more than anyone ever had.

"Come on, princess, I'm going to give you a lift home," he finally said.

"I think it's best if I take a cab. You have done enough for me and Clara today," I said in a harsh tone. I wanted to be mean, to make him resent me and drive him away, because that would be easier to deal with.

"All right, but someone should call Elaine. She's going to find out sooner or later and then she'll kick up an even bigger fuss. Last thing you need," he reminded me, brushing his fingers lightly over my cheek, caressing over my faded, yet still visible, scar. I sucked in a breath, but let it slide because he was just being kind. Nothing more.

"I'll do it in the car."

"Okay, princess," he said. "She's going to be okay."

"Thank you," I said, my eyes stinging with unshed tears. My heart was crushed to a pulp, but with a nod, I walked away, knowing we had reached some kind of understanding, but choices had been made from which we couldn't backtrack. His gaze burned into my back, but I resisted turning around.

Everything was broken.

The man I longed for—always would—was about to be my stepmother's husband. I had to move on from this, somehow.

I called Elaine when I got back to my apartment and explained the situation. Shocked and in a panic, she wanted to go to the hospital straight away, but I assured her that Clara was all right and just needed rest.

That night, when I was unpacking, I felt relief that I wasn't going back to New York tonight. I called Robert and told him that I would have to stay in Los Angeles for a little while to make sure Clara was okay. Thankfully, he encouraged me to do what I had to, and I loathed myself for not being entirely truthful. I needed time to figure out what to do. Besides, I decided I had to ensure Emilio ended up where he belonged. He was going to rot in prison if I had to drag him there myself.

I had a germ of a plan forming, a lifeline to grasp, but that meant I had to reach out to some people I'd rather not connect with. The alternative, though, was unacceptable. We needed to proceed with our lives, with some sort of closure. I owed it to Clara.

Over the next few days, I visited Clara every moment I was allowed, making sure she had everything she needed.

I fought with my conflicted feelings and emotions, pushing away my desire for Ivo. I wanted him, and the guilt this created within me was slowly eating me alive. He wasn't going to leave Elaine for me. There was too much at stake—including lives, if the Russians decided to make this territory Hell on Earth.

Clara went through with her psychiatric evaluation. She

was doing better and after several days, she was finally able to go home. She was prescribed some medication and this time, she'd have to go to therapy and take better care of herself. Elaine insisted that she stay with her, and I agreed because I didn't want her to be alone. She needed support from both of us.

"Good morning, Merry," Elaine greeted me when I arrived to see Clara early the next morning. "I haven't managed to find a decent attorney just yet, but since you're going to be here for a little while longer, I won't bother. I think you can take care of a couple of matters for now."

Typical Elaine to hit me with these ridiculous demands without preamble. "I'm here to look after Clara. In fact, I was planning to take some time off work," I countered.

I wondered where Ivo was. I'd seen his car outside, so I knew he was here, too. Elaine had no idea he'd been with me in the hospital and it would be easier if that stayed between us. Hopefully, I'd avoid seeing him. It hurt too much, and I didn't have the headspace for that at the moment.

Elaine gave me a bright smile. She often ignored me whenever I mentioned I wasn't working for her. The business always came first and yesterday, she'd arranged a meeting with some of Victor's relatives. Apparently, they were interested in buying some land from us. I wasn't even a real estate attorney, but Elaine knew I had experience with these matters because of who we were and what we did. She wanted me around to help smooth out things. Whether she wanted to or not, though, she'd need to hire a legal professional in the state to take care of the final paperwork. Elaine would likely never stop fighting me over my decision to step back from our business.

"Well, don't get too comfortable because I have some ideas to get the Russians off Ivo's back," she said, smiling sweetly.

I didn't doubt she did. She was known for being tough and an ace when it came to securing deals. I wondered if it would be easier just to get up and leave. But I couldn't. Not now, or ever. I might though, if I didn't have Clara to think about.

"I don't know how you manage to get them to sit down with you, but this isn't a good time, Elaine," I told her. I found out from experience that I always had to be firm with my stepmother and it was time to set some boundaries. "And when it comes to Clara, you need to understand that she's not your responsibility anymore. She's not going to get married anytime soon."

For years, I let Elaine do what she pleased only because I didn't want to be involved, because I hated this world, but now I understood that I needed to intervene.

Ivo approached us, carrying two cups of tea and giving me an intense look that caused the butterflies to flutter in my stomach.

Meanwhile, Elaine raised an eyebrow at me and I smirked, pleased that I finally had her full attention. It was time to be clear and let her know that Clara was never going to be her puppet, at least not while I was still around to protect her.

Chapter Eighteen

Ivo

Tension hung in the air. Merry was done taking Elaine's shit and I wanted to see how the latter was going to react. Clara had tried to kill herself, and Elaine should have taken this as a sign to back off from her Machiavellian ways.

"I don't think this is up to you, my dear. I have been making decisions for this family for a very long time and Clara eventually would have to think about securing an advantageous marriage. I tried to arrange one for you, too, with Lorenzo. But you've always been hard-headed," she said, her tone cold as ice.

She hated being questioned, but Merry wouldn't let this go. It was almost amusing to watch.

I wondered who the fuck this son of a bitch Lorenzo was. This must have happened a good while back.

The women stared each other down, neither of them

backing away. As always, seeing Merry felt like a punch in the gut for my yearning for her never ceased. Would it ever?

The day of the wedding was slowly approaching, but all I could think of was Merry. And the way she almost screamed my name when I made her come at the police station.

Merry eyes narrowed as she took a small sip of water from her glass. Her mouth twitched at the corners.

"Maybe you've taken care of my father's business, but you shouldn't make any assumptions about Clara. She needs time to heal and pull herself together," Merry pressed, her tone still sweet and calm. "I don't care about your connections and plans, Elaine. Clara is going to choose her own potential husband when she's ready. I'll make sure of that."

"You're suffering from some delusion, Merry. You of all people should know how we do things. Strategic marriages are how we keep the peace. My cousin Dominic was shot because he too wanted to marry a nice, normal girl from a small town, and then paid for it," Elaine continued, tapping her long nail over the table.

"I think Merry is right, Elaine. This is none of our business. Clara is fragile and unfortunately, Emilio is still out there, probably scheming to find more ways to hurt us, too," I interjected, suppressing a frustrated growl.

Nothing good would come out of a conflict between Elaine and Merry. Elaine was older and not stupid—she needed Merry's support to thrive, and aim higher.

My son was the thorn in my side. His mother was back in Bulgaria and had no interest in getting to know him. Sometimes I wondered if he was already dead. Victor's niece had been badly hurt and Emilio was to blame. I had no idea why Victor would keep him alive unless he planned to use him in some way. I wouldn't wish Victor's wrath on my worst enemy, even Emilio himself.

Elaine frowned, clearly not happy I'd interfered.

"Emilio will get what he deserves, Ivo. But fine, I won't dictate what should happen in Clara's life anymore. She's all yours, Merry. For now," she said, and then pulled me toward her. Merry's stare felt like an arrow piercing right through me. "And I will deal with Emilio too, Ivo. You have so much on your plate with the club and the new shipments."

Merry snorted and shook her head. I was glad when she turned around to do something else because then Elaine leaned over and started whispering some dirty shit in my ear.

Fuck, I didn't want to do this in front of her, especially after I thought we'd mended things between us in the hospital. I believed she was going to forgive me because she understood what I had to go through, but I wasn't helping myself when Elaine was whispering how much she wanted to suck my dick in front of her own stepdaughter. I'd managed to stay away from her for a while, but for how much longer would I be able to avoid sex with Elaine? With Merry present, it was becoming harder and I just wasn't able to perform like I should.

I walked away from Elaine when Merry turned around and announced she was going to check on her sister upstairs. I bet she wanted to stab me and maybe this would have made me feel better about myself.

Clara was out of the hospital but I didn't want sit here pretending that everything was peachy when it wasn't. All my problems weren't going to magically go away if I married Elaine.

"I think I should go. I don't want to make things awkward

when Clara comes downstairs," I told Elaine, but she was already beside me.

"Don't be silly, darling. None of it was your fault. Emilio had gone off the rails. This is all in the past now," Elaine said.

"No, Clara is proof that it's not. I think you should take this more seriously. I'm going to head to my old apartment. Emilio used to stay there a lot. Maybe I can find something there," I snapped. I was fed up with Elaine being so dismissive.

"You're right. I'm aware that sometimes I can be insensitive, but it's just because I want to be proactive and positive. I do love Merry and Clara, as though they were my own children. I'll ask Ricardo to see if he can find out anything about Emilio's possible whereabouts."

"He's a devious coward. I have to go, Elaine. I will see you later," I told her. My mind was racing and then her phone started ringing, so the timing was good, because I needed to get out of there.

When I was outside, I pulled out my phone, deciding to call some of my old contacts. I'd been too passive about this, letting the police handle things and almost washing my hands of the whole situation. But in doing so, I'd done Merry and Clara wrong.

My pulse spiked when the door suddenly slid open and Merry showed up.

"Everything okay? I thought you were going to spend the day with Clara?" I asked as she approached.

"Yeah, but then I overheard what you said to Elaine and decided I want to come with you," Merry said, folding her arms over her chest.

"And where is that exactly, princess?"

"To Emilio's old apartment. And you're not going to stop me because I have promised Clara that he's going to be behind bars soon enough," she spoke firmly.

I took out a cigarette and lighted it.

Unfortunately, I knew Merry well enough to know she wasn't going to listen to me and stay put. She was way too stubborn.

"It's too dangerous. The Russians are not to be trifled with," I warned her, taking a drag of my cigarette. I had quit some time ago but being around Merry made me nervous.

"I don't fucking care, Ivo. You owe me, so I'm coming with you."

"What about Clara?"

"She is watching some TV show and she's fine at the moment. Someone will check in on her often, and this time will be different. I will force her into therapy if I must," Merry said, visibly swallowing.

I wanted to protest, to put my foot down, but she was already walking toward my car.

In moments, she was sitting next to me in the passenger seat, staring out the window while I ignored the rising tension in my groin at having her so close. This was wrong in every respect because I wasn't supposed to desire her, but the nights we spent together flashed in my mind, reminding me that there was never any other woman who made me feel this way.

"Why did your father marry Elaine? Someone told me that she wasn't connected to our world?" I asked her, because I wanted to kill the awkward silence between us.

"Well, he saw her in Rome when he was on holiday and apparently, it was love at first sight. It took a while for everyone to accept her. It was pretty brutal at first." She laughed.

"Guess she can be quite the charmer." I snickered.

"She was determined to prove everyone wrong, and show that she could be a mobster's wife. My father was crazy about my mother, but she died when Clara was only four," she explained. "She had a rare brain tumor and that sort of broke him. He was never the same afterward, and he needed help with us. So he returned from his trip with Elaine and she settled into her role as our new mother."

I wanted to say something about my past, but I liked listening to her voice, so I let her keep on talking about Elaine when she was just settling into her new life in the Camilleri household.

Almost forty minutes later, we arrived at our destination. I'd bought this place almost twenty years ago when this area wasn't so infested by drug addicts and hookers, but it got worse over the years. When Emilio turned eighteen, he'd insisted on moving there, so I let him. He had always been a problematic kid, but I often dismissed it, thinking he would sort himself out eventually.

"Just keep close to me at all times," I told her, looking around. Several people were standing outside their homes, and a group of teenagers hung around nearby, smoking and horsing around.

I'd done well since the time I'd bought this place. I might not be as wealthy and well-connected as Merry's father and Elaine, but I'd made a name for myself over the years and my business was doing well. I liked to stay low-key and under the radar, never going for the flashy lifestyle.

"How long did Emilio live here?" she asked.

We walked inside the neglected building, walking past trash bags piled on one side. It had been a while since I'd been here. Emilio used to throw parties all the time when he lived in this apartment, and I generally stayed away.

"Since he turned eighteen. He always wanted to be independent," I said as we walked on the second floor. The smell of mold and stale air wafted around as I opened the door.

"It looks like someone has been here recently," she said, looking at the empty pizza boxes lying around on the coffee table and a couple of beer bottles. The scent of my son's aftershave lingered in the air.

"Maybe he stays here periodically," I said. "I doubt he'd linger too long. Too risky. I'll look around the bedrooms and you can check the living room here."

The last time I'd seen Emilio, things hadn't ended well between us. Blood was shed, and bonds had been irredeemably broken. He was too troubled, and as much as we're supposed to support our children, I was at a loss. He seemed beyond help.

The words we said to each other, we could never get back.

The damage Emilio caused, he could not undo.

He'd broken the woman I loved—yes, *loved*—and called her a whore. Hurt her sister to a point where she didn't want to live anymore.

During our last encounter, I'd encouraged him to leave this city for good. I never wanted to see him again. But now I realized, that was a mistake. What he did to Merry and Clara, he could do to others. He was never going to change.

"You're not my father," he'd spat out, and I laughed. He was deluded and dangerous. I was his father. Dona had been faithful and Emilio had some of her features. He was my flesh and blood.

"Have you found anything, Ivo?" Merry's voice pulled me back to reality. I glanced around the empty bedroom, wondering how on earth I'd managed to create a monster.

"Not yet. What about you?" I asked as I started opening the drawers, looking for anything that might be useful.

Merry didn't reply so I called her name again.

Nothing.

I went to the living room to see why she wasn't responding, and stopped in my tracks.

Maybe I was seeing things.

Maybe Emilio wasn't really standing in front of Merry, smiling at her.

Chapter Nineteen

Merry

I'd been searching through the old kitchen cabinets and suddenly, I had this feeling someone was watching me, so I turned around. My heart stopped when I found Emilio standing in the room, staring at me.

My worst nightmare, come to life.

This couldn't be happening, and yet there I was, staring at his gleaming eyes filled with madness and rage.

Fear slithered down my spine. I wanted to scream but any sound caught in my throat. Ivo was in the next room. He had no idea...

"Hello, Merry. I heard you guys have been looking for me," Emilio said, glancing around. "I was hoping you'd come. I missed you." He grinned, and I had no doubt then, he wasn't quite right in the head.

My palms were damp with sweat, and my nape tingled. I felt queasy, for his words cut through my skin and I started shaking uncontrollably. I was pounded with a vision of him touching me when Jack was forcing me to suck him off. I had done my utmost to block these memories but too often, they resurfaced.

Just then, Ivo rushed in and his gaze landed on his son.

"Emilio?" Ivo called out, then stopped when the younger man reached inside his jacket and produced a knife. The blade flashed as he turned it to and fro. Was it the same one he'd slashed my face with, I wondered?

Hate like I'd never felt before consumed me. All I wanted was for the bastard to suffer a slow, painful death.

With his free hand, Emilio pulled a cigarette out of a pack in his pocket and slid it casually between his lips, then lit it, taking his time.

"I heard that congratulations are in order. You finally managed to pull your head out of your ass, *Daddy*," he said, staring at Ivo with detachment in his eyes, as though he had no soul to speak of. The man felt no remorse whatsoever. Rooted to the spot, I tried to keep from passing out when the smell of blood hit my nostrils—another memory manifesting in the present.

"I hope you're here because you're planning to turn yourself in?" Ivo stated, looking at me and giving a small nod, as if to assure me he'd protect me.

Emilio laughed and then started coughing from the cigarette smoke.

"No, that's not why I am here, and no one is going to touch me while I'm under Victor's protection," he sneered. I shuddered again when he quickly added, "Did you know that you're not my real father, Ivo?"

What? I gasped out loud, but Ivo seemed unfazed, acting like he didn't just hear the bomb Emilio had just dropped. The man had to be lying through his teeth, as always.

Confused, I threw Ivo a questioning look, but still, I couldn't read anything from his expression. He wasn't buying his son's bullshit, either.

"So you ran over to Victor then? You were always a coward, Emilio. I didn't expect anything else from you," Ivo replied coldly. "And you're my son. I know you wish you weren't, but you're my legitimate son."

Emilio let out a sarcastic laugh, shaking his head and shuffling his feet.

"My mother was fucking Victor long before she met you and told me that she lied to you. I am not your son. She sent me a letter recently. Take a look at this picture yourself, *Dad*," he said, his voice full of contempt. He threw a white envelope at Ivo and it landed at his feet.

Ivo picked it up and pulled a picture out. Frowning, he stared at it while the seconds ticked by. Emilio glanced at me and licked his lips. My skin crawled.

"How are you, little Merry? Are you still fucking him even now that he's with your stepmother? Seems like he's going to be your real daddy very soon. That's pretty hot," he taunted, his leering gaze traveling up and down my body. "See, I'm not the only one that's perverted, you whore."

Tired of him and his games, I reached behind me and pulled my gun out of my belt, where I'd hidden it after sneaking it out of my bag. Luckily, he'd never noticed what I was up to.

I pointed it at him—at his head.

"Don't move, you sick scum! I can put a bullet in you quicker than you have time to use that thing in your hand."

I was glad I'd decided to carry it with me when I made up my mind to come over here with Ivo. I had a feeling something would happen—only, I didn't think he'd be so stupid as to be found here, now. Had he intended to confront us? Or at least, his father?

If it was down to me to shut down this menace, then I would. As long as he wouldn't hurt another living soul again.

"Merry, please put the gun down," Ivo's voice reached me then, but I shook my head.

"No one is going to tell me what to do anymore. And you deserve to rot in hell for what you've done to me and my sister, you piece of shit!" My hands were shaking but I gripped that gun tight. Tears brimmed in my eyes but I wasn't going to back away. If I had to kill that bastard, then I was ready to pull that fucking trigger. My father had taught me how to use a gun when I was in my teens. I was a pretty good shot, and this target was easy.

So easy...

"She's not going to shoot me. She doesn't have the guts," Emilio said, but he didn't sound too arrogant then. A chip in his armor.

"Merry, I'm begging you. This is it. He's not going anywhere now, but if you kill him, it might be hard to cover this up. What do we do? Buy everyone in the whole building?" Ivo urged.

I held my ground, longing to wipe that fucking smirk off Emilio's face for good.

"Why did you hurt my sister, Emilio? She was just an innocent girl and didn't deserve this!" I shouted because I wanted to make sure he heard me.

A dark shadow passed through his eyes, quickly replaced by fury. Ivo was silently pleading me not to take matters into my own hands, but all I could see was Clara's face as she lay on the floor, numb and violated and so, so terrified. He had broken her and I wanted him to admit that, to acknowledge what he had done.

"Because I wanted to hurt him." He gestured toward Ivo. "To hurt my father for not letting me take over his business when it was my right because I put in most of the work. I was done being treated like a second citizen. I was done not being taken seriously! And you bitches are not worth a dime," he scorned.

And that was when I shot him.

Time stopped, and I dropped the gun on the floor, feeling dizzy as Emilio stumbled and screamed like a banshee. I covered my ears and tangled my fingers in my hair as the weight of what I'd just done sank into me.

Ivo was now beside Emilio, who had blood gushing from his lower thigh. It was a small bullet and I only wanted to graze his flesh, not hit the femoral. Of course, it had been a risk...

"Merry, you need to leave so I can call an ambulance. Call Elaine to come get you. You can wait round back, on the next street over," Ivo ordered, tearing off a strip of material from one of the curtains to fashion a tourniquet with it. "And for heaven's sake, tell her not to come up here. I'll stall as much as I can."

My head spinning, I grabbed my phone from my bag and

called Elaine, giving her the address and ending the call before she started bombarding me with questions.

I glanced at Emilio in disgust. He was lucky that I hadn't aimed at his heart, head, or farther up his leg, or he'd probably be close to death or already gone.

"I'll call the ambulance in a moment, so go downstairs now! You need to get the fuck out of here before the police show up and start asking questions," Ivo ordered.

I was still in shock, feeling lost and staring at the blood pooling on the floor.

"I don't need to go anywhere. I will tell them it was self-defense," I said.

"Just go, dammit! I will deal with this. Emilio won't talk. I'll make sure of it," Ivo pressed.

I flinched and crossed my arms. Then, as if realizing what a jerk he'd been, he stood and gathered me in his arms. Pulling back, he cradled my face in his palms. "I'd rather stay with you right now because I believe you need me, but I must take care of this mess. For you. Do you think you can handle going down by yourself?"

I nodded, my mouth suddenly going dry.

"Fine. I will come to the house when this is taken care of, okay?"

"Yes," I said breathlessly.

"Good. Now go." His tone was gentle, but firm.

I went downstairs when Elaine called to say she was a few minutes away.

Inside the car, Elaine kept trying to get me to talk, asking a barrage of questions—especially what I was doing over there with Ivo—but after a while, she gave up. I just wanted her to shut up so I could retreat into my world, and when what I did started to sink in, I just couldn't face her. I couldn't face anyone. I needed time alone.

Would this hurt my career?

Would Robert understand?

What did Ivo plan to tell the police?

What would I tell Clara—or should I tell her at all?

I'd left my gun there, and it had been my father's. Oh my God. Had it been worth it? I know Clara would be relieved to know Emilio was going to prison. But would he make sure to bring me down with him?

So many questions swirled in my brain.

Like what Emilio said about Ivo not being his real father, but Victor Poroshenko. Clearly, his mother wasn't in the picture anymore. I wondered if she was even alive.

When we arrived, Elaine urged me to keep Clara in the dark. I rolled my eyes at that. Did she believe I didn't know what my sister needed to hear?

Entering the house, I went straight upstairs and didn't wait after knocking on the door. I found her in her room, at her computer.

Turning, she smiled faintly at me. "What happened, Merry? You look like a ghost."

"Funny you should say that," I said. "I should be the one to ask how you're doing." I smiled, pleased to see her out of the bed.

"I'm doing better," she said. "I took my medication."

This was huge. Had she decided to finally take her health seriously?

I sat on the edge of the bed near her, and reached out to

clasp her hand. She let me, and squeezed my hand back. Clara had a right to know.

"I want to tell you something, sis. I can't give you all the details yet, but I went with Ivo to his old apartment and Emilio showed up," I said cautiously. "I shot him in the leg and he squealed like an animal. Ivo is with him now, but I'm not sure what's going to happen."

Leaning forward, I took her in my arms. Her jaw dropped, and it was like she'd lost her ability to speak. But I sensed, it wasn't because of pain this time. She was happy that at last, vindication was here. "Guess what I want to say is ... we got him, Clara. He's finally going to face justice for what he did to you and me!"

Chapter Twenty

Ivo

I stared at the photograph Emilio had given me in the apartment. He must have been only four years old and back then, he looked like the spitting image of Victor Poroshenko. The similarities were so strong—how did I never notice? Dona had claimed that she got pregnant when we were together and I never questioned it. I was young, stupid, and fucking thought she was good for me at the time.

Everything sort of made sense now but I still didn't get why she lied to me. She'd claimed she loved me and I would have taken care of him either way.

But now, I wondered why she'd told him the truth. Did she want to ensure that Emilio got his fair share of wealth, after realizing it wasn't coming from me? Of course, once he found out, he ran right to Victor. It could have backfired, but the man took him in, accepting him as his son. Perhaps he'd wanted proof, or he just relished the opportunity to take something from me. I'd always thought he held a grudge for me because of Dona, but why take it so far?

No matter what, there'd been bad blood between us, but to take Emilio in when Victor knew he'd attacked the club and hurt his niece was the most depraved act I could think of. Unless there was something else and he was just using Emilio...

I had been sitting in my office for hours now, trying to piece together certain memories from the past. I glanced at my elder son, wanting to give him an answer, but didn't know what to say. He had been working hard in the past several days, running the club for me. After the doctors took care of Emilio's wound, he ended up behind bars.

Morales showed up at the scene after Merry left and then questioned Emilio in the hospital.

"It was an accident, Detective. My dad and I had a heated argument and I shot him. He wanted to call you, and I had to stop him," Emilio said gruffly, grimacing with pain and anger. "Then he shot me back."

I'd told him what to say. If he didn't co-operate, I'd hand him right in the hands of Catherine's father, and he'd be done for. I doubted Victor had disclosed his son's identity to the man, and if the shit hit the fan among the Russians, there'd be a bloodbath. Nobody wanted that, but I'd be prepared to stir the pot if Emilio decided to act cute and implicate Merry.

Merry, who'd brought a gun with her, was prepared to make trouble. Why did I let her come with me?

Also, I let him know that the woman who drove me insane

would not hesitate to come back and finish the job, even if it meant losing her life, freedom, and independence.

I had no doubt Morales didn't buy Emilio's story, which I backed up, but there was no way to prove otherwise. I'd told them I always carried one of the Elaine's late husband's guns with me, and that's what I'd used.

To make my story jive with the facts, I'd cleaned Merry's firearm before holding it in my hand. Luckily, I also had my gun. Using a silencer, I fired a shot in a strategic spot in the wall, then put Emilio's prints on the weapon. I wasn't taking any chances. It was self-defense.

Victor had me by the balls because he was supporting my alliance with the Maltese mafia. Maybe Emilio was his insurance that I'd follow through with my commitments. He wouldn't hesitate to throw me under the bus with Catherine's father and finally bury me for good. Besides, it was a point of pride. Victor had Dona first, and I raised his son like a fucking chump.

I stared at Gregory, who sat across from me in silence, clearly giving me time to work through things. "So what are you going to do now?" he asked.

"I'm not going to do anything. Your brother is in prison and I'm marrying Elaine in a few months as the Russians want."

"What did he say about the Russians?" Gregory questioned.

"That he was finally treated with respect amongst them. He had been working for Victor all this time when he was hiding, so they are all one big happy family now," I snapped, dragging my hand through my hair. "Where did I go wrong with him?"

"Don't beat yourself up, Dad. Emilio has always been a twisted son of a bitch. Probably Victor's genes," Gregory admitted, fully aware of his brother's warped fantasies. "And are you seriously going to marry the razor bitch?" Some in the mafia world called her by that nickname because she was sharp and ruthless. "She's probably screwed half of Los Angeles. We both know you don't want to stay miserable for the rest of your life."

"I have to honor the deal. Victor will kill me this time around for screwing him over," I said, and perhaps Elaine would cut off my balls, too.

When I spoke to Merry yesterday, she told me that Clara was doing much better. She finally agreed to see the therapist. Merry wasn't going back to New York yet, so I had some time to figure out how I was going to proceed in regard to this engagement. I knew Merry was still determined to move and be with that lawyer. My time was running out.

"You're getting weak, Dad. That girl is crazy about you," Gregory muttered, shaking his head.

I didn't say anything but fuck, he wasn't wrong. I'd created nothing but one mess after the other. Maybe I was losing my touch, or age addled my brain.

Ryga suggested that we should reach out to the Russians and discussed what had happened because a thought occurred to me. What if Emilio hadn't told Victor he was involved in the Sputnik attack? Sure, there was video evidence, but he wasn't visible on it, only some of the men. Which in essence, pointed at me as the guilty party. What if Victor's shenanigans to frame me had to do with that?

Suddenly, a few pieces of the puzzle seemed to fall into place. Emilio was simply using his heritage to get with Victor ... but the man might still be in the dark about the truth. Emilio was clearly unstable, but now I needed to worry about Victor's long-term plans, too.

Notwithstanding, I didn't think I could bring myself to throwing Emilio to the Russian dogs. They'd kill him in the most horrific way, and they'd get someone on the inside to do it. He might not be my true son, but he'd lived as such all his life. As evil as he was, I just couldn't do him like that.

After some time, Gregory left to go downstairs, muttering something about loyalty and love. And most of all, regaining control.

Over the next few days, I buried myself in work and tried not to think about my desperate situation, but my encounter with Merry at the police station kept playing on my mind. The fact that she had let me touch her filled me with confidence and positive thoughts. But what did that change? I didn't want to accept that soon, she could become my stepdaughter. Holy shit, this even sounded wrong.

On Friday night, I had to get myself ready for a garden party at Elaine's mansion. She'd invited Victor and a few of his associates to smooth things over between us. I wasn't looking forward to that at all, but Merry was going to be there and I really had to see her.

Morales hadn't actively pursued my case due to lack of evidence, but I had a hunch she wasn't done with me yet.

Elaine asked me to stay with her for a couple of days, but I told her I needed to work after the meeting because we had special events lined up. I had no idea for how long I could keep this up.

If I was going to marry her, I had to give her what she wanted, and Elaine liked sex. She liked it a lot.

I got changed in the club and then asked Ryga to drop me

and Gregory to her place. It had been a hell of a week, and I hoped I wouldn't be getting any more bad surprises.

A housekeeper opened the door, and I found Elaine entertaining her guests by the pool. I had roughly six weeks to figure out how to break the engagement and stay alive. If I failed, I was doomed.

I instantly spotted my princess, but she wasn't alone. Some asshole's arms were wrapped around her waist. Had that asshole, Robert, flown all the way over here? Whatever the case, I needed to be on my best behavior. I came here to play a good fiancé and network with Victor, but I couldn't take my eyes off her.

"Ivo, let me get you a drink... I was just telling Mari about our theme for the wedding reception. I am so excited," Elaine chirped, passing me a glass of whiskey.

I smiled, murmuring something inane, but the man standing next to Merry was getting on my nerves. If he didn't back off, I'd punch him in the face.

Eventually, Merry must have noticed me staring at her because she finally looked at me. Our gazes hooked for a long while until Elaine started talking about the wedding again.

"Maybe we should focus on the business at hand today," I said with a sigh.

"Well, once we get married, we are going to be one of the most influential couples in Los Angeles," she purred, while I took a generous sip of my drink. I wanted to drink the whole bottle but I needed to pace myself. She had this idea in her head that with the Russians on board, she was going to be a celebrity. "So we're going to be set."

"Whatever you say, Elaine. How is Clara?" I asked, wanting

to direct this question to Merry, but it was best if I stayed away from her for now.

"She's much better. I think the therapy helps," she replied dismissively. "Does Emilio have his date scheduled for court?"

"Yeah. The hearing is in about a week or so and I'm expecting him to stay locked up for the foreseeable future," I replied, finishing off my drink. I didn't want to think about Emilio, but once I got to chat with Victor, I'd need to find out what he was planning to do about him.

"Well, I wouldn't be so sure. I have a feeling Victor might have other plans in mind," she said, and a bunch of bricks cascaded down to my stomach. Fuck this bitch and her predictions. I truly fucked myself over agreeing to marry her.

"We shall see, but Emilio is where he belongs."

"Victor won't want to see his own son in prison. It's bad for business, dear," she continued, driving me crazy. Family was always important in our world, but where did one draw the line? "Anyway, come. I will introduce you to Robert, Merry's boyfriend. I think they look so cute together, and I hope they get married. Robert is a pretty brilliant business lawyer."

She didn't actually give me any choice. Taking my arm, she forced me to follow her. Damn it. I wasn't ready for this and clearly, I wasn't drunk enough to talk to them. Merry was wearing a pale pink jump-suit that showed off her curves and amazing, perky tits. I didn't think I could control myself being around her, inhaling her scent and knowing that I couldn't fucking touch her. I couldn't even afford to get a hard-on because Elaine had insisted I wear slim leg white pants tonight. She even tried to control what I wore.

This couldn't end well.

"Robert, this is my fiancé, Ivo Sergei. I've meant to introduce you two for a while now," Elaine sang as she pushed me in front of the dark-haired, bearded guy. He grinned like he'd just won a million dollars and reached out to shake my hand. I already hated him and wished I could break his bones for touching what was mine.

"It's good to meet you, man. Merry has such a huge family. I'm staying here until Monday, then unfortunately duty calls," he explained, as though I was fucking interested in his boring life. At this point, I stopped looking at him and turned my attention to my princess.

Immediately, my dick stirred, so I linked my hands in front of me, hiding my crotch. Damn it.

She looked positively radiant and when she bit on her lower lip, giving me a heated look, I almost groaned out loud.

"Oh, you're such a busy bee, Robert. Just like our Merry," Elaine commented.

When Elaine stopped talking, an awkward silence ensued, during which time I had a hell of a time dragging my gaze away from Merry. How could I, when all I wanted to do was undress her, rip her panties off, tie her to a bed, and fuck her hard until she couldn't take any more of my cock? And then do it again, and again, reducing her tight, sweet pussy to a wet pulp.

"Merry told me you own a club, Ivo. How's it doing?" Robert asked.

"Yes, that's right. It's going great," I snapped.

"I just need a refill. Will be back in a second," Merry muttered, then threw me a warning glare before excusing herself, leaving me alone with the other two. They got to talking about Elaine's extensive art collection and I was ready to slit my wrists. Several long moments later, I told them both that I need another drink when I spotted Merry heading upstairs.

I went to the bar and refilled my glass, contemplating whether I should follow her. Gregory winked at me as though he could already see what I was planning, and more than that: encouraging me. Asshole. He was chatting to Clara, who looked much better, and that cheered me up.

When I realized Elaine was still immersed in her conversation with Robert, I went for it and hurried upstairs. I couldn't find Merry at first, so I figured she must have gone to her old room Elaine had maintained for her. I heard her moving around in the bathroom when I shut the door quietly, so I could surprise her. This must have been one of my biggest fantasies—to take Merry on a wild ride while a party was in full swing downstairs. I knew she wanted me. She could deny it as much as she wanted, but as I always thought, her eyes didn't lie. She'd always had expressive eyes.

I waited for her to come out and then I ambushed her, pushing her against the wall and lifting her hands above her head.

"We're done playing, princess. Daddy's missed you."

Chapter Twenty-One

Merry

Elaine could throw a great party, but I was bored and exhausted. I had been somewhat looking forward to it, until Robert arrived in the morning unannounced. He said he'd wanted to surprise me because he missed me so much.

We'd kept in touch almost every day but I wasn't expecting this. I felt guilty because the truth was, I didn't want to see him.

Deep down, I knew we were never going to be an item but I didn't want to ruin his weekend, so I took him to Elaine's party. It was too late to cancel and if she heard that he was here, she'd insist that he come, anyway.

Then, Ivo showed up and I couldn't breathe when I saw him. He looked furious when he noticed Robert's hand possessively around my waist. The heat from his stare trickled into my veins, holding me in place.

This whole situation was complicated and plain wrong. I never wanted to cheat on Robert with Ivo, but I turned into a different person when my stepmother's fiancé was around me.

I nervously wet my lips when Elaine dragged Ivo over to where we stood and introduced the two men. I wished I'd had the opportunity to prepare him regarding Robert.

My boyfriend was a good and decent man, but he didn't know anything about my past. He had no idea who my father was and it was better this way, even though I was sure Elaine had other plans in mind. The only way she'd bless this union so enthusiastically was if there was something in it for her.

Ivo had protected me, kept me out of the scene of the shooting with Emilio. He'd kept his promise, and the thought of him taking responsibility for it just for me did something to me. My heart ached for him, and my body suffered without him. I just didn't know what to do. How to get through this.

At least, Clara was glad that everything worked out, but I had to make sure she continued going to therapy, otherwise it would be a wasted effort.

Ultimately, I had to get away from Ivo. I had no choice. These strong emotions were slowly tormenting me. For this reason, I'd had to excuse myself and leave the three of them downstairs, while took a breather and made sense of my thoughts.

I hurried upstairs and found refuge in my old room. In the bathroom, I stared at my reflection in the mirror for a little while. My cheeks were flushed and I was tense. Ivo had this effect on me.

Then, I washed my hands and decided to face my demons, so I exited the bathroom.

That was when someone grabbed me and pushed me against the wall. I gasped, ready to scream when I realized it was Ivo. He pushed my hands above my head, bringing his lean, hot body flush against mine, and that mad gleam in his eyes told me he was up to no good.

"We're done playing, princess. Daddy's missed you," he said, and my knees buckled.

I looked around him at the door.

"Door's closed, like you had it," he said, as if reading my mind.

I looked into his eyes, and suddenly, I was tired of fighting.

Tired of pushing him away.

Tired of denying how much I wanted him.

This was wrong on so many levels, but at one time, for a few unforgettable nights—before Elaine, before Emilio—Ivo had belonged to me. If only...

I needed something more to remember him by because living this lie was slowly destroying me inside.

"This is dangerous, Ivo. Someone is bound to notice that we're both missing," I whispered while my heart pounded a loud rhythm inside my chest. I felt the bulge in his pants, pressing against my navel. Ivo was absolutely gorgeous and all he had to do to make me wet was stand in my presence. After our indecent encounter at the police station, I couldn't stop thinking about him and what else he could do to me.

"You have been a naughty girl, princess, and you deserve to be punished," he growled, causing my nipples to stiffen.

He wanted to play games. I should slap him and get out of this room while I was still ahead, but my heart wouldn't let me.

Warmth spread over my chest, then down between my legs, and I drew in a shaky breath. I wanted him to touch me, to punish me and talk dirty. I wanted him to do whatever he wanted to me.

What was wrong with me? Robert was downstairs, none the wiser. He loved me and I was betraying him with a man twice my age, in my old room Elaine had kept crisp and clean—unlike my feelings.

The man in question regarded me as though I was good enough to eat. "What are you going to do to me?" I asked, my voice hoarse.

His gaze roamed over me, stern and disapproving, pausing on my lips.

"Take off that jumpsuit. I can see your ass in it and I noticed a lot of men have been looking at it. You know how much that displeases me," he ordered, moving his other hand over my cleavage and gently caressing my nipple. I shut my eyes, trying to breathe, but I was struggling to stay still.

"I have no idea what are you talking about. My boyfriend likes this outfit very much," I finally said, angry that he was being so possessive. He was never going to own me so I could wear whatever I wanted.

He pinched my nipple then, and I gasped, desperate for more.

"You're mine. I want to drag you downstairs and let everyone know that no one has ever made you come like I have, princess," he whispered, then moved his lips gently over my neck, kissing and caressing it.

Goosebumps appeared on my arms and heat spread between my legs, igniting a fire inside me. He was so fucking gentle but his touch was driving me insane. Savage desire kept me locked in place, and I knew I was losing this war.

"No, you can't because we are not together, Daddy. We are just fucking," I said crudely, knowing that he was going to be mad about it.

Just as I expected, he bit into my neck, painfully hard. I cried out, already throbbing for him as he massaged my breasts. I needed to have him inside me. He always knew how much pressure to apply and where to touch me.

Then, he pulled away and just stared at me. He was so hard, his erection heavy and throbbing.

"You have to get rid of this asshole, Robert. You're not marrying him, princess," he growled, and I gasped when he buried his lips between my breasts. We were separated by a thin layer of material and I was ready to tear everything off us both. I needed him to slide into me and start that maddening rhythm, over and over, until I couldn't take it anymore.

"I might get rid of Robert when you leave Elaine, but we both know you won't," I sneered.

"Get on the bed and lie down on your stomach," he ordered, and I giggled.

"Make me," I challenged, excited about all the possibilities this situation was leading us to.

One corner of Ivo's mouth lifted in a lopsided smile.

"You forgot to say: Make me, Daddy," he murmured.

I tried to pull away from his tight grip, but the bastard was bigger and stronger than me. Kneeling down, he moved his arm between my legs and threw me on the bed, so I lay face down.

"Someone is going to look for us," I hissed, but he was

already unzipping my jumpsuit. "At least lock the door, asshole."

"No, because I want that wimp you're dating to hear you scream my name, from all the way downstairs," he said, then I lifted my ass so he could take the jumpsuit off me. Okay, I was wet for him, ready to play, but we both knew we couldn't afford to get caught. "And you have been naughty so you're going to be punished."

"Whatever—just get on with it," I growled, frustrated when he ran his hands down my spine, sending tingles of warmth through my core. Once he got rid of my jumpsuit, I was left wearing a black lacy thong and strapless bra.

I hated being in this position where Ivo had all the control—well, maybe hated was too strong a word. All right, it wasn't even true.

My skin prickled with awareness as he hovered over me. I looked back at him when I felt him hesitate. He was taking something out of his pocket, then dangled it in front of my face. A pair of handcuffs.

"Oh, no, you're not—"

He didn't even let me finish and seconds later, he was tying my hands behind me.

"Daddy. Every time you forget to say 'Daddy' you will get a spanking, princess. So far, you missed saying it four times," he stated.

I bet he was so happy about the fact I wasn't very compliant. His body heat was a living thing, sinking into my skin and urging me to lift my ass, so he could touch me. My breathing was erratic and all my senses were hypersensitive.

I thought about how Robert had wanted to have sex when

he'd arrived, but I told him I wasn't feeling well. I wasn't sure I could even sleep with him again. At least not in the same state where Ivo lived.

Ivo pulled my knickers down over my legs, so nothing would separate me from receiving his cock—the ultimate prize.

With each touch, each caress, we were sinking deeper into a hole we couldn't dig ourselves out from. But then, Ivo smacked me on my bare ass and those dark thoughts flew away. The burning pain left me breathless.

"Count for me, princess," he ordered, caressing my raw skin on my rear end.

"One, Daddy," I said, feeling so aroused and wet.

"Good girl. I bet you're already soaking wet for me," he said, and then slapped me two more times after that. Each time harder than the other.

Lost in these incredible sensations, I obeyed his commands.

He moved his fingers along my ass crack and caressed it until I panted for breath, then slid them down all the way to my pussy. I yelped, praying for release as he pushed two fingers inside me, fucking me gently. This felt so good and my pussy was pulsating in rhythm with the steady beats of my heart.

"Oh yes, I was right. My princess is coming all over Daddy's fingers. Shit. You have no idea how much I want to take you right now." He started ramming the fingers in and out of me.

In this uncomfortable position, I buried my face in the duvet, trying to suppress my moans. He was right. My heart raced and if he continued like this, then I would be reaching the peak very soon. He had all the control and could punish me like this for hours.

I cried out, but then he suddenly stopped, withdrew his

fingers, and delivered his final slap. This time I shrieked when his palm landed on my ass. I felt numb all over and my skin burned with raw fire. Ivo didn't hold back—he pulled out all the stops and hit me hard.

A moment later, when I was still panting, he released me from the handcuffs and flipped me around, so I was lying on my back.

"What was that, princess? I didn't hear you?" he asked.

"Four, Daddy," I said through gritted teeth, staring at his huge erection that was visible through the white fabric of his pants. My throat went dry with need and desire. I needed him to stop playing around and just get me off.

"Such a good and obedient girl. Now lie still, princess," he ordered. I didn't even know why I was obeying his every command, but my hope was that he'd make me come soon. "And spread your legs wide for me."

I inhaled sharply and did as he asked. My pussy was fully exposed then, and he could probably see how much I desired him. Groaning, he pressed his hand over his shaft, then pulled me closer to the edge, so he'd have better access to me.

"Such a pretty pussy, Merry. I won't let you leave this room until I hear you screaming my name."

His lips curved in anticipation as he greedily eyed my body. My breasts were tender, nipples perky and hard. He only had to touch me, but I was too stubborn to ask for it.

Then, he stuck his face between my legs, licking me there like a furious animal, as though he couldn't get enough. I cried out with pleasure, getting closer to the finish line. I wasn't going to last long, especially after the spanking—the pleasure-pain that almost drove me over the edge.

Ivo licked my clit, moving his hand over my thigh gently, to make sure I stayed still.

"Do you like that, princess? Are you going to come for your daddy?"

I nodded, unable to offer a coherent response when he sucked on my nub with such enthusiasm. My whole body shuddered as I arched my head backwards.

"Stick your fingers inside me, Daddy, please," I begged, needing this release so much, I didn't care that he'd won and got me where he wanted. Pressure and tension filled my body as he kept licking every part of my throbbing centre.

"Of course, my princess," he rasped before thrusting two fingers again inside me. He proceeded to lick, suck, and pinch on my clit all at once while his fingers worked their magic.

"That's it, just keep going like that. I'm going to come, Daddy!" I shouted, ignoring how desperate I sounded. He sucked on my clit again and again, until my breaths came in long, ragged pants.

And then, when I was just about to explode with my orgasm nearing, he stopped moving. He withdrew his fingers and I collapsed on the bed, sobbing. He grinned at me.

"I'll make you come if you promise you get rid of that asshole downstairs!"

Chapter Twenty-Two

Ivo

She had no clue what she was doing to me with all her moans and Daddy talk. I was so fucking hard, my dick was straining in my pants and I wanted her to suck it, to wrap her beautiful lips around it, or better still—I wanted to come between her tits.

She smelled divine, exactly as I remembered, with a hint of honey and vanilla. But there was also something else, something extra: rose petals. I had her exactly where I needed her. She was under my mercy and she was only going to come if I allowed her to.

"What?" she protested, her eyes wide and telling me I'd lost my mind for withholding her climax. "No, I'm not going to get rid of him. We are almost engaged, just like you!" Her indignant tone grated on me.

Maybe I was pushing this too far, because she was staring at me with such venom in her eyes, I thought she might actually slap me. And I deserved it—maybe even secretly desired it.

"You're soaking wet, ready to come," I reminded her, playing with fire.

"Don't you bloody dare give me an ultimatum. You're marrying Elaine, you jerk. Is this how you want me to forgive you?"

Truth be told, I wanted to see her come for me. I didn't know why I stopped. Probably because I was furious that she was with someone else.

"Do you really believe I'm going to marry her?" I asked as she tried to get off the bed, but I pushed her back down. She wasn't going anywhere until she got her orgasm. Her eyes widened even more in shock and bewilderment. Fuck, I wasn't going to let her go until she was truly satisfied.

"We both know you don't really have any choice. But we do have now..." She smirked, then moved closer, reaching out for my dick.

She was right. In this moment in time, I didn't really have any other options—not until I spoke to Victor and figured some things out. I needed to see if he could be convinced to consider another perspective.

I caught her hand and dragged her into my arms before she could touch me. There were so many wonderful things I wanted to do to this woman, but we were running out of time.

"You are not to touch my dick, but I am a man of my word. Daddy wants to punish you badly, but Ivo is a bit more lenient," I said before kissing her hard, devouring her mouth. She still had that bra on, so I unclasped it and then I had her naked, her pretty breasts flush against my chest. Our mouths moved in sync and I wanted more—I wanted all of her.

Moving my hand to her hip, I cupped her pussy, so she was trapped. We were both breathless when we finally pulled away from each other.

"You're dripping all over my hand, princess," I murmured, then shoved two fingers inside her again, the way she liked. She shut her eyes and moaned so loudly, I knew someone would hear eventually, especially if they climbed to this floor. These walls were thin and there were plenty of people downstairs. Lost in a wave of desire, I started massaging her clit with my thumb.

With my other hand, I traced the shape of her stunning ass, then teased the slit between her cheeks. She was so delicate and I was obsessed with making her come, indulged by her sounds of pleasure. This time she would reach her peak, so she'd remember how well she responded to me.

She was panting, gripping my neck and digging her nails into my skin. This was beyond wonderful—and then, when I thought it couldn't get any better, she was coming for me and only me. Her body started to spasm as she screamed my name, telling me that I was the only one for her, the only one who made her feel this way. We cocooned ourselves in our own bubble as that delicious orgasm rocked through her.

I felt pre-cum oozing from my dick and wetting my pants. I lived for this moment when she proved she was mine, and I wanted to kill any other guy who'd dare touch her. I was massaging her beautiful breasts, bending down to draw a nipple into my mouth, when we were both startled by a knock at the door.

Her eyes shot toward me and a moment later, she scrambled

off the bed and vanished inside the bathroom. Cursing under my breath, I picked her clothes off the floor, cracked the bathroom door open, and threw them to her.

"Just don't let them in here," Merry hissed.

Trying to calm my huge boner was a feat unto itself. The material around my crotch was damp and if anyone looked, they'd figure out what I had been up to.

"Who is it?" I asked, pushing the door open a bit.

Clara flinched when she saw me, and her cheeks were flushed.

"Hi, Elaine is looking for you. Victor is here," she said. She strained her neck to peek in the room, as though knowing Merry was in there, somewhere.

"I'll be right out," I said, clearing my throat. She giggled and I wondered if Merry's sister still hated me after all this time.

"Tell Merry that Robert has been looking for her too," she said with a wink, then headed back downstairs.

I shut the door and exhaled a ragged breath. That was fucking close, all because my princess made me do crazy things.

"Who was that?" Merry asked in a tiny voice. She was almost dressed and had gone so pale, but then she caught sight of my prominent boner and her expression morphed to amused.

"Clara. Does she know about us?" I tried to think about Elaine, just so I could get back downstairs without the hard on.

"Probably. So, what did she want?"

"The Russians are here and your *boyfriend* is looking for you," I said, making plans to secret away somewhere and jerk off my pent-up energy. Merry had her jumpsuit already on and she was fixing her hair, but her hungry gaze kept drifting to my cock, which made things worse.

"Let me blow you. I can be super-fast," she offered, and I raised an eyebrow.

Well then, how could I say no? Without saying a word, I communicated what I wanted.

She went down on her knees and quickly undid my pants. Merry was so damn addictive, and this was a thousand times better than dejected old me taking care of myself in some bathroom on my own, like a fucking teenager.

"Just be quiet and take it. We don't have much time," she said as my cock sprang out of my boxers.

She immediately took it in her mouth and I had to lean into the wall to brace myself. She was right; this was going to be quick. I'd be exploding in no time. Her mouth was perfect, moving over my shaft with eagerness and a good rhythm. She was well acquainted with my cock, but she must have been practising because now she took it all the way back to her throat.

"Fuck, Merry, you're going to kill me. I want you to swallow me whole like the good girl you are." She trailed her mouth up and down my shaft, tickling my balls at the same time with her fingers. She had all the control, and it drove me wild. She sucked me effortlessly, relishing the act of satisfying her daddy.

I arched my head back, grabbing the back of her neck and tangling my fingers in her soft hair.

She licked the tip so eagerly, so expertly, I wondered where she'd learned these tricks. Last time I'd ordered her to blow me, she barely knew what shew was doing. My balls were getting so heavy and my orgasm was nearing

"Have you been taking lessons, princess?" I growled, suddenly thinking that she was sucking that fucker like that? The thought alone triggered a rage inside me that I found hard to contain.

The pressure around my groin area was mounting as Merry almost gagged on my length. Letting out a groan, I came inside her mouth and she took it all—every last drop. It took me a moment to recoup, after which I pulled out and freed her, completely wiped. Merry had just sucked the life out of me.

She got up and wiped her mouth, a goddess walking the earth. She was incredible and what we had between us was solid. No one was going to change that because it was real.

"Now you go first and I'll come down a bit later. I know I've said it before but this cannot happen again, Ivo. We just can't," she said.

Without saying a word, I went to the bathroom to quickly clean myself, trying to look presentable again. I wanted to go tell her that she was wrong, and what we had was too important, not purely physical, but just then I heard the door open and shut.

I thought about Elaine. She wanted me to sleep with her tonight, to stay in the mansion and pretend we were one big happy family. I'd told her I was busy, but knowing her, she wouldn't take no for an answer. Releasing a sigh, I exited the room several minutes later. The floor was empty, but I could hear the chatting and laughter downstairs.

With the presence of the Russians, I could already sense a lingering tension, a more mellow party atmosphere. It was hard to explain and difficult to decipher, but there, nonetheless. I made quick work of going downstairs, trying to mingle with the crowd, and hoping no one had noticed me gone for too long. Gregory gave me an all-knowing look. He wouldn't be fooled. I quickly grabbed a glass of champagne from a tray one of the waiters was carrying, ignoring my son. Where the fuck was the hard liquor?

Elaine was standing outside, talking to two men of large build. I recognized one as Victor, but didn't know the other one. From a distance, I realized how much Emilio looked like him, now that I was focusing on similarities. The proof had been right in front of me, but I never noticed because my dealings with Victor weren't a frequent thing. He was always in the background, moving around like a shadow. Slowly, the reality of this tangled situation started weighing on me. How had I been so blind?

I headed to the bar, needing a fortifying drink before facing Victor. Elaine hadn't spotted me yet, so I went to the kitchen where she kept her Scotch. I found the bottle and poured myself a few fingers, neat.

Merry wasn't anywhere to be seen and I hoped she hadn't left yet. I glanced around and was just about to walk away when I heard noises outside, behind the patio doors that led out to the garden, just off the kitchen. From where I was standing, I could clearly hear what they were saying.

"What do you mean you're not sure? What changed in the past half hour?"

"A lot of things, Robert. You wouldn't understand. I mean, things work differently with my family and I have obligations ... I might have to stay here for a while," Merry replied.

What was she doing? Breaking up with that clown? It sounded like it and I was suddenly in a very good mood.

"That doesn't change the fact that I love you. If it becomes necessary, I'll move to LA, Merry. My father has a firm here, so the transition wouldn't be that difficult. He's been asking me to work with him forever, anyway," he said, and I clenched my fists. I was going to cut that motherfucker up like charcuterie, then burn him, and destroy him. That was how far I was willing to go with this.

They couldn't see me because I was hidden between the doors, but the moment I sensed he was getting closer to her, I thought I might lose my fucking mind.

"Stop it, Rob, please. I don't want you to move. I am all over the place, but the truth is that I ... I don't love you. I've been thinking about this, and I'm sorry," Merry said in a sad tone, and my heart literally danced inside my chest.

Yeah, motherfucker. She was doing exactly what I asked her to do—getting rid of him.

"I know your family background. You don't have to hide it from me, and your stepmother's fiancé is involved in some shady business, too," Robert continued. I held the bottle in my hands, wondering what exactly he knew about me. "I am aware you want to escape this life and I can help you with that. We are good together and I can't get enough of your perfect body, Merry."

This wasn't good and now I had to fucking see what he was doing. I leaned over to catch him in the act of kissing her. The rage soared to new heights, so potent it turned my blood to arsenic. If he didn't get his dirty hands off her...

So then, I did the only thing that came to my mind. I threw the bottle of Scotch at the patio doors and shattered the glass to pieces.

They backed off each other like skittish cats and Merry screamed, hopping away from the door. They both stared at me in shock as I shrugged my shoulders.

"Sorry about that. The bottle must have slipped through my hand."

Chapter Twenty-Three

Merry

"Oh my God, you're bleeding!" I cried, shocked as my now ex-fiancé cradled his injured hand in the other. "Come on, let's go find the first aid kit."

I gaped at Ivo, wondering what the hell was wrong with him. He must have overheard what I was telling Robert. God damn it, why did men have to be so obtuse? Robert belted out a curse, glaring at Ivo like he wanted to rip him a new one.

Staff came running to the kitchen and saw the shattered glass on the floor as I handed a paper towel to Robert. Did Ivo really have to throw that fucking bottle and smash the patio door to pieces?

"No, leave it. I don't need your help," Robert snapped, pulling away from me when I tried to look at his hand. His grey suit was ruined.

Elaine barged in then and started fussing around, being all dramatic.

"I'll take him upstairs and look after the hand there. Oh, poor Rob. I am so sorry about that," she finally said, giving me a questioning gaze.

Ivo was still standing in the same spot and my blood was boiling.

Some of the wait staff started cleaning the floor, taking care of the glass. I grabbed Ivo's elbow and pulled him to the side after Robert had left with Elaine.

"What the fuck is wrong with you? A bottle of whiskey? You could have killed him!"

His eyes were sharp, focused on me, and there was no sign of remorse in them. I shouldn't have had this conversation with Robert now, during this party, but I didn't want to lie to him and let him believe there was a future for us. He deserved better.

"He put your hands on you," he snarled, vicious as a snake.

This wasn't even remotely funny anymore and I was so done with all this confusion. Being the other woman, pretending I was happy, caving in to Ivo's charm—I had had it up to here...

"Ivo, I've been looking for you. Can I wrestle you away from your future stepdaughter for a moment? We have so much to discuss." The man in the black suit I'd pegged to be Victor showed up in the kitchen and gestured to Ivo to follow him. My throat went dry because he looked so much like Emilio, but scarier and fairer, with dark blond hair. With broad shoulders and a large, chiseled jaw, he looked like someone who could easily destroy you.

I felt a little unsettled, despite knowing that Emilio was

locked up. This man, with whom the filthy rapist shared his genes, gave me the heebie-jeebies.

"We can talk business with Merry. She's after all the Camilleri family attorney," Ivo said unexpectedly, measuring the man with a sharp gaze.

Victor seemed irritated at that response, and I felt even more uneasy in his presence. I hoped they remembered this was neutral territory and they needed to act civil.

Victor sized me up and I stood still, giving him time to make up his mind. He knew my father well—they'd done plenty of business together at one time in the past. I remembered being at one of their meetings when I was younger.

"I'd rather talk in private," Victor finally said, growling like an angry tiger.

Ivo surely realized how dangerous the man was. I had heard about his penchant for violence and murder.

"It's fine, Ivo. You guys go ahead. I have something to attend to, anyway," I said, throwing a pointed glare at Ivo before walking away. I was too upset with the man right then, and I needed to be somewhere else. Some place he wasn't.

The gall of the motherfucker to feel jealousy toward Robert and hurt him when *he* was fucking my own stepmother and planning to get hitched with her. Let him deal with Victor, the man he was currently at war with. This was their business and Elaine's business, and I honestly wanted to stay out of it.

I got myself a drink and tried to find Clara. Around twenty minutes later, I was ready to disappear with her, to ditch this party altogether, but she was talking to Gregory outside. She looked relaxed and laughing, so I didn't want to ruin her day, too. I probably needed time alone, anyway.

"And where do you think you're going, Merry?" Elaine asked, catching me on the way out.

Coming face-to-face with her so soon after Ivo gave me that explosive orgasm had me feeling flushed from the top of my head to the tips of my toes. How did I get myself into this mess? Why could I not resist him?

He's not the man for you. He belongs to your stepmother.

"I'm leaving. I think I'm done with parties for a while," I said, trying to push through the guilt. As manipulative and overbearing as Elaine could be, she didn't deserve this kind of betrayal. She put her hand to her mouth as though not feeling well, but then frowned. She'd probably had a few drinks too many.

"You need to take Robert home and talk to him. I patched him up but he seems upset. What on earth did you tell him earlier?" she asked, and I inwardly groaned.

"That I wasn't planning to marry him and this wasn't working. He kept pushing me and I wasn't ready, so I had to let him go," I said, hoping she wouldn't start asking questions or pressuring me to take him back. But this was Elaine. I wouldn't expect any less of her.

At the same time, I was angry with myself because I let Ivo dictate how I should live and what decisions I make. This was my life and yet, I'd listened to him and broke up with Robert. Granted, I knew how I felt, and that Robert wasn't the man I wanted to be with, but that was beside the point. I didn't have a future with Ivo, either.

"Don't be absurd. He's perfect for you, so take him home and sort things out," she said, and I almost laughed. Elaine was deluded if she thought I could just take Robert back. It seemed she lived in a different universe.

That was when Robert showed up with his shirt off. The jacket was ruined but the shirt had been badly stained with blood. Elaine must have taken care of the wound on his hand as it was bandaged. He looked so defeated, and it was all my fault. Ivo had turned my life upside down and I was making one bad decision after another. Oh dear.

"Come on, Rob," I told him. He hesitated, reluctant to come with me, but Elaine practically shoved him out the door, telling him that he had to listen to what I had to say.

She wasn't helping me in any way.

"I'm going back to New York tonight, so don't worry, you won't have to pretend any longer, Merry," he announced when I got into the car and started the engine. I hated that he was so hostile towards me, but I understood. I never meant to hurt him.

"Please stop it and come in. You can stay as long as you want. I'm sorry for bringing it up tonight, but I can't take that back. Now you need to rest. I can go and stay with Clara so you have my apartment to yourself," I admitted, feeling like the worst human being in this world.

He was suffering now because I thought I could have it all. Power and a good life beyond the reach of the mob, but nothing was ever that simple, especially with my family.

Robert looked broken and for a while, he just stood in front of the car, staring at me. He must have done his research about my family, yet he still wanted me. I was the one holding things back.

"No. I just want to go home. Please take me to the airport," he said firmly, getting in the car.

Heavy emotions clogged my throat, and I found myself unable to utter a word. What should I say? He couldn't bear to stay a moment longer, and I had to respect that, so I nodded. This was hard for both of us. I was a coward and an idiot. Ivo was never going to leave Elaine and yet, I still let him get close to me. I must be a glutton for punishment.

Punishment...

The entire drive was awkward and long. First, I took him back to my flat, so he could change into a clean shirt and grab the rest of his things. He was still angry with me and didn't want to talk at all, which I didn't blame him for. Part of me wished I could go back in time and change everything. Maybe then I would have never walked into that club and met Ivo. The moment I decided I needed to experience a proper orgasm, I unlocked a chain of events that led to Clara's rape.

"I'm sorry once again. I never once meant for this to happen," I said when we were almost ready to leave. I just needed him to know that none of this was intentional, that deep down I cared for him very much. He finished up and I had him sit in my living room, offering some coffee, but he declined. He was wounded and I wanted to make sure he was all right before he decided to travel today.

Robert was going to be fine, I knew that, but somehow, I needed him to forgive me.

"It's my fault, too. I was pushing you too hard. I thought you were ready, so don't beat yourself up over it, Merry," he finally said, sighing heavily. "I really can't stay here any longer but you don't need to worry about me."

Then, he picked up his luggage, his mind made up. We left the apartment and I drove him to the airport. I watched him walk inside, at last feeling like a heavy weight had been lifted off my chest. We were done and now I had to move on with my life.

But how?

That night, I went back to my apartment and called my sister, asking her to come over. When she arrived, I told her everything that had happened. We stayed up until late, drinking wine and talking. I was so happy she was finally opening up to me. It had been such a long time since we'd done that. Her new medication worked wonders, yet I also believed something within her had clicked, and she'd finally come to the realization she was worthy of love, and most importantly, worth fighting for. The mind was such a mystery.

In the days that followed, I threw myself into work for my firm, attending remote meetings with clients and colleagues to wrap up some cases, and then put in my notice to leave the job. I wasn't sure where I was destined to be ... where I'd lay my hat. One thing was sure: I couldn't go back to New York and face Robert every day. I had a license to practise in California, so that was one road I could take until I made a decision.

The biggest issue was that I didn't want to stay here because of Ivo. I needed to be away from him unless he found a way to break his ridiculous deal with Elaine—and even then, it would be awkward and wrong. How could I face my stepmother ever again?

If he did marry her, there was no way I'd stay in LA to torture myself.

I closed my laptop and stretched on the chair, feeling a little peckish. My back hurt like hell and I needed a nap, but my mind was whirling. Sooner or later, I would need to make a decision. I could go to New York and find a position at another firm, but maybe it wasn't for me. That part of my life was over—there was a finality to it, and it wasn't just about Robert.

My cell started ringing, and my sister's number flashed on the screen.

"What's up? I thought you were at your meeting with Doctor Johnson?" I asked.

Clara had made huge strides with her new therapist, and I was so proud of her.

"Ivo was just in the mansion," she said, and I had to roll my eyes.

Clara was rooting for us but she didn't understand how complicated things were. She did make it clear that she didn't hold a grudge towards Ivo or Gregory, and she was slowly healing. Emilio was a different person, she said, not like the rest of his family, and he was the guilty one, along with his friends.

Her recovery was going to be a long process, but I would stand by her every step of the way.

"So what?" I asked in an amused tone. I was hurting, yet I couldn't burden my sister with it.

"Yes, at first I thought nothing of it, but then I overheard Elaine and Ivo talking in the garden," she said, sounding oddly calm.

"Right."

"She wants him to move in with us, and she's not taking no for an answer," she said, and my heart squeezed inside my chest. "And don't even say you don't care because I know you do. He has never been responsible for Emilio's actions. You need to accept that, Merry, and fight for him. He's not right for Elaine."

I didn't say anything, but thousands of emotions swirled inside my head. From anguish to pain and finally, desire. I rubbed the back of my neck, utterly exhausted.

"This is natural. They are engaged and they are going to get married soon. It's obvious they are going to live together," I told her.

"So you're just going to stand by and do nothing? Robert is gone and he's not coming back. You have to tell Elaine that Ivo has always been yours, that you met him first," Clara insisted.

I liked that she was so enthusiastic about this, but Ivo was risking too much, for a lot was riding on this union. I'd be damned before letting innocent people get hurt.

"This is not as simple as that and you should know this, Clara. We are the daughters of a mob boss," I said.

"Bullshit. He's crazy about you, so stop denying it. Elaine has been acting strange lately, more than usual. She nearly flipped when Ivo told her he needs some time to adjust to the idea of living with her," she divulged.

Just when I was about to respond, I heard a knock on my door. I groaned into the phone because I wasn't expecting visitors.

"Hold on, there's someone at the door. I'm going to have to call you back," I said to her.

She called me a chicken and then hung up. I smoothed my hair and opened the door, thinking it might be a delivery man but instead, I found Ivo staring right at me. He must have come straight here after seeing Elaine.

He looked so serious, I started to dread what he must have come here to say.

That he was choosing Elaine.

Chapter Twenty-Four

Ivo

Things were spinning out of control and I couldn't think straight. I had lost control at the party and I shouldn't have, but I couldn't stand by and let another man touch my woman. I destroyed Elaine's patio doors and then nearly blew up the meeting with Victor.

Merry had been right all along. I had to sort my shit out with Elaine first. That woman had me by the balls but I hoped against hope she could be reasonable. She needed to understand that I had never planned to fall for her stepdaughter, but I'd met her first.

Merry deserved all of me, not just the scraps I could give. She had too much self-respect to be the other woman, and I felt like a moron for even suggesting she should.

And then there was Victor, getting concerned about Emilio.

I told him straight that I wasn't planning to get him out, that he needed to stay behind bars if Victor wanted me to honor my agreement and marry Elaine. This union would be insurance the Bulgarians would not stir up trouble with the Russians. To be true, some thought me a sell-out and they wouldn't be wrong.

But I was sick of bloodshed and violence. What would be so wrong about being a simple businessman? The club generated enough revenue for me to live a comfortable lifestyle. I didn't need backroom negotiations and shady deals to get by.

Our conversation had been short and brief. Apparently, Elaine had promised him some of her own territory. She also wanted to work closely with him to make sure to prevent any conflict of interest. She was licking his boots, trying to keep him happy.

Elaine would think me an idiot for thinking these thoughts about the future, which was why I never mentioned them to her.

"Emilio had grown restless after your empty promises, so that's why he did what he did in that club. He lost control and my niece paid the price," Victor said, holding my arm when I was ready to walk away.

Of course, the man would always put the blame on me for anything. Even for the way he'd hurt Gregory. Even for the way he believed lies as they suited him.

The sheer audacity of his words infuriated me. I had never promised anything to Emilio. He was only helping me with security in the club and I encouraged him to continue his studies. I never thought he could survive in the mafia world because he was too impulsive and hot-headed. Case in point, he was telling everybody I'd made him some sort of special promise. Lying through his teeth—even to my face. He needed help, because he was delusional.

Elaine benefited from this whole arrangement with the Russians, too. I'd never cared about expanding my business. All I wanted was peace.

"I always thought he couldn't handle what we do," I responded, trying to get a hold of myself because Victor ticked me off.

What was he trying to achieve? A good father award because he kept Emilio close when he was supposed to be locked up in prison?

"That boy is smart. After all, he has my blood in his veins. He needs to be kept busy. I just need you to realise that he's no longer your problem. I take care of my own blood. Just don't complicate things for me or him," he warned me, and then I shook his grip off my arm.

Victor was a piece of shit, and a lunatic. He didn't even care about what Emilio and his men had done. That was the problem with some of these two-bit thugs—they had no morals to speak of. No boundaries they live by. No honor.

I was suddenly tempted to drop everything and let the chips fall where they may. Would the Russians truly start an all-out war? After all, it wasn't in their interests, either. If I backed away from the business, Victor could deal with whoever my successor was, and if there wasn't one... well, all the better for him.

There was one person I could turn to in an emergency though: Sebastian Dimitrei, my Serbian cousin, who was killing it in Chicago as a mob boss. We spent much of our childhoods around each other, our families ignoring we were supposed to be natural enemies. He'd be a solid ally, which I needed, but I'd only use that card as an absolute last resort. My preference was to clean my own messes.

Besides, as far as I knew, Sebastian had been lately dealing with some shit of his own. The last thing he needed was my bullshit piled on top of his.

The party ended late that night. Elaine vanished in her room and I was glad she stopped bothering me. Victor left and promised to be in touch, so over the next few days, I had my men watch the Russians closely, because I didn't trust them. What were their plans with Emilio?

In the afternoon, Elaine called me and asked me to go see her because she wanted to talk to me about something important. Things were stagnant between us because of me, so maybe if I appeased her, it would go some way toward clearing the way between us. I needed her to convince Victor to keep Emilio where he was.

We started talking about this business at first when she suddenly blurted out to me that she wanted me to move in with her.

"What?" I asked. I was holding a glass of seltzer water half way to my lips when her words blindsided me. She'd asked me this before, but her tone this time around gave me pause.

I had to admit, she was looking exceptionally radiant today, with the sun filtering through the window right over her face. Such a shame I didn't feel anything for her but perhaps some admiration.

"I need you to make a commitment. It will look good if we are living together, Ivo," she explained, yawning, and I frowned.

What the hell was wrong with her today? She couldn't have been serious. "People talk, but when you move in, then this should ease the rumors."

I just stared at her, because she knew I didn't give a damn about rumors. Annoyed at her wasting my time, I told her she better help figure out what was going on with Victor and Emilio first. She needed to get her priorities straight.

And then I left without giving her an answer, telling her I needed some time to figure things out. She was pushing me and I couldn't deal with that shit, especially today.

Was Victor planning on using his connections to free Emilio, somehow? Maybe even on bail, despite the seriousness of the crime? That was the question, and I believed he was.

I also wondered if the police were ever going to find who'd planted drugs at the club.

No matter where I looked, trouble stared me right in the face.

After I left Elaine's, I decided to visit Merry. It was time to have a serious conversation with her. Elaine wanted to move forward, of course, and life was closing in. She likely questioned why I wasn't sleeping with her as I used to, and I was surprised she hadn't brought that up.

Merry opened the door and stared at me, surprised. After what happened at the party with Robert, I was probably the last person she expected to see.

"Ivo, what are you doing here? I don't think we have anything left to say to each other, and I won't be your side piece."

She started to close the door in my face but I stopped her

and pushed it back open. She looked so damn sexy in an elegant suit, her dark hair spilling around her shoulders.

"We need to talk," I said, walking in.

"Yeah, come on in. It's not like I have nothing else to do today," she muttered, following me to the living room.

She was mad at me. But there was no point in denying this any longer. I had made up my mind, and I was done with hiding and sneaking around.

Her apartment was cozy and stylish. Merry's distinctive perfume lingered in the air, and I closed my eyes for a moment, savoring it. When I turned back to her, she folded her arms over her chest and stood there, waiting for me to say something.

"Elaine asked me to move in with her," I said, not wanting to beat about the bush. Merry's expression was more disappointed than surprised. "And I'm going to say no. Tomorrow night, I am going to tell her about us."

Shock settled on her face. I bet she wasn't expecting me to say this. We were both struggling to stay away from each other and I couldn't keep lying and pretending I didn't care about her. She could deny it as much as she wanted, but I couldn't let her throw away what we had without a fight.

"Why would you do that, Ivo? Victor is expecting you to honor the deal. This will ruin everything for you and Elaine, and it's downright risky," she said.

"All Elaine wants is power, and what I want is peace. There is another way, and I can handle this on my own." I stepped a little closer to her. "You belong to me, princess," I said. Being so close to her and not touching her was the meanest form of torture.

I should have been straight with Elaine earlier on. No—I

should have done this a long time ago, but fact was, I didn't have a plan. Putting my people in the line of fire by antagonizing the volatile Russians wasn't an option I was willing to take, but now I had an ace I was willing to play.

I took another step toward Merry, tired of playing games and denying myself. Tired of catching a few stolen moments with her. She seemed speechless, but her eyes glossed over, overwhelmed with emotion. Honey and vanilla mingled and drifted to my nostrils, filling me with comfort and hope and lust.

I clasped her face in my palms and bent down to press my lips to hers, softly, until I was lost. After the slightest resistance, her delicate hands settled on my arms and she returned my kiss, letting me devour her, claim her as mine, connect with her soul.

She kissed me back, her tongue stroking mine until I longed to rip both our clothes off and take her right here, on the living room floor.

Once we pulled away from each other, we were breathless and I had a giant erection.

"This is such a bad idea, Ivo," she rasped. "How are you going to get out of this?"

Her eyes held both bewilderment and sadness, but a smile was trying to break through. I hooked a stray lock of hair behind her ear.

"Princess, I want you to know that I am willing to do anything for you, because you're worth it," I stated. "And now I'm going to do it."

With that, I took a long, deep breath, pressed a tender kiss to her forehead, and walked back out the door.

This wasn't what I wanted, but she needed time to think, and I had to show her I was serious about us.

As far as I was concerned, Victor was my biggest problem. He was the wildcard, but I was willing to go out of my way to make it up to him. Elaine might pitch a fit, but she could do so much better than me in the grand scheme of things. All I had to do was point that out, and tell her the truth about my and Merry's history.

I drove through busy roads back to my club and called Elaine to tell her I'd meet her tomorrow for lunch to continue our discussion. Thankfully, I managed go through the evening without any hiccups.

That night, I barely slept. I kept dreaming about Merry and Emilio. I was seeing him with her in the bar. He was holding her hand while challenging me to make a move. I tried to get to them, but I was chained to the floor and Emilio was laughing, mocking me. I remembered waking up early, drenched in sweat and disoriented.

Maybe I should go see him, talk to him, try to get some answers. He might not be my blood son, but I had raised him the best I could, just like I did Gregory.

In the morning, I decided to visit him after my lunch with Elaine. This was going to be a difficult conversation, and she wasn't going to like what I had to tell her, but this whole charade would be over soon. It wasn't like she was in love with me.

I had to offer her something in exchange—something worth her while.

It was just after one pm when I walked into the restaurant. I saw her sitting at the back, wearing a crimson dress that emphasized her tan. She was a beautiful woman and apparently, had never gone under the knife. She deserved someone who adored her as she was.

She waved to me and greeted me with a smile and a peck on the lips.

"Can I have a double whiskey with plenty of ice?" I asked the waiter who came to hand us the menus.

"Drinking so early? If I didn't know you, I would say you're feeling nervous," she teased.

"Guess we should get to talking," I said, wanting nothing more than to get it over with.

"Right. Anyway, I have something to tell you," she sighed. "Yesterday, we both said some things we shouldn't have, but I still believe you should move with me. After all, we're getting married, so I don't see the problem."

"Yes, I apologize, but you caught me off guard," I explained.

The waiter brought me my whiskey and I sipped on it while Elaine ordered herself an entrée. Then, I quickly picked something off the menu. Elaine was a vegan, and this was her favorite place that specialized in the cuisine, so I wasn't going to get a fat, juicy steak here today. Once she handed the menu to the waiter, we stared at each other in silence for a moment. Something in her gaze made me pause.

"You're unnerving me, handsome," she finally said, taking a sip of her water.

I knew she was going to lose her cool once I revealed the reason for my hesitation at accepting her proposal. The fact I was in love with her stepdaughter.

"Well, I do have something important to tell you as well," I stated, finishing my drink. I was driving so this wasn't wise, but I needed the fortifying liquor to get on with it and say what I needed to say. I imagined Merry's face, and me licking her wet pussy until she was screaming my fucking name. That was a good distraction for a moment. "But you go first."

"Okay, well ... I am just going to say it, Ivo, because there's no point in hiding it anymore. I'm pregnant. You're going to be a father again," she said, and I gaped at her, having no doubt that she was fucking with me, so I started to laugh.

I laughed because it was so damn funny—until I noticed Elaine's disturbed and angry expression. My mirth subsided but I still thought she was pulling my leg.

"Oh, Elaine, you really got me, but we need to get serious for a moment," I said. "Can you imagine us as parents?"

"I'm not joking, Ivo. I went to the doctor today after doing around five tests. I'm expecting your child," she said, and I nearly choked on my water. I coughed and coughed, covering my mouth and breathing in to stop the bout.

"What the fuck, Elaine? Didn't you clearly tell me you couldn't have kids?" I asked, thinking that this was just another nightmare like the one I had last night and I was going to wake up soon enough. "And just in case, we always used protection."

No fucking way. She wasn't pregnant. We hadn't even slept together that often, especially the last few weeks. I could barely get my dick hard when I was around her.

"You're a son of a bitch, you know that, Ivo Sergei? I thought you were going to be happy for us. I mean, I am forty-two after all and I was never planning to have children, but this just happened. It's a miracle," she said with a sigh.

Chapter Twenty-Five

Ivo

I was slowly losing touch with reality. The world was spinning and I felt like my chest had cracked open. I couldn't get any oxygen down to my lungs.

For a second, I thought I might throw up on Elaine. I came here to end things with her and she was telling me she was pregnant. This woman had trapped me and this wasn't possible, because she'd clearly told me she couldn't have kids. I was trying to remember when was the last time we'd had sex.

Since Merry, I hadn't been with many women. And with Elaine, I always used a condom.

Emotions clogged my throat. I just couldn't comprehend how I'd been such a fool.

"Frankly, I can hardly believe it," I managed to say when I found my voice again. "I know we've never discussed this but fuck, my kids are adult men and you ... well, you're in your forties and told me you weren't able to..." I probably sounded like a jackass, but my world was crumbling around me.

"Emilio isn't even your real son, so now's your chance to start over," she said. "And the girls will be ecstatic, I'm sure."

Did she even hear herself? She lived in a fantasy world—pretending what we had was real, and we were just a normal family. I had a hell of a time keeping it together.

"I hated all the secrecy," she continued. "I had to pretend I just had a bit of a stomach bug. Twelve weeks in, I can start telling people."

Blood drummed in my ears while Elaine rambled on. I stared at her moving lips, thinking how the life I'd planned with Merry would remain a fantasy. She'd never forgive me for this, and this thing between us was over before it even started.

We were done. I was done.

I had to let her go, but my selfish need wouldn't allow me to move on.

There was no future though, and nothing mattered.

"You should wait," I finally said, interrupting her mid-sentence, then added, "Are you a hundred percent certain you want this baby?" I wasn't that kind of guy who'd shirk his responsibilities, but the words left my lips before I could stop them.

"What is that even supposed to mean? Of course I'm keeping it," she snapped, sounding furious. Rising from her seat, she gave me a hard look. Again, I felt like a total asshole. "I'm going to the bathroom and when I come back, I'll pretend you didn't just say that."

She walked off and I took a deep breath, raking my hands

though my hair. Everything was falling apart and I was going to stay miserable for the rest of my life.

Just then, my phone vibrated inside my pocket. I didn't recognize the number, but instead of letting it go to voicemail, I answered it.

"Mr. Sergei. This is Detective Morales, have you got a minute to talk?"

"This is not a good time, Morales," I said, sounding rough. My own voice felt alien.

"I'll just cut through the chase," she said. "Do you have any idea where your son Emilio might have disappeared to?"

"As far as I know, he should be inside his cell, waiting on his trial and—"

"He's been released today," she interrupted me, and my chest heaved.

No, she was messing with me just like Elaine had earlier on. The judge wouldn't have granted him bail, right?

"What bullshit are you talking about, Morales?" I shouted into the phone, attracting the attention of some of the other patrons.

"You must have people in very high places who could pull this off. I know you helped him out. Emilio was released around two hours ago. He's a very dangerous young man, so this won't end well for either of you," she ground out.

"I had nothing to do with any of it. I actually want him behind bars," I growled, and then hung up because my temper was getting the better of me. I tried to put some coherent thoughts together, but my mind was spinning.

Elaine came back, looking so fucking happy.

"God, Ivo, what's wrong with you? You're so pale. What happened?" she asked.

Stress wasn't good for the heart. Maybe it would explode and leave me reduced to mush.

"I just had a phone call from Detective Morales. Seems Emilio was released today. Do you happen to know anything about that?" I asked, my head throbbing.

It was like I'd been totally and utterly fucked in the ass with a giant dildo.

Her eyes widened and there was a twinkle of excitement in them. She couldn't have been happy about that. The whiskey didn't help. Emilio was a psychopath, and now he roamed free.

"Why would you ask me that, Ivo? Maybe it was Victor. He must have found a way to get him out," she calmly pointed out.

"I have to go," I said, standing up abruptly. I needed to get away from Elaine and think things through.

"What? Where are you going? I thought you had something to tell me?"

I shook my head, and the throbbing pain amplified. "Never mind. It doesn't matter, Elaine. I need to get some fresh air."

"Oh, honey." She tried to grab my hand but I was out of reach. "We will find Emilio. I will send Cody and the others to look for him," she assured me.

"What?" I asked, having no idea what she was talking about.

How was I going to give this news to Merry?

"You're stressing way too much over this. We have a lot of important things to discuss now," she pressed on.

"I haven't got time for this now, Elaine. I have to find my son before he does something bad, before he hurts someone else," I said firmly, and walked away before she could say anything else.

Through the pounding in my head, I decided I needed to speak to Ryga about this problem. I called him and left a voicemail to call me back. I'd given him a day off but he was good with returning calls.

The first thing I did after that was drive around aimlessly. Then, I found someplace to park with a view of the ocean and sat there, staring at the water. I had no clue what I was doing and didn't care.

I just knew that at some point, I needed to speak to Merry. She deserved to know about Elaine and Emilio. I was such a fucking idiot for thinking that this could work, that I could have the cake and eat it.

Later, when I resumed driving, I almost got hit three times. I should have taken an Uber. Everything was spinning out of control and in that moment, I fucking hated my life so much. The life I'd manage to royally fuck up with the best of intentions.

***

Merry

I was out and about, trying to stay busy and waiting for the phone to ring. Elaine had text that she'd be calling me in a while to give me some news. She probably wanted to tell me off for how I handled Robert, then she'd go on and on about how I should make better decisions and why I insisted on making her life difficult.

I was used to her dramatic rants, easily forgetting how she could be a cold, calculating woman who knew her way around tricky situations. I believed Ivo was slowly discovering what a snake she could be. No doubt, she didn't love him. He was a means to an end, and for some reason, she thought she needed him.

After walking around the shops for over three hours, I decided I was done waiting around. It was three pm in the afternoon and her lunch with Ivo was likely over. I'd show up at the house so she could tell me in person what was going on. Hopefully, I'd find her there. I could have called, but a drive with the windows down would do me good.

It took me twenty minutes to get there. Elaine's white Lexus was parked in the driveway, not yet in the garage, which meant she recently got home. My heart skipped a beat, then started racing triple time. Either way, this conversation was going to be awkward.

A few security people were patrolling the property, carrying walkie-talkies and guns in holsters. I wanted to laugh at how Elaine did everything in a flashy manner. Although my dad had people, he'd been quite discreet, and wasn't a big fan of Hollywood-style parties.

"Hello," I said when I walked inside, my stomach in knots.

"We are in the kitchen," Elaine called out, so I headed there.

The space was huge and after the renovation, the kitchen was even bigger, likely able to fit and feed an army. Elaine was sitting on a stool with Clara.

I was a little taken back to see her eating pickles straight from a jar. I thought she loathed the things. I glanced at my sister, but she shrugged.

"Merry, come here, darling. I have something important to tell you," she said, popping another pickle into her mouth.

Clara sighed loudly.

"Hey, what's up?" I asked. Elaine looked way too happy and relaxed. I thought this break-up would make her miserable, but she was so radiant. What the hell was going on?

"I just had lunch with Ivo, so I thought I would share the good news with him first since he's my fiancé," she said with a chuckle. "Unfortunately, he left shortly afterwards. It would have been better if I made this special announcement with him by my side, but it is what it is."

I frowned, chancing a glance at Clara but she seemed as confused as me.

"Right, so what is it?" I pressed.

Elaine laughed and then started patting her stomach in such a strange way.

"I'm pregnant! Ivo and I are expecting. I thought I couldn't have kids, but there you go."

I thought she was joking, but then caught her enraptured expression and realized she was serious. Clara's jaw dropped and disbelief hit me hard. My heart threw itself over my chest when it all sank in.

Pickles and that fucking glow. Granted, not every woman had those cravings but this wasn't normal for Elaine. She had to be telling the truth.

"Pregnant? Are you sure this baby is Ivo's?" Clara asked first, and I was so glad she did because I was at a loss for words.

Elaine's eyes narrowed and if looks could kill, my sister would be dead.

"Of course it is. I haven't been with anyone else since we got engaged. Who else would be the father, Clara? I don't know what you think of me. I was loyal to your father when he was alive."

I was going to be sick, so I quickly excused myself and ran to the bathroom, hearing Elaine telling my sister that I had always been the emotional one.

Once I got to the restroom, I threw up my whole lunch. My chest heaved and my vision turned blurry.

How could Ivo have done this to me? I remembered Elaine saying she couldn't have children but maybe she'd been wrong?

I flushed the toilet and washed my face, holding myself steady and staring at my worn reflection in the mirror. The world had gone off the rails, but this was my new reality. Ivo was going to have a baby with Elaine, so the wedding was going ahead as normal. She must have told him during lunch, so that was why none of them had called me.

Ivo had probably crawled into some hole to avoid facing me. I hoped he'd drop to Hell and rot there.

My heart ached as I dried my hands and my face. We were so done. Ivo couldn't leave her now. She needed him by her side because she was carrying his baby. This was completely fucked up and I felt like someone had pried my heart with a long needle. I just couldn't bear being in this house any longer. I had to leave.

As I exited the bathroom, I found Clara waiting for me.

"Merry, are you all right?" Her hushed voice made me shudder.

"This can't be happening," I said to her, but my voice was barely audible. She looked crushed, too, lost and confused. Damn it.

"I'm sorry, but she's completely serious. She is about ten weeks in and she showed me the ultrasound photos," Clara explained, and I wanted to howl.

No, I wasn't going to cry. Ivo wasn't the kind of guy worth crying over. All he'd done was get inside my head and wreck my ordered life, which I'd worked so hard to maintain.

"Oh my God." I let out a whine and sat on the toilet, breathing hard and burying my face in my hands. How could I face Elaine now?

"But that's not all." Clara placed her hand on my shoulder, and I felt her tremble. "Merry ... apparently, Emilio was released earlier today." The tremor in her voice was also evident. She was terrified.

That was the final straw. Standing, I embraced Clara and we sobbed in each other's arms.

Why? Why couldn't we catch a break?

Chapter Twenty-Six

Merry

When we were done crying, I tried to reason.

"How did that happen?" I asked, trying not to freak out, but it wasn't easy, especially with all these overwhelming emotions clogging my insides.

Baby

Ivo

Elaine

Emilio

"Well, someone got him out, Merry. Elaine just confirmed it. It seems Ivo got a phone call from that Detective Morales," Clara said, as much in shock as I was.

It was a nightmare, but Ivo couldn't have done it. He wouldn't have gotten Emilio out. So, who had it been? Had his blood father paid someone off? Who else?

"Clara, listen to me. He's not going to hurt you and I'm going to make sure he returns to where he belongs. Please, don't do anything silly," I begged her, taking her hands and making sure she understood. "I'm here now. We'll get through this together."

A flash of irritation crossed her eyes but then, her shoulders drooped and she gave a sigh of resignation. She squeezed my fingers.

"Oh, Merry, that asshole doesn't scare me anymore," she said. "Well, he used to, but he doesn't really care about me. He wanted to get back at his father, and I just happened to be in the way." I sighed with relief at her reaction, because it sounded reasonable and genuine. Clara was not dumb but most importantly, she was healing. "Are you going to do anything about the situation in the living room?"

"What situation?" I asked.

"Ivo and Elaine, obviously."

I huffed, waving a hand dismissively, even though I wanted to scream. "He should have been more careful and I'm not a home wrecker. There's nothing left to do," I said, resigned.

Clara seemed deep in thought. "I tell you, Merry, I have this feeling... I don't think that baby is his. Elaine is lying and you shouldn't be giving up on him just yet," she said.

She probably meant well by being overly optimistic, but I had to face the truth—and it wasn't in my favor. Also, although I was glad Clara was recovering, a person like Emilio shouldn't be out on the streets, wreaking havoc. Too many growing problems, and we hadn't solved one fucking thing. Except maybe my sister and I were getting close again now.

Silver linings.

"Sis, let's be honest. I don't think Elaine has been running around on Ivo. She's too busy. And even if he doesn't go ahead with the wedding, I can't imagine us being together. Elaine would destroy me first before she gave us her blessing," I said, because this was the reality of this situation.

Clara was trying her damnedest to think of a counter to my argument, but from her silence, she was coming up short. I had a lot to think about, particularly the Emilio problem.

"Merry, he loves you," my sister insisted weakly, and I laughed. At this point, I was out of both tears and fucks. Ivo had made his bed and now, he had to lie in it.

We should have never met and most importantly, I should have not let him back into my life. That had been my biggest mistake.

"No, he doesn't. It was just physical, nothing else," I argued. We returned to the kitchen to find Elaine on the phone with someone. Thank goodness, I didn't have to talk to her. "I have to go. I need to look into Emilio's case and figure out what happened."

"What about Elaine? What are you going to tell her?" Clara asked, and I sighed.

Elaine was happy and I wasn't going to take that away from her. She didn't need me by her side.

"Just tell her I had to go because I wasn't feeling well," I said, walking to the foyer. Clara followed me there. "Just don't go anywhere and wait for my phone call, Clara. Is that okay?"

She nodded. She understood why this was so important and I had faith in her. Her mental health might be fragile, but she was stronger than she realised.

I don't know why Clara was so obsessed with me and Ivo.

Maybe it was compensation for her shutting me out the last few years. But in my mind, Emilio was a much bigger problem. He was a psychopath and a sadist who deserved to be locked away. In an ideal world, the key to his cell would be thrown away until he kicked the bucket.

I left in a hurry and jumped in the car, knowing just where I was going. Elaine loved being the entertainer, so now with the baby she was overjoyed because she was going to get a lot of attention from everyone. Thinking about this made me sick, and if I had a choice, I'd move to the other end of the Earth so I wouldn't have to see everything play out.

Ivo took fatherhood seriously, so he was going to take responsibility. It was one of the things that attracted me to him. And the very thing that would separate me from him—forever.

I kept thinking about that first night at Club Top D—the first time I'd met Ivo and his sons. Emilio couldn't get me to come and that had likely injured his pride. Fast forward to Sputnik, he was in control, but he attacked me and Clara because he wanted to get back at Ivo. I swallowed hard, moving through the traffic, telling myself that this was the past and I had to look forward, not backward. I wanted to see justice done.

For his part, Ivo had accomplished something no other man could with me so far. He played my body like a violin, and I'd never met anyone like him. However, that didn't mean I couldn't find someone else in the future who'd make me feel just as good. The world was big and full of alternatives.

To make sure I covered all the bases, I tried to get more information from the DA about the release, but they wouldn't give me a name as whoever had posted bail wanted to stay anonymous. Exactly the response I'd expected.

So, I drove to a part of the city where good girls like me didn't normally venture to, but this was necessary. I was going to there to see one man who might give me clues. None of the night clubs were open yet, but one particular restaurant would be serving customers at this time. The place was often occupied by Russians.

Several individuals, mostly young and rough-looking, were eyeing my car when I parked outside. I had no choice but to leave it there. I wasn't going to be long. It was early afternoon, so the lunch crowd would be in full swing. The whole eatery was decorated in dark colors, which made it more dingy-looking. I spotted a few people sitting in one corner. Several heads turned to look in my direction. It wasn't as crowded as I thought it would be.

Then, the woman behind the bar asked me if I wanted a table.

I shook my head and she didn't look happy, but I didn't come here to eat. Instead, I walked toward a group of large men who sat behind the biggest table at the back. Two of them stood right away when they saw me.

"Victor, I need to talk to you. We met at my stepmother's party the other week. I'm Merry Camilleri," I said, when his two bodyguards blocked my way. They were taking this job way too seriously.

"Let her through," he said, and they instantly obeyed him. I recognized one of the two Russians with Victor. I'd heard he was well connected to Senator Bailey.

I was never very good with small talk, so I decided to get straight to the point.

"I need to talk to you about Emilio," I said, folding my arms across my chest. This wasn't wise, but I wasn't scared of him for, in this situation, he was all bark and no bite. I was no threat and he wasn't going to hurt me, probably out of respect for my father.

Victor was an odd-looking man. His face was scarred, but it wasn't an injury. Word was he'd suffered some kind of skin condition when he was younger. He tilted his head to the side, then muttered something in Russian. In moments, the other two fellows left us alone and Victor gestured at a chair.

I hesitated, but then I sat next to him, feeling a little less brave now. Elaine was going to freak out if she found out what I was up to, but Clara's health and safety was my top priority. I didn't give a shit about her business deals. That motherfucker Emilio needed to understand that he wasn't above the law—well, some of us were, but there was a limit. This might sound awful but in truth, Emilio was a nobody. I refused to believe he mattered to someone in the grand scheme of things.

"I'm listening," Victor said. I tried to ignore the fact that I was sitting very close to one of the most dangerous mobsters in Los Angeles. He controlled most shipments coming through the California coast and had connections in high places with the Columbians. Everyone was afraid to get on his bad side.

Why the fuck had I talked myself into coming here?

"How did you do it?" I asked him, and he frowned. He was probably going to pretend he had no idea what I was talking about. Either way, he was going to tell me everything he knew and more.

"Did what? I am sorry, Ms. Camilleri, but you must be a little more specific."

I shook my head, not in a mood to play games.

"I'm talking about Emilio. How did you manage to get him released—the man who cut my face and raped my little sister?" I ground out. Ivo's men had beat his niece and Emilio had raped her. I'd heard it was so bad, she had to have reconstructive surgery on her jaw. The man in front of me had to take the responsibility for his actions, for freeing a man who was not only dangerous, but also crazy. Maybe I was insane myself for doing this, but I didn't know where else to turn.

Victor sighed, then flashed a small smile, which totally creeped me out.

"I still have no idea what you're talking about. I had nothing to do with Emilio's release. At your stepmother's party, I asked Ivo to take care of it. He refused but maybe he had a change of heart, so you should ask him," Victor said, and my stomach curled with unease.

Ivo couldn't have done it, could he? He wouldn't have betrayed me like that, but he said had sent Emilio to that club only to put the fear of God in the people there, not to hurt them—yet, what if he had lied about that, too?

"Emilio wanted to hurt Ivo, so that's why he did what he did." Was I trying to convince Victor, or myself?

Maybe Victor was the one telling stories and he was hiding Emilio somewhere.

"Merry, I haven't the faintest idea where Emilio could be." Victor studied me dispassionately. "But I am looking forward to the wedding. Your stepmother will be a beautiful bride." He gave me an intimidating stare—one loaded with unspoken words. Victor's power was expanding and with Elaine in his pocket, as well as Ivo on a leash, nothing and no one could stop him.

I stood from my chair, feeling like an idiot for coming here. "Thank you for your time," I said, and rushed out of there like the hounds of Hell were after me.

I found a few of the young men from before still eyeing my car with interest. They started to back away when I got inside and frantically started the engine. When the familiar revving sound ensued, I drove out of there like a bat out of Hell.

If Victor didn't get Emilio out, then who did?

None of this made much sense to me, but I needed to get some answers. For a moment, I considered talking to Ivo, but then I changed my mind. We had nothing more to say to each other and I didn't want to complicate things further.

I got back home and had a quick shower, trying to calm down. The smell from the restaurant and Victor's presence had somehow attached to me and I tried to wash it off. Part of me wanted to forget about it, but Victor was Emilio's biological father and he no doubt loved to rub it in Ivo's face, so I'd naturally suspected him first.

When I was out of the shower, I thought I heard a sound coming from the kitchen area. Picking up my gun from the dressing table drawer, I wrapped my towel tightly around my waist. I trod carefully out of my bedroom. When I made it to the living room, I found the man who'd caused much turmoil inside my heart standing by the window.

"What the fuck are you doing in here, Ivo?"

"We need to talk," he said, not turning around to face me.

I sighed, knowing he was right but hating every word when I replied, "Yes, we do need to talk."

Chapter Twenty-Seven

Ivo

After everything descended into chaos, and time passed during which I found no comfort in any single moment of the day, I knew I had to do something. As I drove around today, I tried to calm down and eventually acknowledged all my thoughts had led me to this place: Merry's apartment. I had to be the one to tell her that her abuser had been released from prison.

Deep inside, my frustration was getting the better of me. Emilio would disappear again, so I had to find him as soon as possible—by tonight.

I had a dream where Merry and I lived in a good neighborhood with great schools. We'd have children and live a perfectly normal, vanilla life. But this dream was only an illusion. Elaine was pregnant with my child and I was destined to live the life of a mafioso until my last breath. All I had was today to sit with her and wipe away any bad blood between us—the most I could hope for.

I still remembered the code to her building, so I let myself in. When I got inside, I found her front door unlocked, and that ticked me off. When was Merry going to start being more careful? She was a single woman who lived alone in the city and Emilio was free, roaming the streets.

She was in the shower when I shut the door behind me. My head was banging and I had countless missed calls from Elaine, but she had to fucking wait, because this was much more important.

Several minutes later, I heard her getting out of the shower.

"What the fuck are you doing in here, Ivo?" she asked, pointing her gun at me—not the one she'd used to shoot Emilio, which the police had confiscated after I told them I'd used it on my son. She'd gotten herself a new one.

Her dark hair was wet and she had a white towel wrapped around her lush body. So beautiful. My imagination went wild, but I told myself this wasn't right or even fair. I had no right to even look at her that way.

"You shouldn't be here." She lowered the gun and walked into the kitchen, putting the safety on and placing the weapon on the countertop.

If only I could go back in time. If only I'd waited for her to finish her studies... waited for her to spread her wings... waited... waited... and then waited some more. Since the first time I'd laid eyes on her, she'd become my obsession, my sinful addiction. I didn't think I could ever have enough of her.

She stood behind the counter, the large slab of quartz a

barrier between us, and I looked into her eyes, finding endless pain and also guilt.

And in that moment, I knew Elaine had beat me to the chase. Of course she did. She couldn't wait to share the good news with everyone.

"I know, but I had to see you and it seems you already know about Elaine," I said, swallowing hard and taking a step toward her. Her expression changed, becoming deeply resentful. I wanted to touch her, maybe place my hand on top of hers, but I didn't dare invade her personal space. I could sense the anger cutting a swath through her. I was going to have a baby with another woman—her fucking stepmother.

She was devastated, and this was one emotion she couldn't hide. Somehow, I could read Merry like a book.

"Clara called me, so I went to see her since you didn't contact me," she said, her voice empty and emotionless. Too much so. "I soon found out why."

Remorse ate at me. As much as I wanted to embrace Merry, I couldn't bring myself to do it. She deserved better than me.

"I'm not going to marry her, Merry. I can't. She might be carrying my child in her womb, but she's not the woman I love and care for. She was never supposed to be that. I don't know how I'm going to get away with this, but I'm going to do my utmost." I looked away for a moment, trying to find the right words.

"Ivo, don't you even dare play this shitty game now!" she rebuked, pointing her finger at me. "How can you say that? You cannot suddenly pull out of this and abandon what's yours. There isn't any other way around this."

"Merry, please—"

"No!" she roared. I wanted to say this wasn't fair, that I never meant to hurt her, but it was too late. She was crying and my heart was being ripped from my chest. "Don't. You have people to protect. I think you owe it to me and Clara, at least!"

"Okay, do you want me to be honest? Huh? Okay, here goes: I don't believe that this is even my child!" I admitted, and this was the truth. I couldn't deny the possibility, but it was just a hunch that she had to be fucking someone else and pinning this on me. I just needed to figure out who.

Merry started laughing and shaking her head.

"That's ridiculous! Are you serious? Who else's could it be?" Putting her elbows on the counter, she slid her hands down her face in a frustrated gesture.

I raked my fingers through my hair and released a breath. "I'm not going to abandon any child of mine, Merry. What do you take me for? But I need to be sure. And most importantly, I love you and only you. I have never loved any other woman like this before. You've always been mine, since we met."

My emotions were so raw, simmering inside me for weeks.

"And Victor? What are you going to do with him? He expects you to go through with this." When I didn't respond, she continued, "Emilio is out and about now. Someone helped him go free. Do you know who that could be? I even went to see Victor because I thought he was the one who had him released."

I couldn't believe what I'd just heard.

"You did what? You went to see Victor, one of the most dangerous criminals in Los Angeles, to ask him that question?" The woman had lost her motherfucking mind. The man had likely been the one to get Emilio out, but her going there could have had any manner of terrible outcomes.

She folded her arms around her chest and shot me a defiant look.

"It was fine. He did say he wasn't the one that got him out," she claimed.

"We both know it's bullshit. He lied to you and I'd bet my right arm and left testicle that it was him." Victor had probably told Emilio to lay low in one of his locations until things calmed down and no one was looking for him anymore.

After what he said at Elaine's party, I knew for sure that he needed Emilio to be free for whatever reason.

"Why would he lie about this though?" Merry pursed her lips. "But now I'm worried about Clara because she won't feel safe."

She slammed her head on the counter as I approached her, a sob escaping her, then bit her lip. Tentatively, I reached out and covered her hand with mine. She flinched, but at least she didn't pull away. She stared at our joined hands.

"I'm going to find him before he hurts anyone, I promise you, but I swear to God I wasn't the one to get him out. Victor was lying to you," I insisted, wishing that I could just wake up from this nightmare.

She nodded, and I let our touch linger a little until her phone rang. I wished I could comfort her, take the pain away, but this was it. There was no future for us.

As she took the call, I saw myself out. I'd head to the club and speak with Gregory, then get to working to find the bastard who had us by the balls. Emilio wasn't my blood son, and although I still saw him as my child, he had to pay for what he did.

My driving force was Merry. I wanted to worship her body, touch her, taste her all the way to ecstasy, but I loved so much more than her body. Her sense of honor, the love for her family, her beauty inside and out—she was one of a kind, and I wanted her to be mine not just in my mind. The world had to know this amazing woman belonged to me.

But first, I had to do what was right.

By the time I got back to the club, I was strung out. Elaine kept calling me, so I eventually answered and told her I was busy searching for Emilio.

"If he doesn't want to be found, then you won't find him," she said with a sigh, and I ended the call before I said something I regretted. Elaine had no fucking idea about my son. He was going against me because he believed I wasn't important enough, and he could easily take what was mine.

We had finally reopened the club and patrons were already flooding the place. The music was loud and people were having a great time.

Gregory was watching the screens when I walked into my office, ready to smash something.

"Emilio is out," I snapped, pacing around the room.

Gregory's dark eyes followed me. He didn't look surprised.

"It was just the matter of time. Victor has a lot of people in his pockets," he said, and I slapped the table.

"We have to find Emilio before he does something unpredictable, dammit, and knowing him, he will soon enough."

"I'm going to call a few of our people," Gregory said, standing. "But is there something else that is bothering you? Emilio wasn't the one that got you so worked up."

I tried not to think about the baby, Elaine, and Merry, but Gregory had a right to know what was going on.

"Elaine is pregnant, so the wedding is going ahead as planned," I blurted out.

Gregory raised an eyebrow in question. "You're fucking with me," he said, and I swore. "Are you telling me you've been so careless?"

"She told me she couldn't have children," I muttered. "But I did use protection, most of the time."

"Condoms can break," he said.

"Yeah." I sat down, feeling defeated.

"Then you're screwed," Gregory said.

He wasn't wrong.

Chapter Twenty-Eight

Merry

In the five days that followed, I hadn't made much headway in getting information about Emilio. I'd put my feelers out, making contact with my father's old friends, but so far, nobody had called me with any news.

Ivo was in the same boat as me, and he seemed exhausted. Clara was unusually quiet, every now and then telling me that it wasn't bothering her, but I knew better. She just didn't want to worry me. I did think Emilio wasn't going to bother us again, but how could I be sure what went on in his fucked-up head?

Clara had gone back to work, and at least, that was a distraction. This situation was hard on everyone, especially when Emilio could be so unpredictable.

Meanwhile, my stepmother lived in her own bubble, going on and on about the baby shower her friends were planning months in advance. I had to admit, she looked healthy and her excitement was only natural. Besides, she'd had no idea about my history with Ivo, and I shouldn't blame her for it.

"So I am planning a big party this weekend to announce the date of the wedding," she said when I came to pick up Clara. She was sitting in the kitchen, stuffing her face with strawberries.

Last night, I made a decision that I needed to leave. I was aware I'd been waffling about this, trying to hang on to hope, but I was done with Los Angeles, done with Ivo. Yet, I wanted to ensure Clara was all right first. I would hang around until Emilio was located. Considering the worst-case scenario, I wanted to talk to her about making the move with me this time, at least until Emilio was no longer a threat. Meanwhile, I would work on getting Ivo out of my every thought—easier said than done. I missed him too much and, deep down, I was hoping I'd catch a glimpse of him here.

"Great," I replied, trying to sound thrilled. "Where is Clara? We are going out."

"She's out by the pool." After a slight hesitation, she added, "Are you okay, Merry? You seem down."

I gave her a weak smile. I had to pull myself together, because I didn't plan to stay miserable for the rest of my life. "Don't worry about me. I'll be fine."

At least, she seemed satisfied with my answer, at least for now.

I didn't plan to keep having nightmares, and getting minimal sleep because of them. After the incident at Sputnik, I had them for a while, but now, they'd returned in full force. In these twisted dreams, I kept seeing Emilio come at me with a knife. I was on the floor, tied up, sitting in a dark and dingy cell. Every night, I had the same recurring nightmare, each time more intense than the last, and I kept waking up covered in sweat.

I headed to the living room to get away from Elaine and go outside through the French doors. Before I could exit, Clara walked in with my friend Tasha. I was surprised, because I hadn't seen my friend in months. She was busy with her new career in advertising and we never had time to catch up.

"Girls, there is some wine in the fridge. Help yourselves. I can't drink at all and I am so tired, I have to go lie down," Elaine said, leaving the room.

"Thanks, Ms. Camilleri!" Tasha shouted before hugging me tight. "Damn it, girl, you really look terrible. Clara, I think you were right about her."

I frowned, staring at my sister who looked so innocent, but she wouldn't fool me. I knew she'd probably called Tasha here to cheer me up. After what happened in the club with Emilio and Clara, we started to drift apart a little. We were all dealing with our own demons the best we could. That night changed so many things in our lives.

I lobbed my gaze between the two of them. "What have you two been conspiring about?"

"Fine. I'll just go out and say it," Clara said, her expression serious. "We are going out to a club where no one knows us tonight, far away from our usual haunts, so you can finally find another guy."

Tasha put her arm around her and gave me a big smile. "Yeah. Your sister told me about your little dilemma and I think it's time for us to party like we used to," she said.

"This is crazy. Clara—"

"I'm perfectly fine! I want to have fun again," she insisted, her brows gathered together. "I want to live a normal life." Her voice broke, and then I realized, this was her way of trying to move on, past the hurt.

"What about Emilio? This is too dangerous, Clara, and you know it," I said, hating to be the voice of reason, but it was the truth. A few weeks ago, Clara was trying to kill herself and tonight, she wanted to be out. I thought it was all too soon. Besides, I had no intention of fucking anybody.

Having some fun without a care in the world sounded great though. If only we could.

The look of determination on her face told me she wasn't going to back down. I couldn't believe she was suggesting this.

"Emilio doesn't care about me. He just wanted someone to bully that night, and to use us to get back at his father. I know that now. I am so done with living in fear and you need a good night out," Clara said, and Tasha patted her on the back.

"Exactly what she said. You're young and available. Ivo's not going to ruin your life," Tasha added.

"I'm fine, and I've accepted that we are not going to be together," I told them.

"Good, but we are still taking you out. Wear something black. I'll pick you both up at eight with my Uber. Nobody's a designated driver tonight." Tasha headed out then, whistling a tune.

"What exactly did you tell her?" I asked, turning to face my sister.

"I haven't told her everything obviously, but enough. She knows you need to forget about Ivo and move on. Robert was very handsome, but he wasn't the one. You guys didn't have any chemistry. We are not going to be hiding anymore. We are the Camilleris, and our father was one of the most powerful businessmen in Los Angeles," she said proudly, and she was right.

Our father would have turned in his grave if he witnessed me being afraid to live my life. He would have encouraged me to face my demons.

"Fine, but promise me you'll be careful," I told her, and she nodded, smiling. She poured some lemonade for us and then Clara even agreed for me to take her shopping.

We had lunch in town and talked about our father, who we both missed terribly. I was finally able to relax, just spending quality time with my sister, talking and laughing about pointless things. For that one day, we could both pretend that Ivo and his two sons weren't a part of our lives. I returned home a few hours later with many shopping bags, exhausted but happy. Clara had helped me forget about Ivo and I knew there were plenty of other men that would be interested in me.

Later on, I relaxed in front of the TV, then did a bit of work for a client. At close to eight-thirty, I started to get ready for the evening with the girls. Robert had been right about me. I was so invested in my sister's life, I often forgot about my own needs.

Tonight, I was going to have fun, and maybe I'd meet somebody special. It didn't matter that Ivo had smashed my heart to pieces. I was going to fall in love again, with someone who would love me for who I was. I pretended I hadn't heard him when he confessed he was in love with me. This wasn't real love. Ivo simply loved the idea of being in love with me.

"Looking hot, Merry," my reflection in the mirror told me

once I put my new dress on that I'd bought earlier on when I was out with Clara.

Short with tiny straps, it showed off my curves well. I went for killer black heels that emphasised the red of the dress. Clara and Tasha were going to love this outfit, although they still hadn't told me where we meant to be going out tonight. I took a small glass of the wine I had in my fridge, and then waited for them to pick me up.

At nine-thirty, Tasha was banging on my door.

"Hey, girl. Woot, you look hot! First things first, you need to put this on when we get to the club," she said, handing me a carnival-type mask.

"What?" I asked.

"Trust me." She grinned. "And just saying, it was Clara's idea. Apparently, she knows some guy who organizes events in nightclubs."

We went downstairs, and Clara squealed.

"Who are you and what did you do to my little sister?" I asked her as soon as we arrived at our destination.

"Just have fun, forget about the Sergei men, and have a few drinks. No one knows anyone here and this place is safe. Trust me for once," Clara said, looking genuinely excited. She was wearing a black skirt and a shiny top. Her mask was similar to mine.

"Fine," I said as she dragged me along with Tasha inside the loud club. It was a theme party where everyone was wearing masks. The club was very busy and I loved the tunes that were being played.

We headed straight to the bar and before I knew it, I was sipping a raspberry mojito sitting in a booth with my sister and best friend. Clara went quiet every now and then, but I was glad to see she was overcoming.

"This guy in a white shirt is totally checking you out," she told me, sipping her drink.

I really had to stop worrying about her. She had clearly made great strides in her healing.

I glanced in the direction she was indicating. My stomach tightened with unease as I stared at the tall guy wearing all white. He smiled at me while talking to another guy.

"He gives me Hispanic vibes and I think it's time for you to move away from Eastern Europe, don't you think?" Tasha laughed, and I had to agree with her.

Several moments later, the man was right by my table. He had dark eyes and a nice smile. When he asked if I wanted to dance, I didn't hesitate to take his hand.

"Wish me luck," I told the girls when I left with him.

"You don't need luck. You need a good orgasm," Tasha whispered with a giggle.

He dragged me to the dance floor, grabbed my waist, and started moving to the rhythm of the music. My eyes widened and my heart kicked me in the chest.

"You're beautiful. *Hermosa*," he murmured in my ear as we danced.

I told myself it was time to let go and put Ivo in the past.

"Thanks. What's your name?" I asked him as his cheek brushed mine. He was leading and he was a pretty good dancer, carrying me like I weighed nothing at all. When I glanced back at the girls' table, I could see they already had company. Clara was chatting to someone and Tasha was laughing her head off.

The fact my sister was talking to a man without freezing up was a huge improvement.

"Manuel," he replied, moving his hand over my back. I liked how he smelled and the way my body responded to his, but then I felt another body behind me. Someone was pressed against my back and then, a familiar voice chilled my blood.

"Leave, before I break every bone in your body and feed your insides to the sharks."

Chapter Twenty-Nine

Ivo

I was barely coping, my mind all over the place. The situation with Emilio had me all over the place, speaking to my people day and night. I had lookouts all over the city, ready to give me a call if they spotted something. Meanwhile, Elaine was all agog about the wedding and, of course, the baby. Soon, I'd have to accompany her to the doctor for her check-up. I was never one to shirk responsibility, but I just couldn't shake that this wasn't my child. I couldn't explain it, but I just wasn't feeling it.

I hadn't seen Merry in the last five days. Anyway, she'd made it clear it was all over between us, and seeing her without being able to touch her would be the worst form of torture.

Today, when I was with Elaine in the living room, I stepped to the French doors to look out at the backyard, and the pristine pool area. The doors were ajar to let in the breeze, and I overheard Clara talking over the phone about a club she was going to attend with Merry and some friends of theirs.

So Merry was going out to party tonight. I kept telling myself that I had to let her go and move on. But thoughts of her consumed me, bringing me down as the day wore on.

By the time evening rolled in, my mind was made up. Letting Gregory take over at Club P, I arrived at the Axis Lounge around ten in the evening. I should be focusing on Emilio, but I couldn't do anything unless somebody gave me the call I was waiting for. I'd set the stage, and at this point it was a waiting game. I'd already scoured all of Emilio's known haunts and came up with nothing.

He didn't have any friends, which was telling. The men who'd gone on the rampage at Sputnik with him were all dead. Sooner or later though, I'd ferret him out. He believed he was above the law, especially after he found out about Victor, so he was bound to make a mistake at some point.

I stood across the street from the club, watching and waiting. I'd been there about fifteen minutes when I spotted the group walking inside the establishment. This little outing was probably that girl Tasha's idea. I remembered her from Club Top D, and she was always the wild one.

I could barely believe it had been over three years since I met Merry for the first time.

I had been with a few women afterwards, but I could never get her out of my head. Sex was never the same, because it wasn't with my princess.

When I mentioned to Gregory where the girls were heading tonight, he said I had to wear a mask to get inside because they had a special event. This worked well for me because I didn't want her to recognize me. At the same time, I was furious because I was sure she planned to hook up with someone.

This whole experience was going to be torture because Merry wanted to forget about me. She was doing everything she could to move on. She was going to flirt and even possibly go home with some other guy and I couldn't fucking allow it.

She wasn't mine, but I treated her like my property, and at that moment, I was fine with that. I sat at the back and watched them laughing, ordering drinks, and scoping out the men. Merry looked fucking stunning in her red dress and I had been hard ever since I saw her get out of the Uber. She was the only one who did that to me.

It was obvious men were noticing her, and I wanted to kill them all. Every. Last. One.

They ogled her, all wanting a piece of her. But she was still fucking mine. Even though I was set to get married in a couple of weeks.

I told myself I was here only to protect her and watch from a distance, even though she was one of the strongest people I knew and could take care of herself. But when she started dancing with one of the assholes, I saw red.

I nearly broke the glass I held in my hand when he maneuvered his body close to hers and brushed against her, again and again, running his filthy hands over her hips. She was an adult, and we weren't together, but this was bullshit.

In moments, I was crossing the floor, ready to beat the shit out of the bastard. Clara was chatting to some guy by their table. She looked happy and relaxed. Maybe she was truly healed, but Merry should have known better. Emilio was out there, ready to strike, and the girls were out partying. This was irresponsible and frankly, stupid. I could come up with all manner of reasons as to why they shouldn't be there.

The guy was standing way too close and she was going to fucking kiss him—some stranger that she didn't even know.

Like she knew you when you made her come.

My blood boiling, I approached them and grabbed his arm before he could grope her again.

"Leave, before I break every bone in your body and feed your insides to the sharks," I said through gritted teeth.

Merry's jaw dropped and she stared at me through her mask, clearly livid because despite me being masked, too, it didn't take long for her to recognize me. I could see it in her eyes. So much for anonymity. The guy automatically backed away as though licked by fire. He lobbed his gaze between me and Merry as if trying to figure out whether my threat was real. The air was static with electricity.

I was certain she would tell me to go to hell or maybe even slap me, but for a long moment, she just stared at me, bringing me to my knees. I fucking missed her and I knew she felt the same. I loved her, and sensed the same with her.

I'd never love another woman like this. It was the worst. If I couldn't have Merry, I'd just drift through life, fulfilling one obligation after another. Putting myself on the backburner. What else could there be?

If I ever saw her shack up with another man, it would kill me.

I was inside a cage, trapped with a lion, waiting for its teeth to sink into my flesh.

I broke our gaze and looked around. The guy must have

figured out that he didn't want any trouble because he'd disappeared.

I was wearing a black shirt and pants so I could blend well with the shadows while watching her. But how could I fool my princess? She stood there, unmoving, and I took a step forward, transfixed by her. A sensual dance track pumped through the speakers, urging us to get closer and move to its beguiling beat.

Forgetting all the promises I'd made to myself to stay away, to give her space, I couldn't follow through. I grabbed her by the waist and pulled her close. Her warmth seeped into me as she pressed her body to mine. We moved in rhythm to the music, her cheek against my chest, a silent understanding passing through us.

This thing between us would never end. Just like gravity, it just was, in spite of everything.

How could I let her go?

She'd come here for a wild night, and I would give it to her. We couldn't keep pretending, fighting our emotions.

But this game of desire, we could both understand. We were both good at it, her and I, when it came to each other.

I yearned to take her there and then, to lower her to the floor and fuck her brains out where we stood. My cock strained in my pants, weeping with every bump and grind, pulsing with each brush of her body against it.

She was so fucking sexy. I held her close while other people danced inches away, occasionally bumping into us. Her breathing was laboured, her eyes gleamed with desire and need when I moved my fingers over her cleavage. Her scent was intoxicating but I wanted so much more.

So much…

There were VIP rooms beyond the bar area and I was ready to take her there, to punish her for being so reckless, for coming here without me ... but I hesitated. This was beyond sick, because I had Elaine to consider. Maybe she'd never been a true hindrance, but the situation was highly complicated now.

"That guy wasn't worth your attention, princess. I couldn't let him keep on touching you," I whispered in her ear. I moved my hand to her throat, squeezing it gently. The skin there was soft and sweet-smelling. When she gasped, I smiled in satisfaction, knowing she was handing the control to me. My cock grew harder as I imagined how she would moan my name when I licked her drenched pussy.

And just like that, our problems disappeared in the here and now. Our chemistry was through the roof.

Nothing else mattered but us, together, on a wild ride.

Did she want me enough to forget reality?

To set everything aside and let nature take its course.

Because I was ready. I was here. With her. All of me. There was no place else I'd rather be.

I would fuck her until she couldn't walk or remember her name. We'd make new memories tonight to tide us over on the cold nights to come.

Tomorrow, we'd go back to pretending. I was done apologizing for the past. She had to know I wasn't the villain in her story.

She looked up at me, bringing her lips to inches from mine. "You shouldn't have come."

"And you shouldn't have done the bump and grind with some punk," I said, the thought making me angry all over again.

"You're worth my attention, then?" she said, looking back

at her sister.

I knew what she was truly asking. She was worried about leaving Clara alone, so I took out my phone and texted Ryga to ask him to keep an eye on her through the evening while I was busy with Merry. He replied instantly and said he'd be there within the hour. Meanwhile, I arranged to have Clara and Tasha taken to a VIP room and get served appetizers and drinks until my man got there. "One of my people will watch your sister and friend," I said.

Merry nodded, then went to let them know she was only a phone call away.

"Come on, Ryga will be here soon. I got us a private room. This wasn't a sex club but we wouldn't be disturbed unless we wanted to order something. Taking her hand, I walked her to the back of the building where some of the VIP rooms were located. With our masks on, I felt like we were strangers who met out there and got carried away. The possibilities were endless...

I led her inside a room decorated from floor to ceiling in red. The couch was so wide and big, it looked like an enormous bed taking up the majority of the space.

When I came back, Merry was sprawled on the couch, her sexy, figure-hugging red dress hiked up her hips to reveal a pair of black lace panties. She kept the mask on, which turned me on even more.

For a while, we wouldn't think about our problems. Tonight, it was just me and her.

"You have no idea what you're doing to me, Merry," I said, thinking about all the positions we could try. The room smelled of roses and spicy perfume, adding to the allure.

She straightened on her seat and removed her dress all the way, revealing a bra that matched her panties.

"I have an idea," she said in a sultry tone. "Sit on that chair. I'm going to dance for you," she instructed. She stood on her high heels, giving me an all-knowing smile. What a long way we were from that time in the club when she didn't have the confidence to know what she liked.

I did as she asked, relishing the fantasy.

Merry turned around and started moving her hips, swaying her ass back and forth to the sexy beat of the music that filtered in the room.

"Shit..." I slid my hand to my groin to still my dick, which now made its presence known. I growled when she suddenly turned around and moved her hands up and down her body to the rhythm of the song.

She inched closer and soon, she rubbed herself all over me. I had no idea where she fucking learned any of these moves, but I was lost in my own flaming desire. My groin was burning and I needed to have her now because she was sucking me into a dream and I was hypnotized by her movements.

"I am here to please you, Daddy," she purred, leaning her ass over my hard on and lowering herself just enough to graze my erection. I wondered how much more I'd take of just watching her, without touching.

When she swiveled around and straddled me, all bets were off. I placed my hands on her hips. I wanted to take that nipple into my mouth and torture her a little bit.

She leaned toward my ear and whispered, "I'm going to take your hard and beautiful penis into my mouth and then I'm going to suck it until you come all over my face, Daddy."

Chapter Thirty

Merry

This was completely crazy but I was so turned on, I couldn't back away now. Ivo had showed up, stealing me away from that stranger. At first, I was furious with him that he followed me all the way here, but when he touched me, I was lost again.

At this themed event where everyone had to wear masks, we could pretend we didn't know each other, and we weren't going to meet again. This helped ease the guilt that burned through me for what I was about to do. I wanted to go through with this, no matter if the hounds of hell were chasing me.

I thought I could dance for him, take control, and forget about the problems we faced.

I'd been prepared to fuck someone here tonight. A stranger, and I'd have asked him to make me come, to prove to myself that I didn't need Ivo to orgasm. This whole plan had fallen to pieces.

Instead, I ended up here for him and only him, primed to do anything in my power to make this moment unforgettable.

Ivo let me lead, so I told him exactly what I was going to do to him. He was so hard and that made me instantly wet, thinking about his hard cock moving inside me after I gave him the best blow job in history.

I went down on my knees and started unbuckling his jeans, staring directly into his eyes. My hands were shaking a little, my pussy throbbing with need. I was so wet for him, eager to take him into my mouth and make him come all over me. The tiny voice in my head kept telling me this would be the last time, that we were never going to do a repeat. But this wasn't the first time I'd pondered the exact same thing, and each time I'd failed.

"Fuck, princess. Touch me," he breathed when I had his cock out. It was thick, hard, and veiny, so I clenched my thighs together for the sight of it made my pussy weep. I wanted him to fuck me hard after this. I'd demand he would.

I took his massive size into my mouth. He moaned, fisting his hand in my hair and telling me I was so good to him. The mask was a little restrictive, but I didn't want to take it off. I'd feel bare without it, and too much like the real me—riddled with guilt and regrets.

I moved my mouth up and down over his hard shaft.

It took me several tries to get it all the way to the back of my throat. Ivo loved it; he could barely sit still on that chair.

"Princess, who the fuck are you and when did you learn this? I am so fucking close, this is unbelievable," he gasped as I thrust his cock into my mouth, cupping his balls.

Ivo was so tense, so I kept licking the tip and savoring this moment, making it last forever. He groaned when I finally started picking up the pace, making us both crazy with need.

"Yes, that's right, princess. Keep sucking that cock like a good girl. You're doing such amazing job, you filthy whore," he said, and all that praise and dirty talk just made me wetter and needier.

My nipples were stiff and my pussy was dripping for him, throbbing for more. I was going to come again for him like I had the first time in his club. Back then, he was my teacher, my master, and now we were equals.

I kept licking his shaft, fucking him with my mouth until I felt the pressure rising fast. His cock expanded and then he was coming, releasing a wild, animalistic roar.

His semen sprayed down my throat and I took it all in, swallowing every drop as he fisted my hair so hard, I winced in pain. By the time I pulled away, we were both out of breath, but for the first time in a long time, I was proud of myself. Proud that the mask had stayed on my face the entire time.

My throat felt raw, my jaw ached, and my neck was burning, but it was worth it.

"Fuck, princess, you made me come in seconds. You sucked the shit out of me. You deserve a reward now," he said, taking my face into his palms and squeezing it gently. He wanted to make sure that I was looking into his eyes when he kissed me. Ivo always kissed gently and with such a passion that I felt it in every cell of my body.

Tingles of heat spread over my arms, my chest, all the way to my core. This energy we shared, the connection, touched me in places I didn't know existed.

"So, what are you going to do to me now, Daddy?" I cooed.

"Just get on that big couch and take your panties off. I want to see your beautiful ass in the air," he ordered. I did what he asked, going on all fours. I couldn't really see what Ivo was doing, but I was too turned on to care.

He finally got behind me, deft hands caressing my backside.

"Touch me..." I begged him, totally into him. Craving this until it hurt.

"You're going to scream for me when the pleasure hits. You deserve to be treated like a princess," he said, and then slid his fingers down my ass crack to my wet centre.

He growled in approval as he dipped two fingers inside me. Soon after, I felt his wet tongue on my backside, tracing where his fingers had traveled. The feeling was so strong, my skin was blazing with heat. I cried out, wanting more, needing to come.

Ivo was licking my butthole while easing his fingers in and out of my pussy, slowly taking me to the edge.

"Shit, this feels so good," I panted when he started fucking my ass with his tongue.

I gripped my left breast and massaged it to amplify the sensations as my vision got a little blurry.

Ivo kept going, his mouth licking and fucking my butthole while his fingers thrust in and out of my pussy. It was rough, but I loved every second of it.

Pressure built up in the pit of my stomach. He sped his pace, finger-fucking me harder, caressing my clit at the same time.

"Come for your daddy, princess. Come now," he commanded, and as my brain was wired up to obey, I exploded, my hips trembling as I screamed his name, coming so hard I thought I might reach the stars. The orgasm rocked through my core, and for a second, I couldn't catch my breath.

My whole body trembled as I finally collapsed on the couch, feeling completely exhausted.

I wasn't planning on moving for a while. I needed to rest. The sudden volcano of sensations wrecked me.

"I'm not done with you. Now, I'm going to fuck you so hard, you won't be able to walk tomorrow." He forced me back on my all fours and I groaned in protest. But when he drove his cock inside me, gripping my hips from behind, it felt like home.

"I can't..." I mumbled, so many unbelievable sensations rocking through every nook in my body. He wasn't joking when he said that he was going to fuck me hard. It was raw and brutal, but I didn't want him to go easy on me.

We both needed this release.

He pounded me until I was seeing stars, moaning and pleading with him to slow it down a little because I couldn't take it anymore. Ivo laughed and just kept going, fucking the shit out of me while digging his nails into my skin until I bled.

And then I came again, over and over. After a while, I lost count of how many times he made me come.

It was sometime later when he finally slapped my ass and collapsed on the couch next to me.

The world around me was spinning and I just lay there drenched in sweat, in the comfort of his arms, feeling completely and utterly taken. My breathing was coming in short, ragged pants, and the music was still going.

"This was unbelievable, Daddy," I whispered to him, and then forced myself to get up. It was time for me to go back to the party. Clara was probably looking for me. I wanted to sleep so badly, but I couldn't stay here. "I need to go now... This was fun, but nothing has changed. We both know that," I said.

He got up too, capturing my lips in a tender kiss and making me melt once more in his arms. Tears forced their way to my eyes but I didn't want to break down now, not in front of him.

We didn't speak as we got dressed. "I have done what I intended to do tonight, but this isn't over, princess. Not until I say it is. I will find a way for us to be together," he stated with confidence.

This situation was out of our control, no matter how much he wanted to fix it. The world was against us, and some things were more important than love.

"Just be careful out there, princess," he said, adjusting the mask on his face. Then, he turned around and walked out of the room first, leaving me alone with my jumbled emotions.

I walked back to the others, my heart beating a wild tattoo inside my chest.

My legs were wobbly, and every muscle in my body was aching as I moved. What happened between us in that room was fiery and indescribable. I was passing other people, feeling like I had been dreaming and was slowly waking up.

Why did life have to be so unfair? I wanted him and he wanted me. But that only made my heart break more.

I seemed to lose all sense of time but after a while, I found Clara in the VIP room he had reserved for her and Tasha.

I didn't see Tasha anywhere, but I wasn't worried. She liked to explore and not sit in one place.

My sister looked happy, chowing down on olives and a

martini. After years of struggle, it seemed like she was comfortable in her own skin.

She walked out with me and we found Tasha on the dance floor, dancing with some guy. I pulled them to the side and told them I wanted to go home. After a few complaints about me not meeting anyone yet, they finally caved in and let me be. I asked Clara what she wanted to do, and she was ready to stay with Tasha. Picking up my phone, I called Ivo and asked him if he'd get Ryga to continue keeping an eye on my girls.

"Leave it to me," he said in a rich voice. "They'll be safe."

I took a cab to my apartment and went straight to bed, my head buzzing and my muscles aching. Ivo's incredible scent lingered on my skin, and I never wanted to wash it off. I sensed him everywhere and when my head touched the pillow, I had flashbacks of our evening together.

I couldn't love this man—not the one who was about to marry my stepmother. If I said it enough times, I might even believe it.

I tried to fall asleep but couldn't because every time I shut my eyes, Ivo's sultry voice and his touch made me moan again. I was drained, knowing I had to do something about it.

But what options did I have?

Chapter Thirty-One

Ivo

I tossed and turned all night, thinking about my dilemma. It had been days since I'd seen my Merry. I'd followed her to that club like a stalker and didn't even feel bad about it. I just couldn't stay away from her. When I saw her outside the place wearing that red dress, I thought she looked stunning, but I didn't like that she was using it as bait for other men.

This whole thing was more than fucked up, but she was as frustrated as I was. She could deny it all she wanted, but I just knew.

So I went and fucked Merry like I never had before. Hard, rough, putting my all into it. All my frustrations and despair. All my desire. By the time we were done, she could barely move, let alone walk, and I thought I might have a heart attack.

My time with her was always powerful and precious. She

loved being serviced and she was thrilled with sucking and riding my cock.

Now I had a huge problem though because the guilt weighed heavy on me. Elaine was acting strange, still insisting that we move in together as soon as possible. But I kept avoiding the issue, making excuses and prolonging the inevitable.

Something didn't add up, and I intended to follow up on this to figure it out. Her behaviour sounded odd, erratic, and my intuition needed following through. I couldn't shake the feeling that Elaine was cheating. The problem was, with who? She wasn't known for restraint, and before she'd met me, she'd fucked half of LA already. Merry had mentioned a few affairs once, some with her security personnel. The woman didn't have too many hang-ups when it came to sex. What if she cared for someone and ended up pregnant by him?

I had some ideas about how to approach Victor, but later on in the day, while taking a shower, a lightbulb flashed in my head. I had some suspicions, so I could approach this another way.

I quickly got dressed and decided to head over to the prison where Emilio had been held. Jacob, one of the Bulgarian guys, had been busted dealing on the side and I knew for a fact he was still there. He was serving a few years and had always been loyal, until he decided to steal from me to pay a few medical bills for his mother.

He got five years, but Merry could most likely help him get out early. He was probably going to be surprised to see me there, but it was worth a shot, because he knew Emilio.

Later on, I had to attend another event Elaine was hosting. Something about making our wedding date public. She really did believe she was a celebrity, and everything she did was for show. One of the things that drove me up the wall about her. Our goals didn't match.

I was stuck in traffic for a while and by the time I arrived at my destination, I was in a foul mood. After the normal round of security, I finally sat down in the waiting room. Jacob would see me, and he'd want to help, regardless of what happened between us. What he did had been for a good reason, and for a long time, he'd served me well. If anyone could find out any information about Emilio, it would be him.

Jacob walked in, a big, intimidating guy with a dark complexion and tattoos on his neck.

"Ivo Sergei. This is unexpected. What brings you here?" he asked, getting straight to the point. I'd always liked how he was a no-bullshit kind of guy.

"Emilio—he was here for a little while. I just wonder if you can tell me anything useful. I need to find him before he does something really, really stupid," I told him.

Jacob smiled as though he understood what I meant, then silence stretched between us. I didn't mention Merry just yet, but I knew she'd go with it if it meant getting closer to finding Emilio and putting him behind bars.

"Yeah, he was here, but not for very long and he wasn't particularly chatty," Jacob replied. He sounded bored and I bet he wanted to be out of here. I could use that as leverage.

"All right, listen up, Jacob. I know there has never been bad blood between us, but I need to know things about my son. For example, who he was hanging out with, who he fought with, that sort of thing," I said, rubbing my hands together. "And particularly, who visited him. I think that's more important than anything and I am willing to help you. I happen to know a very good attorney. She can study your case and maybe help you get out on parole so you won't have to serve a full five years."

He dragged his hand over his unshaven jaw and mulled my words for a short while. I could tell he was tempted.

"And you're sure about that? You won't screw me over once I tell you what I know?" he asked, pointing at the both of us. When he was arrested, I had washed my hands of him, and he was likely referring to that.

"Last time, you were guilty of stealing from me and I wasn't particularly inclined to help. This is different," I said. "You have my word." I reached out to shake his hand. He relaxed a little, but I could see the guards were staring at us.

"He kept himself to himself and yeah, he had several visitors. You know my woman comes here often, so I was present when we all had visitations," he explained, and I shifted on the chair.

Emilio didn't have many friends. He hanged around a few of my men in the club, but he often did his own thing.

"Do you remember who visited him?"

"Well, I only saw him a few times, but one time I remember a woman was with him. They looked pretty cosy together," Jacob stated, dragging his hand through his dark hair.

A mystery woman. Now we were getting somewhere. Excitement prickled at my nape.

"Can you remember what she looked like? Blonde or brunette?" I questioned.

"She was stunning, to be honest. Very done up, slim and elegant. She was probably a little older than him, but beautiful, you know. Long blonde hair, long legs, big titties, and all the guards were checking her out. I only saw her once. I was with my woman so I couldn't look over at her too much, but this woman was really something," he explained with a grin.

I took off my phone and started scrolling through my pictures, annoyed that I didn't actually have any pictures of Elaine on my phone. She probably had plenty of mine. She also tried to avoid social media as much as possible, so I couldn't look her up online. As much as she fancied herself important, she only cared about mixing with people in our world, or those who had something she coveted. Otherwise, she was super private.

This was a long shot, although I had no idea why Elaine would come and visit Emilio. She did always dismiss my theories when I started talking about the need to apprehend him.

But she barely knew him, so this didn't make much sense.

"Elaine... She's pretty and looks quite young," I muttered, more to myself than to him.

"I have no idea, man, but she was really out of his league," he stated.

"Do you remember how many times she came here?" I pressed, but he shook his head.

"I've only seen her with him once, but she must have visited him more often," he said.

I thanked him and then told him that I would talk to my lawyer friend about his case. We were going to have to work together if I wanted a shot at finding Emilio.

I headed to the club straight from prison, hoping that Gregory could shed some light on this whole arrangement. Elaine was supposed to be on my side. Merry had claimed she had looked after them well, that she always wanted the best for them. This wasn't a Cinderella story, but maybe I was wrong and this wasn't Elaine that Jacob had been seeing with Emilio. If that was the case, I was fresh out of ideas.

The club was busy today, and by the time I got to my office, I was sweating like a pig.

"Why are you so pale? What happened?" Gregory asked when I entered the office. I didn't really have to be here tonight because he had everything under control, but I needed to talk to him.

"Shut the door," I said, and he did. "I went to prison and talked to Jacob. He told me something very interesting. Apparently, Emilio had a female visitor when he was locked up. According to his description, a beautiful blonde, impeccably dressed, tall and slightly older, perfect make-up. Big tits."

Gregory looked confused, and then he started to laugh.

"You're telling me that Emilio, my dick of a baby brother, had some chick who looked like Elaine visit him and possibly get him out of prison?" He laughed until he cried, and I wanted to punch him for it.

"I didn't have her picture so I couldn't confirm if she was the one Jacob had seen," I told him, and he started laughing even more, shaking his head.

"You don't have a picture of your fiancée on your phone?"

"Fuck off," I snapped, dragging my hand through my hair. "This isn't fucking funny. I'm going to talk to Elaine at the party and confront her about this."

"Wait, hold on. You're not sure if it was actually Elaine, so you're going to make a fool of yourself," Gregory pointed out.

He was partly right, because I wasn't convinced Elaine

would do something like this. She wouldn't risk being caught and then having to cancel the wedding.

"I'll just find a picture of her and go back and show Jacob. I looked online, but I can't believe she doesn't have any of her on social media or the internet. She's such a show off, celebrity wannabe, but then likes to stay off the general public's radar. Go figure. What a major pain in the ass." I huffed, then continued, "It has to be her. Emilio has never had female friends. He usually fucks them and leaves them. That son of a bitch has perverted fantasies, so he always scares them off."

Victor was going to be at the party and I was planning to pull him to the side when Elaine was busy elsewhere and talk to him about a different kind of deal. If I approached him in good faith and convinced him he didn't need Elaine as a go-between to trust me, we'd have something to work with.

I was ready to take care of this baby for better and for worse, but only after I had a DNA test in my hand which confirmed I was the father. Besides that, I had no idea how Merry was going to act around me, especially after that evening in the club.

"Good plan," Gregory agreed with me. I still had so many questions, especially the fact I didn't see Emilio getting involved with Elaine that way. "However, talk to Merry before you do anything."

I mulled all the options, knowing that Gregory was right. I needed to get Merry involved. Either way, if this was my child, I was going to take care of it. There was no question about it, and I had to hope Merry would stand by my side while I took care of these matters. Otherwise, none of this would be worth it.

Chapter Thirty-Two

Merry

I was not looking forward to Elaine's party tonight because I didn't want to face her. It was six pm and I was already running late. Clara had been texting me, asking where the hell I was. At least I cleaned up well and looked pretty good for tonight, better than at the club where Ivo had fucked me three ways until Sunday. I was aching all over afterwards, but I would have done it again in a heartbeat. This was the issue—I didn't feel bad about it and I should have because Elaine was family. She didn't deserve this.

I decided that tonight, I would wear a revealing, short and sexy white dress. I arranged my hair in a high bob and went for killer heels. They weren't comfortable at all, but I just needed to be someone else tonight. I'd let Ivo screw with my head, but now we were back to square one.

Yet again I told myself we couldn't keep doing this to Elaine. None of this was fair or right, so it needed to stop.

Tonight, I was planning to flirt with as many men as possible because I knew Ivo wasn't going to do anything about it. It was petty, but my way of showing him that I was ready to move on. This had gone on for far too long.

"Where the hell have you been? Everyone has been asking about you," Clara hissed at me when I walked through the door an hour later. The music was playing, people were drinking and eating. It seemed everyone was having a good time. Elaine invited a lot more people than I expected.

Gregory gave me a nod, standing behind my sister in an elegant white tuxedo. This meant Ivo was here, too. My nerves frayed at the edges, but I pushed the apprehension aside.

"Calm down. I'm sure no one was missing me. I was getting ready. Grab me a champagne, will you? I need something to prepare me before I talk to Elaine and hear another sob story about her condition," I told Clara. I wasn't one to act like such a bitch, but these were special circumstances. I was just extremely frustrated with this whole situation.

Clara looked surprised and then finally seemed to notice what I was wearing, lifting her left eyebrow.

"This dress is short, Merry. Ivo is going to go crazy."

"I don't care. Ivo is not my father and I just felt like I needed to look good tonight. Besides, I can wear whatever I want," I told her, smoothing my hair. I really had no idea what was wrong with me tonight. Maybe my hormones were going haywire as I approached that time of the month next week.

"My my, Merry, you look stunning tonight," Gregory said with a smile. Then he leaned over, lowering his voice, "My father will lose his mind when he sees you in that nightie. Trust me, you won't be wearing it for very long."

My dear sister handed me the champagne and I glanced at Gregory, nervousness rearing its ugly head again. Had I worn it to get other men, or for Ivo? I wasn't his property.

Maybe I should mingle a little and talk to a few lawyers. I bet Elaine had invited a few, likely to find me a suitor.

Truth was, I planned to relocate as soon as I was able. Staying here was not an option.

"Don't worry, I can handle your father, and he's not with me. He's having a baby with your future stepmother, remember?" I said, finishing off the glass of champagne and plucking another one from a tray a pretty waitress was carrying.

This was the only way for me to get through the evening without causing a scene. It wasn't in character for me, being petty, but maybe love made people do insane shit.

Love...

"Yeah, right," Gregory muttered.

I started walking around, hoping not to bump into Ivo just yet. I wasn't mentally prepared to face him. Gregory and Clara were following me, both looking worried, but I tried to ignore them.

I headed outside to the garden and pool area, where I was greeted by a pleasant breeze. Much better than the heat wave we had earlier on.

"Merry ... oh, Merry, darling. I have to introduce you to a few people," Elaine's loud voice spread through the crowd.

I cursed under my breath when she spotted me, waving and trying to get my attention. She glanced at my dress when she finally got to me and her face went slightly pale. I bet she wasn't expecting me to wear that to her party, but I was so through being the good and understanding Merry. Elaine was just stunning and she was glowing. She had an incredible figure and tonight, she wore a pale pink maxi dress that made her look even more radiant than usual. Truth be told, she could show up in a robe and slippers and still look good.

"Why are you so late and why are you wearing this ... um ... dress? People are staring, my dear. It's very inappropriate."

I laughed, pretending I didn't realise she was serious, but from the daggers in her gaze, she clearly didn't approve of my slutty look. Too bad because I wasn't planning to change.

"Well, I love it and the men will be all over me. Isn't this what you want, Elaine, to marry me off to some fancy lawyer or businessman?" I asked in the sweetest voice I could muster.

Her frown deepened. "Don't be absurd, Merry. You're acting weird. Just don't bend over too much and you should be fine," she said, staring in shock as I drained the second glass of champagne.

She truly thought she could tell me what to do. If I looked so good, then maybe I didn't have to care about anyone else's opinion. Shaking her head at what she likely deemed my odd behavior, she gently grabbed my elbow and led me toward a tall guy who was talking to a woman. When she turned to face me, I thought I recognised her from a picture I'd seen. It was that detective who'd arrested Ivo: Lucinda Morales.

"Phil, this is my stepdaughter, the attorney I have been telling you about," Elaine introduced me, showing me off like cattle ready for slaughter. Just great. "Merry, this is Phil Bradshaw, also an attorney."

Phil was not a bad looking man and he was my type, with

dark hair, nice large hands, and a square jaw. He smiled at me and his eyes sparkled in appreciation. I wondered where Ivo was. Maybe he was intentionally trying to keep his distance.

"And this is Detective Morales. She kindly accepted my invitation tonight as she is off duty." Elaine gave a bright smile, showing her pearly whites.

The woman was attractive and fit, but clearly didn't like the way I was dressed. Not surprising, to be honest, and I was past the point of caring.

"I'll leave you to it then. I do need to find my fiancé," she said in that high pitched tone of voice of hers, then walked away.

I felt hot all of a sudden, and chided myself for acting like an immature brat. What the hell was wrong with me? Maybe emotional burnout was having its heyday in my system, making me do the damnedest things.

Or the fact I was about to leave was hitting home, and I just couldn't deal with it.

I wanted to show him what he was going to miss. Petty as fuck, but here I was, holding the last straw in my hand and waving it in the air.

"Yes, I do remember now. I was told you visited the station when Ivo was in custody. I just didn't know who you were when I got your name," Morales stated, giving me a tight smile.

"So, what law firm do you work for?" Phil asked.

"Peeble and Bryce in New York City, but I've given my notice. I'm sort of between jobs right now. I do occasionally work for Elaine and the family," I explained, spotting a tray with more champagne and grabbing a third glass. I took a sip, needing something stronger.

"Well, I can always put in a good word for you at my firm. The partners are always looking for new, talented attorneys," he said, giving me a warm smile.

"So, what do you make of Ivo's son, Emilio, being suddenly released? This must have been a huge surprise," Morales interjected. My stomach knotted with unease. I didn't know what she was trying to achieve by asking these questions, but nothing good was going to come out of it.

"I don't know who would have possibly done it. None of us expected this. Emilio should have stayed in prison," I replied.

My skin prickled when I felt eyes on me, watching from a distance, and I knew it was Ivo. I finished the champagne and directed my gaze to the handsome lawyer who stood by me, ignoring the tidal wave of emotions assailing me.

"So, what do you do when you're not in your shiny armor?" I asked him, hoping he knew what I meant. Morales didn't seem pleased with the fact I was ignoring her line of conversation.

"Excuse me," she finally muttered, leaving me alone with Phil. It seemed she got the hint.

I glanced towards where I felt Ivo might have been standing, seeing that the detective had now joined him. My God, he looked so angry. His eyes were pinning me down and there was violence in them, so I gave him a light nod.

From where he was standing, he had a perfect view of my whole body. He looked like he was just about to lose it, probably because he noticed what I was wearing.

"Oh, this and that. I play a bit of a golf and tennis. Oh, and I see you need a top-up," Phil replied, leaning over to check the contents of my glass. In a flash, he got me a fresh glass—my fourth, and it was still nowhere near enough. I inhaled his spicy cologne and I quite liked it. At least, he was pleasant to talk to.

"Thank you for the drink. Ahh, tennis. I played a bit with my sister..." I said, and then leaned in close to his ear, adding, "Maybe we could play together sometime?"

He gave me such a wide smile, if I had a crush on him, I'd melt. The champagne wasn't strong, but four goblets had taken a toll on me. Someone passed by and pushed me, making me lose my balance, then I felt something wet and sticky all over my chest. I almost landed in the pool before strong hands caught me, preventing me from humiliating myself in front of everyone gathered around.

"Oh shit, sorry. I must have tripped," a deep, velvety voice spoke. A sound that sent a chill down my spine. My heart flipped when I realised Ivo was holding my hand. His eyes were dark and filled with anger. He held a glass of something that looked like tomato juice in his other hand, and when I glanced at my dress, I realized its contents had spilled all over me.

Soon enough the lusty vibrations were replaced by fury as I realized what he had done.

"What is wrong with you?" I blurted out. My dress was completely ruined now.

Ivo's eyes moved insolently down my body, setting me ablaze, and his touch sent goosebumps crawling up my arm.

I detested him.

"Merry, are you all right? God, your dress," Phil gasped.

"She's fine," Ivo snapped, and I shot him a vicious look.

I shrugged his hand off my arm, fuming. Phil seemed utterly confused. Other people were staring, too, particularly Morales. I wanted the earth to swallow me whole.

"You seem ... a little put out," Ivo said with fire in his eyes. He was thoroughly enjoying himself, the miserable jerk. If I pushed him, he might land in the pool...

I started to walk away before my wrath got the better of me and I made an even bigger fool of myself.

"I'll be right back," I told Phil, handing him my drink to hold for me, tempted to smash the glass in Ivo's face.

The man had a temper problem. He ruined my dress simply because he couldn't stand seeing me talk to another man. What a moron. I stormed into the kitchen, looking for something I could clean myself with, but what was the fucking point? The wait staff were walking in and out, witnessing me literally shaking in anger.

I was so done with him and I was ready to give him hell, not caring whether Elaine figured out what had been going on between us. This time, Mr. Sergei had crossed the line.

Chapter Thirty-Three

Ivo

The party was slow going at first. Elaine was acting like her usual self, entertaining all the guests when I arrived. Victor hadn't yet showed up, and Merry was running late, too.

I was fucking tense, wondering what to make of this charade. I had a drink or two, chatted with a few people, and after about an hour finally spotted Merry by the pool, talking to Morales and some guy.

At first, I thought there was something wrong with my eyesight, because she was wearing what seemed to be half a dress, or some stretchy confection made for a much shorter, smaller person. The way she looked should have been for my eyes only.

Was she high on something? This wasn't like her—every fucking man there was looking at her like they were coyotes and she a hapless bird to be preyed upon. Swiftly and lethally, my control was slipping, and I knew I had to do something to stop this madness.

The moment I saw her flirting with the tall man, and Morales left them to it, I was ready to punch a wall. The detective walked toward me and attempted to dredge up the fact Emilio got released, but I had no time for her nonsense. My head was filled with images of Merry bent over my lap, wearing exactly that slutty dress.

Indignation ruffled my feathers, and steam started coming out of my ears.

"Excuse me, Morales, I see someone I need to talk to," I said, interrupting her mid-sentence. I was ready to kill that motherfucker who was eyeing my woman's cleavage as though it was a juicy steak dinner. Merry was fucking with me, fucking with my mind because of what was going on between us.

I burst into the kitchen, doing my utmost to avoid Elaine. I opened the fridge and the tomato juice caught my eye. A mad idea came to me. A risky one, but Merry needed to be taught a lesson. My princess was mine, and she had to be put back in her place.

She was going to be so mad, but I didn't care. I was ready to buy her a hundred dresses like hers, but for my eyes only. I put the juice in a glass and headed back out, feeling a little apprehensive, but when I saw Merry still flirting with that dumb ass right in front of me, all my doubts drifted away. She was baiting him and every other available man present with that dress and her incredible figure.

That fucker was standing too close and ogling the perfect tits I'd been sucking on only a few days ago. She was having fun, keeping his attention. I bee-lined to her so fast, I was surprised I didn't trip on the way there. Then, when I was right by Merry and that motherfucking pretty boy, I intentionally pushed her and threw the entire contents of my glass all over her slutty dress. She nearly dipped into the pool, but I managed to get hold of her and keep her on solid ground.

Well, it was all my fault but she was the one who'd chosen to wear something some whore would wear on a street corner, waiting for some sucker to drive up and pay for a blowjob.

She marched away, probably heading back to the kitchen. As for me, I had done what I needed to do, but I felt guilty, because now she either had to change into something more appropriate, or leave.

People were still staring at me. The man she'd been talking to shook his head and walked away. He was probably sensing that I was ready to kick his ass.

"What the hell happened up there, Ivo? Merry is upset, and what's the deal with the tomato juice?" Elaine asked, cornering me by the pool.

Merry gave me a look that said not to follow her, so I decided to give her some time to cool down. Hopefully, everyone would return to their regularly scheduled programming.

"Nothing. I just tripped, Elaine, Christ. I tried to apologize to her but she was having none of it and the juice was for my stomach," I lied, wanting to ask her what the fuck was she doing visiting Emilio, but I bit my tongue. I needed to wait to be sure that she was truly the one.

I had no solid evidence so I had to keep playing this game for now. Elaine exhaled and narrowed her gaze on me, probably aware that everyone around us was trying to eavesdrop on our conversation. Elaine hated when things didn't go according to her neatly laid plans, and the way she was staring at me indicated that she wasn't buying any of my bullshit.

"What's wrong with your stomach? That juice was for me and that was the last one I had. Oh, Ivo, you're being inconsiderate," she whined.

"Not sure. It's probably a bug," I muttered.

"Honestly, I don't know how you men survive for so long on this world," she said, sounding annoyed, finally leaving me be.

She was onto me and I shouldn't have done that, but Merry knew how to push my buttons.

I circled to the kitchen, but Merry wasn't there. I figured she must have gone upstairs. Apart from the fact that I was ready to punish her for pulling that stunt with the dress, I really needed to talk to her.

This was a little unwise, because Elaine was probably watching me. I didn't know what time she wanted to announce the official wedding day, but I had to find Merry beforehand. Victor had finally arrived, and I needed to catch his attention, too.

I decided to sneak upstairs, hopefully without anyone noticing. At that point, Elaine was having a hissy fit over a flower arrangement.

I heard some voices in the guest room. This house was huge and it was easy to get lost. The door to one of the rooms was ajar.

"It's ruined, Clara, and he planned this the moment he saw me," Merry said. She was mad at me, but she'd known what was going to happen if she teased me like that, with that sorry excuse for a dress. A fucking loin cloth covered more skin than that.

As I stood rooted to the spot, I worked to calm myself down, then knocked and entered the room. Merry had another gown on, this one was long and navy blue. She must have borrowed it from Elaine, because it looked a bit loose.

"Get the hell out of here or I swear to God I am going to kill you!" Merry threatened as soon as she saw me. I lifted my hands in the air in a gesture of surrender, taking her quite seriously. This woman was capable of anything.

Clara shook her head, getting between me and my princess. "Ivo, come on. You should leave," she said.

"All right, hold your horses. It was an accident and I really need to talk to you, princess. This is important," I said. That didn't appease her, and she looked just as scary. The damaged dress was laid on the bed. I didn't even feel bad about ruining it. She'd looked too tempting in it.

Merry's face went purple with rage. She tried to push Clara away, probably to get to me, but her sister held up, not letting her through.

"You don't get to tell me what to do, and this is bullshit. You deliberately sabotaged me, humiliating me in front of all the guests. So now you can go fuck yourself, Ivo Sergei!"

"Clara, please leave. I think I can handle her for a minute," I asked her sister nicely, pleading with my eyes.

She hesitated for the briefest of moments, then walked away.

"Don't you fucking dare come anywhere near me, Ivo. You've gone too far," she snapped, folding her arms over her chest and giving me a hard look.

I smirked—well, I just couldn't help myself when she looked so damn adorable acting like a crazy woman.

"You didn't leave me any choice, princess, wearing something like that for other men to see. It should have been for my eyes only," I told her, taking a step towards her. Her pupils dilated and she drew a shaky breath.

"I can wear whatever I want and flirt with whoever I wish to, so you can fuck right off a cliff. Seriously, I don't want to look at you right now," she said, and then I took another step towards her. These were only baby steps in the literal sense, because I was afraid she might strike me. I knew she wanted to.

"Well, too bad because I'm not going anywhere. We need to talk and you're lucky enough that you're not being punished for letting other men stare at your fine ass and titties," I snarled, blocking her with my body. She walked backwards and hit the wall. Her eyes gleamed with a storm of emotions. She smelled so good and my cock went hard in an instant. She was driving me crazy and I really needed to hurry this along.

She laughed and then, before I could gather my chaotic thoughts, she shoved me, after which she delivered a brutal slap. And my cock got even harder.

"So fucking violent, Merry," I whispered.

I grabbed her hands, ready to throw her across my knee and spank her ass until the skin was red and raw. Instead, I fucking kissed her. Wet and messy and wild and rough at the same time. And then I slowed down, licking and nipping, trying to taste every inch of her mouth. This time around, she didn't even flinch. She stilled, and warmth spilled into my groin and spread around.

She tasted like sweet cherry sprinkled with sugar and honey, as well as champagne. I devoured her mouth slowly, then I forced my tongue inside while holding her face in place, because I thought she would push me away. I kissed her and kissed her until I couldn't breathe anything but her. Finally, she moaned into my mouth and I broke into an inner laugh, proud that I'd managed to break that anger. Break *her*. I kept kissing her deeply until we were both breathless and light-headed.

When I pulled away, the anger in her eyes was replaced by fire. Her lips were swollen and my cock stood at attention. I was ready to rip this new dress off and take her there and then.

"We can't do that and I'm still mad at you," she barked, poking me with her finger.

"Shut up. I bet your pussy is dripping for me already, princess," I said, trying to kiss her again but somehow, she wiggled away from me.

"I'm serious. This is too dangerous. You wanted to talk, so talk. I need to get back to that party," she said, trying to fix her hair, but it was a lost cause.

I pressed my hand over my stiff cock, trying to think about Elaine because as always, this did the trick if I couldn't fuck Merry.

Then I remembered that I was supposed to tell her about Jacob.

"To flirt with that lawyer guy?"

"And what if I am? This is none of your business," she snapped. "Anyway, just tell me what's going on."

I went ahead and explained what I knew as quickly as I could, trying to ignore the thought of her going downstairs and hooking up with that idiot. I relayed what Jacob had told me about Emilio.

"But he wasn't certain it was Elaine, so we can't be sure?" she asked.

"No, but she fits the description. She must have been the one that got him out. She knows people in high places," I insisted, although I didn't have a certainty this was the case.

"I don't know, this doesn't make much sense. Why would she get him out?"

"That's what we need to find out," I said with a nod.

Chapter Thirty-Four

Merry

We needed to leave the room so I forced Ivo to go back to the party. We'd been upstairs for far too long. I was worried that Elaine or even other people might notice us being gone. I went first and Ivo showed up downstairs ten minutes later. The dress that Clara had managed to get out of her wardrobe was old and a bit too big for me. My sister's figure was a little fuller than mine, a lush hourglass, but I had no other choice.

Ivo had acted so childish, but he got what he deserved—that slap had been very satisfying, although the kiss afterwards was mind-blowing.

Then again, I'd been immature, too, so I couldn't point my finger too much.

"Are you okay? Did he do anything?" Clara asked me after I went to get another glass of bubbly. This party was so boring and I had another few hours of getting through it, but my stomach was growling.

Gregory was standing behind her, glancing around as though looking for someone. Lately, he had been spending a lot of time with my sister and I wanted to know if there was anything going on between the two of them. I doubted it, especially since it would be a little odd considering the circumstances, although I would welcome the idea. Gregory was sweet and the complete opposite of Emilio.

"I am fine. I put Ivo in his place," I said, sighing loudly.

Clara giggled at that, then sighed. Indeed, things were never as easy when it came to me and Ivo.

"My father is talking to Victor now and he seemed all right, so maybe Merry is telling us the truth for once." Gregory smirked.

"He's fine, trust me, as long as he won't pull another stunt like that," I reminded him. I wasn't sure why Ivo was talking to Victor now, but whatever it was, I wasn't getting involved.

"We should go. Elaine will probably make the announcement soon," Clara said.

"Really? Okay, in that case I need something stronger," I said, looking at the watch. It was close to eight, and Elaine was nowhere to be seen.

"Everyone is gathering in the garden," Clara pointed out.

"Let me look for her," I suggested, taking a generous sip of the champagne, but I really needed vodka to get through this.

I started going through all the rooms in the house, and there were a lot of them. Elaine had everything redecorated and reorganized right after I and Clara moved out.

I didn't think she'd gone upstairs. One of the household

staff said that she'd checked there already and all the rooms were empty. Ivo was standing in a corner of the living room, talking to Victor. He seemed relaxed but when I glanced at Victor, he appeared almost irritated. I really wanted to know what they were talking about.

People started to gather outside in the large garden, expecting Elaine to make an announcement shortly. This was strange, because my stepmother was never late for anything, but apparently pregnancy hormones were a bitch.

I needed to find her quickly. I circled around downstairs and then noticed that the door to the office was ajar. I was just about to walk in there when I heard Elaine's voice.

"No, you can't. It's not a good time. You need to stay where you are," she said in a hushed tone.

I frowned and stopped in my tracks. Who was she talking to?

"I'm fine, but Ivo has been acting strange. Do you think he might be suspecting anything? He's too tied up in that deal to make a run for it," Elaine continued, and my frown only deepened. Damn it, who the hell was it?

Emilio?

Maybe Ivo had been right about the fact she was helping him, and got him out of prison. And if they were that close, then Emilio must have told Elaine about me and his father. Wouldn't he?

If Elaine knew, though, then she would have said something a long time ago. She wasn't the sort of person to hide her feelings.

"I don't know, but things are getting complicated. We need to keep this hush hush until this whole thing blows over. I really need to go now," she said, and then gasped. She must have realized that she was late, because she hung up the phone.

I quickly backed away and raced to the kitchen, thinking that this whole conversation was just odd.

Maybe Ivo was wrong. Maybe Elaine had nothing to do with this, but this phone call proved that she hadn't been entirely honest with me or him.

Either way, we all had to figure this out. When Elaine left the office, I went back to the garden. My stepmother was a great actress. She was still only in the first trimester so she wasn't showing, but acted like she was at least seven months pregnant already.

"Oh, I'm really, really sorry everyone, but I went upstairs to lie down for a moment and then lost the track of time," she lied when she finally joined Ivo by the pool.

There was something wrong. I could tell she was nervous and Ivo—well, he looked like he'd swallowed something foul. Clara had told me that Elaine had been pressuring him to move in and he was stalling. He had his arms around her waist and from a distance, they looked good together. I averted my gaze for I just couldn't look at them for too long.

Then, I chanced a glance at Ivo and found his gaze on me. For a while, nothing else existed but him, until Elaine started talking again.

"Well, we've talked about this wedding for months and I'm sure everyone is already fed up with it." Elaine laughed and a few people followed suit. "So, after careful consideration, we decided that we are going to get married in about two weeks' time. Save the date everyone, because all the wedding invitations have been mailed!"

A series of gasps and congratulations followed through. I opened my mouth to say something but couldn't really make a sound. Ivo looked as surprised as me and he leaned over to speak to her, but Elaine was busy talking to other people. Her guests started meandering over to her to congratulate her.

I felt dizzy. Where did this come from? They were going to be married in two weeks. Something must have happened since she was in such a rush.

"I swear to God I had no idea she had decided to push the date up," Ivo admitted, finding me in the crowd of people.

I didn't know what to say to him. My anger from earlier had subsided, and now I was just disappointed with myself. Obviously, Elaine wanted to get married before she started showing. Our family was Catholic observant, so she wanted to avoid all the gossip and drama. Even in our world, proper rules needed to be followed.

"It doesn't matter, Ivo. We both know this is it," I said sadly.

"I can and will fix it, Merry, I promise," he said, and I only shook my head.

Clara joined me later and Gregory finally managed to get me some vodka. None of this mattered anymore. I ate some appetizers and tried as much as possible to have a good time.

Sometime later in the evening, I was minding my own business in the kitchen when Ivo caught up with my stepmother right outside on the patio. The party was slowly winding down.

"Wait a minute, Elaine, we need to talk. I don't remember agreeing to any of this. What the fuck were you thinking?" Ivo sounded about ready to burst.

I should have walked away, but I wanted to hear what she had to say to him.

"I just want us to be married and move on with our other plans. I have been telling you that I wanted to get it over with for a long time, but you never listened," she stated firmly. "Oh, I need to ask Merry and Clara to be my bridesmaids."

Ivo crossed his arms and spread his legs apart, in a battle stance. "No, we are not getting married in two weeks, and as far as Victor is concerned, I have been talking to him. I have decided to back away from the business for good, and frankly, I don't really want to go through with this whole charade."

"What?" Elaine's high-pitched voice threatened to pierce my eardrums.

"To be honest, Victor is looking forward to taking over some of my territory, and my men will not be out of a job. The whole setup will be a little unconventional, and we must iron out some details and kinks, but I think it's going to work great," Ivo said, and my heart stopped. Did he really just tell Elaine that he wasn't going to marry her?

Elaine went pale and glanced around. I wasn't really sure what I was supposed to do with myself. If she'd been really talking to Emilio, then she must have known about Ivo and me from the start—but why wouldn't she confront us both about it? He wouldn't have hidden this, especially not after what's happened in that old flat when I shot him.

"You can't be serious." She laughed. "We both know you can't break this deal. Victor is going to have your head. Everyone gets cold feet, Ivo, but you also have a baby to think about."

"Well, I am going take my chances and I will take care of

that child if it's mine, so you don't have to worry about it, but I don't love you, Elaine. This was all business, so there is no need for the wedding."

"What do you mean if it's yours?" Elaine sounded hysterical now, but Ivo walked away, ignoring her question. "You know you're not going anywhere, dammit!"

I had never seen her so speechless. She rushed after him, but he was too fast for her and headed toward some of the remaining guests. She wouldn't make a scene if there were witnesses. Frankly, she didn't look particularly sad or depressed.

I took a deep breath and headed back out again. When all the guests left, Elaine claimed she had a headache so she went upstairs to lie down.

Ivo was fuming because she was truly not taking him seriously. Clara and Gregory were watching him as he paced around the living room.

"I'm going to talk to him," I told them, thinking about that strange phone call from earlier on.

"Just be careful. Sometimes he bites," Gregory muttered. The house seemed quiet, but the maids were still clearing after the party. I grabbed Ivo's hand and dragged him to the office.

"What is it, Merry? I don't want to argue with you right now. I'm not in the mood," he said when I shut the door.

"We are not going to talk about us, but I have to tell you something. I overheard Elaine talking to someone on the phone just before she joined you outside," I said.

"Talking to who exactly?"

"I don't know, but she seemed anxious and she was telling this other person that you might be suspecting something." I kept some distance between us and disregarded the whirling emotions I always felt when he was around.

Ivo stared out the window for a while, then walked back to me. "She was probably talking to Emilio."

"We don't know that, but we have to follow her. Something is not right. Elaine has been acting strange for a while," I suggested, and Ivo smiled, then inched closer to me.

"And you want to do it together, because you can't stay away from me?"

"No, I just want to find out what she is hiding," I told him, folding his arms over my chest. It was better that I acted cold. We were never going to be an item and he needed to come to terms with it.

"All right, we will start from tomorrow. Let Clara know about our plans," he suggested. I nodded. My sister had moved back here for a while after she recovered from her suicide attempt, so now she could keep an eye on Elaine for us.

I headed to the door. For some reason, I felt exhausted all of a sudden. Probably the alcohol.

"Good, see you tomorrow," I said.

"Merry," he called out when I was just about to leave the room. I sighed and turned around. His gaze burned through my core and a shiver ran down my spine.

"What, Ivo?" I asked, a little annoyed. We had nothing else to talk about.

"I love you," he whispered, and something inside me came alive. An indescribable feeling. Why did he have to be so handsome, frustrating, and so incredibly domineering at the same time? I wanted him for myself, and I loved him, too—well, I wasn't ready to admit this to myself just yet, because my emotions were so out of place.

My knees were wobbly when I finally left the office and headed home. Ivo didn't try to stop me again. I really had to take some time out for myself and think about my future.

The man was having a baby with my stepmother and I just couldn't see us together anymore. I wasn't prepared to share him with any other woman or even a child. This was my life and I didn't want to be that second-place person anymore.

I wanted to be the first. I wanted to be the one.

Chapter Thirty-Five

Ivo

Merry wasn't joking when she said we had to follow Elaine. The day after the party she called and told me she was going to pick me up from the club. This was surreal because I was with the woman I wanted to bang for the rest of my life.

For heaven's sake, Elaine had been living a truly tedious life, based on our findings. So much, her entire existence seemed depressing. Merry and I had been following her everywhere for three straight days. She'd always told me she'd dedicated her life to business and the Camilleri family. She was supposed to be this ruthless businesswoman who had everything under control, but all I could see was a woman who was so fucking bored, and she had to eat lunch in an old Chinese restaurant in a rundown neighborhood.

Merry was patient, but she was also distracting me. All I

could think about was sex when I was with her, and this was a problem. We talked a lot and I was trying hard to learn new things about her. I was getting to know her all over again and this was good thing.

We made a deal that we weren't going to touch each other, because we were working and that was fair, but so freaking difficult. I was constantly horny around her, especially when she was wearing tight dresses that exposed a good portion of her breasts. I had a feeling she was intentionally torturing me.

After we'd trailed Elaine for a while, we felt like we were wasting time. Elaine wasn't seeing anyone else. Maybe we were both wrong about her. The fact of the matter was, this baby was likely mine and Merry was leaving Los Angeles for good.

She didn't want to stay here and pretend we were going to be together because it wasn't an option. I didn't blame her, but I couldn't imagine my life without her.

"That's it, I am done with this. I'll get Ryga to follow her around over the next few days," I finally said on the fourth day.

Elaine had a meeting with a few Russians early this morning, but I had no idea what that was about. Victor and I had a serious talk at the party. He wasn't happy at first when I mentioned that I wasn't going through with the wedding. He even threatened me, so I promised him something else. More power. Then, I had his attention.

Merry glanced at me in shock.

"It's only the fourth day. I think we should give her a bit more time. We are onto something," she disagreed, and I shook my head, yearning to kiss her. She was just so beautiful, funny, and intelligent. We had fun together and understood each other without words.

We were in the city where Elaine was getting her nails done. It had been four days and Elaine hadn't called me once. This was odd, because she was always calling me. Maybe she was finally convinced I'd been serious when I broke up with her, but we probably had to have this conversation again at some point.

"Come on, let's grab some lunch. She's going to be in that beauty salon for about two more hours," I suggested.

Merry shook her head. "I need to go back to my apartment. I have a video interview with a firm in Georgia. I'm looking into taking the bar exam there."

"Are you serious? Why so far away?" Panic filled me because the thought of her going to the other side of the country made everything feel so final.

Merry placed her hands on her thighs, then looked out on the street. She looked like she wasn't sure what to do, and I shouldn't have brought any of this up. But I didn't want to lose her. This was happening way too fast.

"I will see you in about two hours. We can meet outside Elaine's house then. You are right. We should let your man handle her from tomorrow. This isn't working," she finally said, dismissing whatever I thought about her new plan.

Then, before I could stop her, she got out of the car and started walking away from me. The tiny, annoying voice inside my head told me I should follow her but I didn't. Merry had made up her mind and I had to respect that.

I went back to my club instead of continuing to trail Elaine. I didn't want to sit in my car for two hours, waiting.

After I was done with my paperwork, I grabbed some lunch from the bar and drove back to Elaine's place at around four.

Merry texted me to say that her stepmother was home so we

didn't have to drive around the city this evening. If she was planning anything or seeing anyone, we would have known already. Tomorrow, I would hand the reins over to Ryga.

Meanwhile, Merry wanted to move forward and I needed to figure out what I was going to do with my life. One thing I knew, I was in love with her, and I was ready to fight for her.

On the way to the mansion, I got a call from Gregory.

"You need to come back to the club. Victor is here and wants to talk to you," he said.

What the fuck did the man want now? I thought I'd proposed a pretty attractive deal at the party, or so I thought, but I must have spooked him.

"Fine, I will be right there," I told him. This needed to end once and for all. Victor wanted to have an alliance with the Camilleri family and he was going to get it, but I wasn't going to marry Elaine. That was a done deal. I'd made my offer to sweeten the pot. I texted Merry and told her that I was running late, and she said that she was all right on her own.

Two of Victor's men stood outside the club. They gave me the once over as I rushed upstairs to my office. It looked like Victor was with Gregory. He didn't bring any other men with him and that baffled me a little, because he normally walked around like a mobile Fort Knox.

"Hey Victor, what's happening?" I asked. He wasn't happy how I left things at the party. He was after Elaine's territory and she had promised him a lot since we were all going to work together. With me being half Russian, that would guarantee him some additional perks.

Victor was excellent at making people do what he wanted.

"Have you spoken to Elaine about the fact you're not going

to marry her?" the Russian asked, sitting with his hands folded together.

Gregory gave me a surprised look.

"I told her I would take care of our child but I'm not going to marry her," I explained, knowing that Elaine probably still believed I was joking.

"*Niet*, you're stepping on a thin line, Sergei. I want what she has, and I don't understand what the issue is here. You're going to have a child together. I want to cut off your fucking cock because you're not honoring this woman for what? For some kind of fling?"

I stared at the Russian, knowing that I was going to lose this battle, but then I sort of went over what he said and frowned.

"Fling? What fling? I have no idea what you're talking about?"

He laughed then and slammed his hand hard on the desk.

"You think I don't know about you and Edgar's daughter, Merry? I'm surprised Elaine hasn't figured out you two have been fucking," he said, and the blood drained from my face.

Victor knew? Gregory also seemed shocked, but then it dawned on me.

Emilio...

"I got to know Merry before Elaine. She has nothing to do—"

"I will give you a few days to think this over, Ivo, and after that it's either yes or a no. You remember what happened the last time you disappointed me?" he warned, glancing at Gregory. I knew he wasn't bluffing. My elder son had nearly died because of Victor's men. He was in coma for a long time afterward and my club was burned down. "You're only alive because your mama was a Ruska. Forget about the girl, she's not for you, and honor the woman who is carrying your child or I'm going to fucking kill you myself."

"What about my retirement, and the fact I offered you everything on a silver platter?"

"I appreciate that and I thought about it, but as I said, I want the Camilleri wealth."

His harsh voice chilled my bones and the truth was, he was the kind of man who followed through on his threats. No one had ever stayed alive long enough to cross Victor twice.

With that, he got up and left the room.

With a frustrated roar, I punched the wall, smashing my hand. I probably broke some bones but didn't feel any pain, only resentment. The air had been sucked out of my lungs and I was winded.

"Are you thinking what I'm thinking?" Gregory asked.

I nodded. "I don't know why it never occurred to me before. Emilio would have told him, most probably."

Then, my phone started ringing and I saw Merry's face flashing on the screen. I answered it right away.

"What's up?"

"I'm texting you an address. Meet me there as soon as possible," she said, and hung up.

I cursed under my breath feeling a little stressed out, but it was good to hear her voice. I knew if I saw her, I was going to be fine.

"I have to go," I told Gregory. "Don't worry. Everything is going to work out. I will handle the Russians."

Then I left, knowing that I had to do better to protect him. This was all my fault because I wanted to be a better father and protect innocent people. Fuck, I had to figure out how to give Victor what he needed without having to marry Elaine.

When I glanced at Merry's text, I was a little shocked. I thought we had agreed to follow Elaine. Instead, she was asking me to meet her on Russian territory.

I drove there and parked the car on the street. I was just about to text her when she slid into the passenger seat a second later. It was raining now and Merry's hair was dripping.

"What's going on?" I asked.

"Something strange happened earlier on. I thought I wouldn't have to follow Elaine after her nail appointment, so instead I went to the mansion. She was there and I thought I would keep an eye on what she was doing without having to be in the car all this time. Then, half an hour later, she left without saying a word to me or Clara. She was all dressed up, so I decided to follow her," Merry explained, and I looked around.

"So where is she now?" I asked.

"She went inside the club. I followed her in, but she went to one of the private rooms. She must be meeting someone there, maybe the same person she was talking to on the phone?" she asked.

This was good. Maybe we were finally onto something.

"Then we have to check this out, princess. I hope you brought your gun because I brought mine." I would normally not want to put her in harm's way, but she'd do it anyway, with or without me. Merry was a badass and I had to work with that.

She smiled and nodded.

"Good girl."

We rushed to the club. I had no idea who owned it, but this

was Victor's territory. He didn't utilize clubs the way I had in the past, but he had other partners for that.

This didn't make much sense. Elaine avoided loud music and she detested going to such places. She usually sent her people if she had to deal with business in a nightclub.

Once inside, we headed straight to the bar. We were both soaked from the rain and Merry's nipples were poking through her dress. That brought back memories of the time I'd first met her. I wanted to recreate that scene one day, but right now we had more important things to worry about.

"So, what do you think we should do?"

"Wait for her to leave to see who she was meeting," I said. "Come on, let's go to one of the booths upstairs." I pointed up.

She nodded, so we ordered two drinks and headed to the first floor. I had my hand on my gun when we entered the booth. Merry was carrying our drinks. She placed them on the table and sat down. I was just about to do the same when I felt something cold pressed to my back.

"Don't move or I will put bullet in you. Follow me and don't do anything stupid," the deep, rough voice ordered, and I froze. I glanced around to see a big Russian guy I didn't recognize. He might have been one of Victor's men.

I grabbed Merry's hand and dragged her with me. She looked behind us, seeing the big guy, and she must have understood what was going on because she didn't say anything. No one else was paying attention to us and the fact that someone was pointing a gun at me. The man told us to keep walking until we stopped outside a white door.

"Get inside," he barked, and I opened the door. We entered a dim office with a large pool table to my right.

Elaine was there, staring out the small window that gave her a great view of the dance floor downstairs.

"It's okay, Mikhail. You can leave now," she said. The guy nodded and as soon as he was gone, I let go of Merry's hand.

"What's going on, Elaine? Huh?" I asked.

She tossed her blond hair behind her and gave me a curious and amused look, wetting her upper lip with her tongue.

"She's with me, Dad," another voice spoke.

Emilio had entered the room.

Chapter Thirty-Six

Merry

We really should have thought things through before showing up in this club. Elaine must have noticed that I'd followed her all the way here. Then the big guy approached Ivo and we were forced to come here. It was a trap.

"What do you mean he's with you, Elaine?" I shot back, rubbing my face. I couldn't believe that Ivo had been right. She was the one who must have been helping Emilio all this time. Fear trickled down my spine when I saw him enter the room.

Elaine glanced back at Emilio in shock.

"What the hell, Emilio? I told you to stay hidden? I said I can handle them," she stated, annoyed, then shot me an apologetic look.

"What the fuck is going on here? I was right all along,

haven't I? You were the one who visited him in prison and the one that was helping him all this time, but the question remains: Why?" Ivo shouted in anger.

"Because we've been fucking, *Dad*, that's why. Elaine was trying to help me to get out of the country after she managed to get me out of prison," Emilio admitted, and my jaw dropped. At first, I thought he was lying to us, because surely this couldn't have been the truth.

Ivo shook his head and then laughed. I glanced at Elaine, waiting for her to deny this, but she just stared down at the floor. Her face went from pale to red. Oh God, she looked embarrassed.

"Don't be absurd, son. Elaine has too much class to—"

"Finish that sentence and I put bullet in your head," Emilio cut him off, pointing a gun at Ivo.

"Elaine?" I questioned my stepmother, and she finally lifted her gaze to look at me. My hands were shaking and my pulse was drumming in my ears.

"Well, we kind of met when I made the deal with Ivo. It was strange, but we started talking and we instantly hit it off. I wanted to keep this quiet because I felt so guilty about the past, about what Emilio had done to Clara and you," Elaine started explaining, and all of a sudden, I felt paralyzed.

Emilio and my stepmother had been sleeping together? How did I miss this?

"This is bullshit. Come on, Elaine, you're fucking with me. Why would you help this piece of shit after what he did to your stepdaughters?" Ivo asked again in utter disbelief.

Elaine cleared her throat. I could tell she looked uncomfortable. Then, Emilio wrapped his free arm around Elaine and brought her closer to him. He was around her height and probably about twelve years younger. I stared at them and thought we must be living in an alternate universe.

"I'm sorry you had to find out this way, Ivo, but things had gotten complicated and I couldn't let Emilio rot in prison, not after…"

She let her voice trail away, looking unsure whether she was supposed to finish what she wanted to say. I gaped, literally feeling like someone had just punched me in the stomach. Fuck, no … this couldn't be possible. And yet, here we all were.

Ivo glanced at me, perplexed.

"Because you found out you were expecting his child," I finished for her.

Then, Ivo's jaw dropped and his mouth parted.

"That doesn't fucking matter anymore because none of you are going to leave this room alive. I asked Elaine to come here today, hoping that you two would take the bait and follow her. Once I get rid of you, Daddy, I will marry her and take over the business. You never had any faith in me, but with Victor by my side, I will be the most powerful man on the West Coast," Emilio ranted.

"Emilio, you're not killing anyone today. We discussed this, so please lower your gun. They weren't supposed to know," Elaine chided. She was speaking calmly and I was surprised he was actually listening to her.

I really had no idea what to say. Butterflies filled my stomach because I suddenly realised that my stepmother wasn't carrying Ivo's child.

"No, Elaine, I'm in charge now and my lousy *father* deserves a bullet. Don't you understand? We don't need them anymore. We can get married and start over," Emilio said, mumbling without much sense now.

"Why do you hate me so much? Is this because of Merry?" Ivo finally asked him, staring at him like he couldn't believe that we were all here, that he had been played so fucking well.

How did I not figure this out? Emilio must have charmed Elaine because he was her type. I wiped the sweat off my forehead, trying to breathe because this whole thing sounded too crazy.

"Because you and my fucking pathetic mother never protected me. You especially left me with strangers—nannies who were supposed to look after me, but they never cared!" Emilio shouted, looking distraught and lost. So much agony in his voice. "And that bastard touched me. Fuck … that scumbag Gino, Valeria's boyfriend, thought he could play with a child. He came over when you were working. He did unforgivable things to me and I had to live with it. He told me if I ever told anyone, he would come back and slit my mother's throat. You should have known, but instead you were worrying about Gregory—your perfect fucking son!"

All of a sudden, I wanted to throw up. I brought my hands to my mouth and stared at my rapist with compassion. I never thought I would feel this way about him, but this was totally fucked up.

Elaine was suddenly so pale, staring at her lover as though seeing him for the first time. Ivo looked broken because he'd just found out he hadn't been able to protect his child, back in

Bulgaria. Damn it, and it had all happened under his roof. Emilio had been abused when and Ivo had never noticed.

"I had no idea, Emilio. Your mother was in charge of the nannies. And then, we emigrated to the US. I'm sorry that I failed you, but this was never intentional. Christ, if only I fucking knew," Ivo finally spoke, and his voice broke. He looked so vulnerable in that moment.

Elaine was crying, shaking her head, and I felt so incredibly sad, mad at that woman he called his mother. God damn it, why had no one noticed? Years had gone by, but the toxic memories stayed. This explained a lot.

"Just shut up, Ivo. I don't want to listen to you anymore. I'm in charge now and I'm more powerful than you. Elaine, honey, he's irrelevant and doesn't deserve to stand by your side. That's why I planted the drugs in his club. Yeah, that was me. I thought Daddy would go to prison, so I could take over the business and rule. I'm in love with you and this child is mine. Victor is my real father and he will be pleased once we seal this alliance," Emilio said, walking over to Ivo with the gun pointed at his head.

Hie eyes were bloodshot and wild. I knew he wouldn't hesitate to kill him. He had so much resentment and anger inside him.

"Emilio, please, I'm begging you not to do this. You have no idea how sorry I am that no one noticed your pain and suffering, but if you kill Ivo, then that's it. The wedding will be cancelled, and you will go to prison for murder," I said, staring at the man who caused so much pain in my life, the man who abused my sister, the man that who broken more than anyone I knew.

"Too late!" Emilio roared, loading up the gun. He was ready to kill Ivo and I had no doubt in my mind that he was blaming him for everything.

"No, Emilio, stop it. Put the gun down. I love you but I can't let you do this!" Hysterical, Elaine produced a gun and pointed it at Emilio.

Ivo backed away to the wall, remaining calm as he kept glancing at me, soothing me with his demeanor.

"What are you—" Emilio asked, then paused, finally turning around and noticing the gun in Elaine's hand. He looked tired and pale. Then, a small smile appeared on his face. "Come on, Elaine, you know he has to die. You love me and you can't choose him over me."

"Give me the gun, Emilio, so we can sort this out. I can't let you hurt your father even if he's not your real parent. Merry is right. You're going to go to prison and I'll be on my own. This baby needs a real father," Elaine said, sounding sharp and confident.

Emilio looked really distraught and now, after all the trauma, the crying myself to sleep, and all the panic attacks, I finally understood what he had gone through. Why he did what he did back in that club.

Ivo was staring at me with worry and compassion. There was love in his eyes and that warmed my heart. I could lose him. He couldn't die when we could finally be together. I wouldn't allow it.

"You disappoint me, Elaine. I thought you were different," he spat, and then charged for the door.

Elaine shouted after him but he was gone within seconds. She lowered her gun and started sobbing.

"Take care of her and call the police. I'll find him," Ivo instructed, and then left to chase after Emilio.

"I have to go after him, Merry. I can't let him kill Emilio!" Elaine cried, and before I could stop her, she raced out of the room.

"Elaine! Wait!" I chased her through a dark corridor, then down the stairs. My stepmother was surprisingly fast. I could barely keep up with her. I had to squeeze through a crowd of people who were trying to enjoy themselves, dancing around.

I pushed through the throng and finally got to the main door. I ran out on the street, where rain was pouring hard and I immediately got soaked. Stopping for a moment to get my bearings, I spotted Elaine running across the road.

"Elaine!" I shouted, and she finally stopped moments later. As I reached her, I noticed her staring to her right. I gasped, seeing Emilio. He was standing in the middle of the busy road, pointing a gun at Ivo amid the cars passing through. Someone was honking, but Emilio didn't move.

They were both soaked and the rain intensified. Ivo had his hands on his thighs and he was breathing hard, staring back at his other son.

"Emilio!" Elaine shouted, and my heart stopped. Emilio wasn't going to miss the shot. His hands were shaking, but he was ready to pull that trigger. A hard expression of pain and resentment filled his features.

"Put your gun down, Mr. Sergei!" someone to our left roared. I glanced to my left, seeing Detective Morales slowly approaching Emilio, pointing her gun at him. I had no idea where she came from, but I felt like time had stopped.

Some cars also stopped, people stared at the scene, and sirens were going off somewhere in the distance.

My heart was falling apart with guilt and regret and powerlessness. Ivo straightened his posture and stared at his son. Emilio must have finally realized that this had to end. He had to know that if he took the shot, his life would be over.

"Fuck off! My father deserves a bullet!" he roared, but his voice was broken and rough.

Fat raindrops hit my face. Everyone was waiting, holding their breaths.

"You have five seconds to put the gun down or I will shoot you," Morales roared, and in that instant, I had no doubt she wasn't bluffing.

Her chest was rising and falling in rapid movements.

Emilio roared with anger and pain, then threw the gun on the ground. He tangled his fingers in his hair, falling to his knees as rain pelted the dark streets of Los Angeles. I grabbed Elaine's elbow as she tried to run to him, but Morales was quicker. She got to him in seconds, pushed him face down on the ground, and started handcuffing him, reading him his rights.

A moment later, two police cars arrived and it was all over. Emilio was dragged inside one of the vehicles.

The rain didn't let up. Some people started to walk away, while others stayed to watch. I looked up and spread my hands, trying to breathe in and out. I knew that nothing would wash away this torment Emilio had been carrying all these years. The world was crying with his sour tears.

"So, you and Ivo? How did I miss that?" Elaine's question burst through my thoughts.

She was now aware she'd made a mistake and chose wrong.

"We knew each other before you two got engaged. It's a long story, but Ivo is the love of my life, Elaine." I said, catching him walking toward us.

Suddenly, I had no doubt we would be all right. Everything was better and brighter because I finally was able to admit the truth.

I was in love with Ivo Sergei.

Epilogue

9 months later

The cool breeze was ruffling my hair as I stared at the turquoise blue sea in the distance, admiring the stunning view. It was the end of May and Malta was already booming with tourists. I had never felt happier and I could stare at that view for hours. The sea always calmed me so much.

"What the fuck are you doing on the balcony? You should be in bed, riding my cock, princess," the rough loud voice reached me from the room.

I smiled and t rolled my eyes, thinking that he was totally insatiable. He woke me up this morning with his head between my legs, licking me like a man starved for oxygen and in minutes, an orgasm rocked through my whole body. Damn, I'd already come three times and it wasn't even eight-thirty in the morning.

I threw him a glance from over my shoulder. He was sitting on the bed, naked and ready for me. He was so tanned—this mediterranean weather was really agreeing with him.

Especially since he'd stepped back from the mob world, leaving Victor a large piece of the pie. Ivo was particularly suited to be a club owner.

Club P—'P' for princess, as it turned out—might soon become a nationwide franchise.

"Oh, come here, Ivo, this view is so stunning. We literally had sex at least three times a day since we arrived," I told him, and then giggled a little, thinking that we were all over each other like teenagers.

"One time is never enough with you, princess, I'm addicted to you."

Ever since Emilio had been arrested, my life changed a hundred eighty degrees. Elaine was distraught that Emilio was going away for a few years. He didn't truly help himself, but he needed to pay for everything he had done. He needed to understand the pain he'd caused and reflect on his life.

I was no longer angry about the past. I came to terms with everything that happened and accepted it. The judge was lenient and Emilio got five years, but potentially, he could go out after two with good behaviour. We would deal with that hurdle when the time came.

Elaine asked me to defend him and after careful consideration, I said yes. Clara knew about everything that happened. I told her about Emilio's past, and she told me she wasn't going to stand in my way. She understood because she was ready to put it all behind her, too.

Ivo was apprehensive. He felt so guilty he hadn't noticed his own son was being abused when he was only a child. Apparently, he'd reached out to Dona, his ex-wife in Bulgaria. She claimed she had no idea and a few weeks later, she flew to the US to be there for her troubled son.

This was a highly complex and sensitive situation. Ivo was going through a lot and trying hard to fix everything. He still considered Emilio his son, even if Victor was his real father. I wanted to believe that Emilio wasn't an evil person, that there was some goodness in him, too. He needed help and time to heal. I truly thought that he was ready to change, but he had a long way ahead of him.

Around three months ago, Elaine gave birth to a healthy baby boy and called him Massimo. She still couldn't believe that Ivo and I were an item, that we were in love with each other. I didn't tell her I'd gone to his club to experience my first orgasm. I just wanted to keep some things private. She accepted it because all of us had a lot to answer for.

Then, after Emilio's arrest, my stepmother asked Victor to sit down with me and Ivo. We told him everything that had happened and Elaine agreed on the terms of the original deal but instead of Ivo, she proposed that she was going to get married to Emilio instead. This way, the Russian got everything he wanted and more—the 'more' being a grandchild to love. Emilio was his legitimate son and once he was released, Victor was planning to put him in charge of his business.

Elaine wasn't entirely happy with this, but it was the best outcome she was going to get.

While Ivo had kept his club, delegating more and more responsibility to Gregory, I stayed in Los Angeles and managed to get another job at a prestigious law firm. Everything was slowly coming together.

Then, about a month ago, we both needed some time out, so we came to Malta on vacation. I had never been happier because I no longer had to hide and sneak around, pretending that there was nothing going on between me and Ivo. I could finally just enjoy loving him.

I walked back inside the room. Ivo was so handsome. Sure, he had a few grey hairs, but his stamina was impressive. Despite his age, he was always ready to fuck me.

Now, I had a soft cotton dress I'd thrown on myself when I stepped outside on the balcony to admire the view. A dress I could easily remove, which I did.

Ivo smiled as I approached him and climbed on top of him.

"No panties. Hmm, you're such a good girl for your daddy," he murmured, and then I slowly guided myself onto his massive erection. He started kissing my chest, cupping my left breast and biting my flesh.

I gasped, arching my head backwards because he filled me so well. So fully. We started moving slowly at first, but Ivo's touch was like fire on my skin. Then, he took my left nipple in his mouth and sucked on it slowly.

"Oh, Daddy, this feels so good," I moaned, dragging my hands through my hair as I moved up and down his shaft.

The heat from his body ravaged my core. He urged me to go faster and the pressure started building.

He just knew how to work me and made sure I came every single time when we made love.

Ivo stopped assaulting my nipple and looked at me as our bodies moved in sync. He smiled.

"I love you, Merry," he said as he thrust his cock deeper, drawing a keening moan from me.

"I love you too, Ivo Sergei."

"Good, so marry me," he asked, and then I suddenly slowed down, staring at him in shock. My heart accelerated, but he continued to move inside me. It seemed that he didn't want to stop on my account and just let me process what he'd asked. I panted, on the edge of an orgasm.

"Fuck, Ivo, I'm coming!" I moaned, losing control of my body and gripping his shoulders tight when he sped his pace again.

Tingles of heat spread through my body when he slowed down once more. I was drenched and my breathing was laboured when he leaned closer, staring at me.

"Is that a yes? Are you going to be my wife?"

I giggled, trying to gather my thoughts and understand if he was being serious. He wanted to marry me—he really did. This was totally unexpected because we'd never talked about it, but I had never been more certain than I was now.

I brushed my hair away from my face, remembering that he was still inside me. Fuck, this was so hot.

"Yes, yes ... I will marry you. Now fuck me hard before I change my mind."

"As you wish, princess."

The End

Bonus Scene Consumed

Bonus Scene

"Do you, Ivo Sergei, take this woman, Merry Camilleri, to be your lawfully wedded wife, to have and to hold, in sickness and in heath, in good times and in bed, for richer or poorer, forsaking all others for as long as you both shall live?"

I held Merry's hands and looked into her beautiful doe eyes as the priest recited our wedding vows.

"I do," I replied, and she smiled brightly.

I had never been more certain of anything else in my life. When I saw her walk down the aisle in her simple silk sheath of a wedding dress, my heart felt like it was going to burst. I was the luckiest man alive, about to share all my days and sultry nights with the most gorgeous woman in the world. Her beauty, compassion, intelligence, and strong personality had me fall hopelessly in love, a condition from which there was no coming back. Nor did I want to.

For a while, I thought we'd never find our happy ever after. The odds were stacked against us, and it seemed as though we'd be living our life apart, miserable, yearning for each other in the worst way yet never be able to act on it.

But the Universe granted us this gift, and now the world would know that Merry is mine and only mine.

We decided to get married on Gozo, an island in the Maltese archipelago where Merry's family was from. They'd emigrated to the United States a couple of generations ago, but maintained a strong love and bond with their homeland. We'd invited only the closest family and friends to the wedding. Merry's stepmother, Elaine, who I was once supposed to marry to keep the peace between rival families, was there with her little baby, Massimo. I noticed her crying, wiping her tears with a fine, monogrammed handkerchief—always so dramatic.

Merry stared up at me with adoring eyes, and all I wanted to do was be alone with her. The priest turned to her and read the vows. We were getting married on a beautiful red-sanded beach, with the soothing sound of the waves rolling gently toward the shore. A constant ebb and flow, manifesting a new future for us both.

"I do," Merry replied, and I squeezed her hand as the warmth of our love swirled around my heart.

She was so much younger than me, but I loved her so much, it hurt. From the first time I saw her, she belonged to me. We were meant for each other.

Gregory was asked to bring the rings. I took one and slid onto Merry's slender finger, then it was her turn. This was exciting enough, but I was already thinking about what I'd do to her afterwards. She was going to scream in wanton pleasure, very, very soon. Maybe even right after the ceremony, as soon as we could get away.

"You have declared your consent before the Church. May the Lord in his goodness strengthen your bond and fill you both with his blessings. What God has joined, men must not divide. Amen," the priest wrapped things up and then, before he added anything else, I kissed her. I couldn't wait any longer —I just had to taste her. People around us started to clap.

"I love you, Ivo," she said when we turned around to face our family and friends that were cheering for us. Even Elaine was shouting and whistling. I wasn't expecting that. A moment ago, she'd been bawling.

"I love you more, princess, so better eat and drink quickly because I can't wait to have you all to myself," I murmured when the guests started approaching us to give us their congratulations.

"Congrats, sister. You will keep him in line." Gregory grinned at Merry, then hugged her.

"I heard that," I told him, swatting him playfully on the arm.

Gozo was incredible. We'd booked a beautiful small villa overlooking the sea, and within walking distance to a quaint seaside town. Our guests had been put up in a lovely, family-run hotel close by. Merry had organised everything and when she showed us the venue, I instantly knew this place was going to be perfect. For tonight, we'd be staying in a luxury suite in the fanciest hotel on the island.

I was tempted to steal Merry away. I wanted a moment alone with her, but we'd have to drive to the hotel unless we found a secluded spot to play in, but I knew she wouldn't leave with me just yet. The ceremony had only just finished and Merry always wanted to please everyone, while basking in all the positive energy around us.

"Oh, Ivo, this was such a great ceremony, but I have to go back and check on Massimo. He's probably missing me, my little cherub," Elaine said after giving me a kiss on both cheeks. Damn, I was a grandfather, and this was fucking weird, but I loved that boy to death.

Even Victor, a ruthless mafia boss I often butted heads with, was ecstatic about the new blood in the family. We agreed to share responsibilities as grandfathers. After all, the whole purpose of our divergences in the past had to do with uniting our families. What best way to do that than with a tiny human —a sign of a united future?

"All right, just bring him down. I'm sure he will enjoy a bit of music," I told her.

Once we were done with all the congratulations and hugs, we were all driven to the hotel in a series of shiny black Mercedes. At the hotel, we'd be having an intimate outdoor, sit-down dinner reception, and we'd booked all the rooms for tonight to keep everything private. It was the perfect weather for the event—not too hot, not too cold. Once we arrived, we were asked to sit at three extra long tables arranged in a 'U' shape, with me and Merry in the center.

Merry had on a simple dress that did justice to her curves and exposed her exquisite breasts amazingly well. I could barely take my eyes off her and my dick was already hard for her, which wasn't good because I was wearing white linen pants.

I remembered another time when I was wearing tight white pants and ended up in this same situation... Merry wearing a sexy dress, me drooling at her ass, her legs, her boobs, and maddeningly perfect curves. She'd always had me by the balls that way. At least, today, the fit of my pants wasn't so tight as to show the entire shape of my aroused junk.

"Can we just go back to our suite and leave them all to party? I really want to fuck you," I growled into her ear when we sat down. Merry had insisted on a small but traditional American-style wedding, which meant we needed to have the speeches, first dance, good food and drink, and an elegant tiered cake, of course.

She stopped laughing and glanced at me on full alert, her gaze traveling to my lips and lingering there. My cock stirred. "Jesus, Merry..." I whispered.

People were talking, looking for their seats, so while they were distracted, I caressed the sensitive skin at her neck and then wrapping my hand around it, squeezing it gently.

"Hmmm," I groaned softly in her ear.

This was going to be a small affair. There were around fifteen of us and unfortunately, Victor had insisted on coming too, so we had to include him. He wasn't the most soothing person to have around. Most of the time, he was super intense; after all, he'd been known to snuff the life out of a person or two, or fifty. One didn't cross Victor and live to tell the tale.

Yet, we were family now, I supposed—long story.

"No, Mr. Sergei, we can't," Merry cooed. "It would be rude of us to sneak out for sex."

"Is that so?" I tightened my grip around her throat, increasing the pressure, and her eyes widened in surprise and excitement. We hadn't played this kinky game recently, and the thought of it turned me on so fucking much. "You know I'm an impatient man, and you haven't been punished for a while, princess," I reminded her.

"What are you going to do, strangle me at your own wedding, Daddy, because you can't get your way?"

"I have other uses for your throat which do not include injury," I said in the sweetest, velvet tone, then quickly pulled my hand away, telling myself to breathe in and calm the fuck down. People were watching.

She slightly parted her lips and exhaled, seeming both anxious and intrigued—but mostly excited. A tiny moan escaped her lips, and I wondered where her mind was going. Merry had a wild imagination and sometimes I struggled to keep up. I bet she was already wet, because now I gave her something to think about.

There were so many toys I was yet to make good use of. Ever since we officially got together, I started introducing a few toys to the bedroom. Merry fucking loved my cock, but when I showed her what I could do to her with a dildo, she went absolutely crazy. Goddamn it, I didn't think I could sit here for another few hours without fucking her. Why do that when there were many secluded beaches in this area that we needed to explore?

"Time for the toast," Gregory announced when everyone was finally seated and the wine and drinks were being served.

I slipped my hand underneath the table, while everyone was staring at us. She would have to let me fuck her soon or I was planning to torture her for as long as we sat here. She gasped when I caressed her upper thigh, moving closer and closer to her delicious and probably soaked pussy.

Gregory started talking, but I wasn't really concentrating

much. All I could think about was how much I wanted to make her come. I needed to have her now, but we had to ensure we'd go through all the speeches first.

"Ivo, you need to stop it," Merry hissed, leaning over. Her cheeks were flushed. She was parting her lips so seductively that I wasn't going to be able to get up because I was so fucking hard.

I pulled her dress up and slid my hand underneath, tracing the edge of her knickers and grazing her sex with my index finger—gently, at first. She was fucking soaked in juice. I grazed her once more and she gasped again.

She caught a moan before it betrayed her when I dipped my finger inside her wet pussy to prove my point.

"All right, you won, Ivo," she said through gritted teeth. "I'm going to the bathroom. Just join me in a few minutes. And make it discreet."

I wanted this woman so fucking much and yes, I was so impatient I couldn't wait another ten minutes.

She hung around until Gregory was done with his speech and for a second, I thought I'd made her come because she dug her nails into the skin of my hand, almost drawing blood, and let go of a few pants as I pumped my fingers in and out of her pussy.

Merry finally got up and excused herself when the waiters began carrying in the starters. The worst torture I'd ever endured was having to wait several minutes before getting up and following along. I just had to pray no one would notice we'd both left.

Luckily for me, the photographer was busy taking snaps of Elaine, who was posing with Clara. I didn't fucking care if people were offended and talked behind our backs. I had to be with my wife and fuck her hard so she would remember this day for a long time.

Gregory was chatting with one of Merry's uncles when I sneaked away. My giant erection was on display and I needed to do something about it. A waiter tried to talk to me in the restaurant.

"Listen, buddy, I'm on my way upstairs to fuck my wife before anyone notices we are both missing, so please cut me some slack," I interrupted him, patted him on the shoulder. At last reducing him to speechlessness, I rushed upstairs to our suite, my hard shaft happily anticipating a good banging.

I burst inside, shut the door, and found my wife lying naked on the bed, moaning as she fucked herself with a giant dildo.

I was paralysed for a split second, thinking that this could have only been a dream.

"What the fuck are you doing, Merry?" I finally asked. She was moaning, massaging her tits with one hand while sticking that dildo inside her soaked pussy, driving me wild.

Seemed I'd arrived just in time for the finale...

"Oh Ivo, I'm coming!" she sighed, pushing that dildo in and out of her pussy in a punishing, super-fast rhythm. It was a beautiful sight, barbaric, sexy, and so fucking wrong on so many levels.

I'd never unbuckled my trousers so fast. My cock was hard as a rock when I stroked it lightly—so much it ached, the skin ultra-sensitive.

Merry needed to be fucked. Walking up to the edge of the bed, I stopped and dragged my hand through my hair.

"Turn around and put your ass in the air for me. You're

going to be punished, princess," I ordered, licking my upper lip. How did I deserve all this lushness in front of me? "Daddy is very angry with you, furious that you didn't wait for him like an obedient little lamb."

She smiled innocently at me, then put her fingers in her mouth and licked them before turning around and going on all fours.

I drew another shaky breath, staring at her beautiful ass that was now at my mercy. She lifted it up, so I had great access to her sex. My mind started racing, but first I went to open the nightstand drawer. If I wasn't careful, I could do a lot of damage with the thick leather belt that I'd just pulled out of it.

My wife came upstairs and used a toy without my permission. She knew this was against the rules, so now she was going to get fucked.

"This will hurt and you will count like the good wife you are. I am only going to spank you three times, princess," I said, moving to the bed and quickly wrapping that belt around her throat, wanting to spice this game up a little.

She shuddered, eyes wide as saucers when I gripped it tightly and squeezed it.

"Yes, Daddy," she whispered.

"Good girl," I praised her, then quickly unwrapped the belt from her neck. I looped the buckle side around my hand and swung it, delivering a quick whip on her ass.

She cried out instantly, traveling the line between pleasure and pain.

Merry's cunt was soaking wet.

"One," she said in a shaky breath, lowering herself a little. I leaned down and kissed the red spot on her ass. She shivered and I blew some air over the red flesh.

"I'm doing this because you made yourself come. We both know I am the only person permitted to give you an orgasm," I reminded her, and then spanked her again, this time harder.

She yelped in pain, so I spanked her one last time, leaving flesh swollen, with red marks on both of her ass cheeks. Merry hid her face in the pillow and sobbed for a bit.

I immediately climbed on the bed and started caressing her skin, blowing some air on her ass, gently touching and kissing where it hurt the most. My groin was burning and I needed to enter her now, despite how much I wanted to stay and soothe her. She was so fucking sexy and primed for me to take her as I wished.

Throwing the belt on the floor, I pulled my pants and boxers down, finally releasing my rock-hard cock.

She turned around to look at me, tense and flustered.

"We don't have much time. You have to be quick, Daddy," she told me, spreading her knees farther apart to give me the perfect view of her pussy. It was pink, dripping and throbbing for me.

I growled like an animal, entering her fast. She was right—I had to fuck her quickly because others probably had already noticed we'd both disappeared.

I really wanted to lick her, devour her pussy, but I could do that later, after the party or when everyone was too drunk to know what was happening. We had all night, maybe even an eternity, so right now this would do.

"Shit, you feel so good, princess," I growled when she shouted out her pleasure, begging me to go faster. I gripped her hips tightly and started fucking her. It was hard and fast, wild and violent, but she loved every fucking second of it. Her juices coated my cock.

I was planning to come inside her without a condom. I was so fucking done with being careful. There was no point anymore because I wanted to be inside her bare, feel her with every inch of my dick. She was my wife and would be a great mother. Her slick cunt swelled as I thrust inside her and pounded her.

Soon enough, she was screaming my name, panting and telling me she was coming for me. I couldn't believe I was fucking my wife while the guests were downstairs, enjoying themselves.

Maybe I'd have a heart attack and die happy, just like I wanted to go some day—hopefully an old-ass man, buried inside my wife in an epic last hurrah.

Chuckling at the thought, I kept fucking her through her orgasm, digging deep, and then I gripped her hair, pulling her head back.

The pressure built in my balls and I came hard, spreading my seed all inside her because we were united and finally together. I pulled her hair again and she cried in pain, following that with a satisfied sigh. A moment later, I was done, collapsing on the bed.

It took me a good bit to pull myself together and catch my breath because I was so wonderfully, utterly drained—to the last drop.

Merry rose to her knees and suddenly climbed on top of me, smiling wide.

"This was amazing, but now I am aching all over and the dinner is still going downstairs. We need to go eat."

"Uh-huh."

She bent down to kiss me gently on the lips, a lingering caress. When she pulled back, love shone in her eyes.

"Well, get ready for more because we haven't even scratched the surface yet. I'm planning to fuck you throughout the whole honeymoon. We probably won't leave this room at all," I said as she got off the bed in all her naked glory. She was fucking stunning and she was my wife. Life couldn't get any better than this.

"You can't go for that long, Ivo." She laughed, picking her underwear from the floor. "By the way, you didn't use a condom and you know I am not on the pill anymore…"

I stared at her, wondering how the hell I'd gotten so lucky.

"You know I can't fucking stand condoms and you're so young. I can be a daddy again. I want to create a family with you, Merry Sergei-Camilleri."

Cocking her head to the side, she went silent for a bit, clearly processing what I'd just said. It was pretty unexpected and totally unplanned, but she was the woman of my dreams. We needed to create something special together. We needed to be a proper family.

"I love you, Mr. Sergei," she finally said, "and I would love to have a baby with you." Smiling, she hurried back and gave me another kiss.

She was perfect and now, my life was just as perfect, with her by my side.

The end

Halloween Games

Chapter Thirty-Seven

Cathy

"To all the ladies that dream of meeting a prince but end up falling for the bad boy."

I read this dedication and cringed, thinking it so damn unrealistic. The truth was, bad boys just didn't cut it in real life —but in romance novels? Give me the mysterious, infuriating villain anytime. So sexy.

Bad boys were always so much more interesting, especially when they put their ladies through the wringer in the beginning, then made up for it with overprotective, borderline stalker and possessive behaviors. Some of the scenes in these kinds of plots were so damn hot and impregnated my imagination with many great potential bedroom scenarios that would probably never come true for me. Which was why they called this genre 'escapist' fiction.

"Cathy, I think your father is waiting for you in his office," Margie's voice broke through my thoughts.

Margie had been a part of our family for a long time. At first, she was hired to be my nanny after my mother passed away, when I was still a baby. She took over without missing a beat, loving me and helping to raise me as though I were her own, especially since she never had kids herself. She was now our housekeeper—a job she wanted to keep hanging around me, no doubt. I had no idea what we'd do without her.

I released a loud sigh and closed the mafia romance book I had been reading. I'd continue the novel later on in the evening when I was safely tucked in bed with a hot chocolate or glass of wine, depending on the mood.

"Thank you, Margie. I will be right there," I replied, giving her a warm smile, even though today, I had to force it.

My father had told me at breakfast that he wanted to talk to me later in the morning, after a Zoom meeting he had to attend. Before I could ask what he wanted to talk to me about, his phone buzzed and as usual, he locked himself in his office.

He'd be leaving on a business trip today, and would be hard to reach. Every November, over Halloween weekend, he attended a Fortune 500 business strategy conference in Jamaica, with a world-renowned add-on program on managing burnout. Pretty ironic, since he was a hopeless workaholic.

While I was going to be on my own. No big deal, since I was an independent adult who currently lived with her father to help him through a few health challenges. Although, the way he carried on with work and other commitments, he seemed fitter than I was.

Him being gone didn't bother me as I'd have the house to

myself. I'd even give Margie extra time off and do my own chores and cooking. Except for the fact that this time, everything was different because I was no longer safe.

I swallowed as the sense of helplessness I'd been feeling as of late laid itself upon me like a heavy blanket I couldn't shake, tendrils of dread woven through the threads.

As a social media influencer—well, Booktoker, specifically—I had over one million followers on TikTok and around half that amount on Instagram. Ever since I could make out letters on a page, I loved reading, and as an adult, my passion for books had allowed me to gather a small following of loyal fans. I earned money doing the best job in the world—a perfect fit for me.

It all started a few years ago when I began to review books on Instagram. I had to post consistently in order to grow my following. At the time, I was in college and hated the idea of busting my ass working nights waiting tables or long days in retail. Nothing wrong with that, but I wanted to widen my options. Since I'd always liked talking about books and technology didn't scare me, this online venture idea came naturally.

Although I was technically an introvert, I was filled with energy when it came to anything book related. At reader events, I'd let my hair down, take pictures with the models, chat the day away with like-minded people.

In life though, I hated the nightlife and much preferred staying in with a good book for company. Most of my friends tried to get me out of my shell, but there was nothing I enjoyed more than to escape reality and immerse myself in a fictional world.

I loved reading romance in general—all sorts of genres.

Fantasy, paranormal, contemporary, fairy tales, reverse harem and of course, mafia romance for starters. I had a small library, but every day, more and more new books turned up. Although I did use my e-reader, I much preferred physical books, especially when they arrived signed by the author.

Over the years, I'd started working with a number of traditional publishers that would send me advanced reader copies of upcoming releases. I was never short of reading material, and I treasured each one.

To my utter surprise, my little vlog review skits started going viral and I was able to support myself with the income earned from promoting authors. These days, I didn't venture out often, but when I did, people in the book world recognized me. Fame came unexpectedly and sometimes, I truly struggled with the sheer enormity of it. I wasn't comfortable being stopped outside event venues or bookstores for random conversations, or asked to take selfies with people.

But now, it wasn't just about discomfort.

This … this situation was something else…

I'd promised myself I wasn't going to live in fear, but the moment I confided in my father, I could no longer ignore the issue. He wouldn't let me. Each step to my father's office felt like my feet were filled with lead for some reason. I suspected he wanted to talk to me about this problem I was having—a conversation which would fill me with anxiety for the rest of the day.

I knocked on the office door, wondering why he had been so secretive lately. After hearing his "Come on in," I entered. The room was situated downstairs and he had his own small book collection there, too—mostly non-fiction books. We had another bigger library where I spent most of my time reading and reviewing books.

Dad was busy writing something in a leather-bound notebook and immediately I realized he wasn't alone.

My gaze rested on a man who sat on an upholstered chair to the side of the desk, holding a glass of water. His muscular legs went on and on, and he was built like a brick house. He didn't have to stand for me to know he was extremely tall—the chair barely contained his form. His huge hams for hands wrapped around the glass, which could easily shatter in his grasp if he squeezed a little. This giant could probably break me in two as though I were a slender twig.

His green gaze met mine and my breath hitched. I'd never seen him before and if I did, there was no way I'd forget that handsome face. Rugged and sharp, perfectly chiseled angles with eyes that screamed intelligence. I wet my lips for they felt suddenly dry, and my heart beat a wild tattoo in my chest.

He was ... gorgeous. Perfection in the flesh. Broad shoulders, defined body—seemingly not an ounce of fat. Dark hair cut short, eyes the color of emeralds. Square jaws and kissable lips. The typical bad boy book boyfriend.

Oh dear. I was in trouble.

Besides, he was looking at me like I was a tasty morsel he wouldn't mind sinking his teeth into. The Big Bad Wolf... I swallowed, aware of how sweaty my palms had gotten.

"Hello, Cathy. Please sit down. Let me introduce you to someone," Dad said, waving his hand at a seat opposite his desk.

"Sure," I murmured.

"I am sorry for the rush, but let's cut through the chase. Cathy, darlin', this is Lennox Carter. He owns LHC Security and is going to be your new bodyguard," he explained, pointing in the direction of the delicious, *very* handsome man whose unwavering gaze triggered all sorts of chaos inside my body. My stomach flipped several times like a circus acrobat in full performance mode as I parked myself in the chair. He cocked his head to the side, regarding me with curiosity now.

Did Dad just say this guy was going to be my security? I could hardly wrap my head around that thought, but my father was dead serious about my safety, especially after everything that happened lately. A stalker was a big deal. Over the past year, he had sent hundreds of emails and showed up on almost every one of my live streams. I ended up blocking him a few months ago because his messages had started to freak me out, but that didn't stop him.

His given name—whether real or fake I wasn't sure—was Richard. He'd even sent countless pictures of himself holding my books.

As if this wasn't disturbing enough, he then took things to a whole different level.

About a month ago, I started getting the sense of being followed while out at the bookstore or grocery store. I was pretty much a homebody, but leave it to a reader convention, or the need to add to my obscene stash of books, dark chocolate, and coffee beans from all over the world to draw me out like an eager butterfly from its cocoon.

I mean, the guy didn't even try to hide as he trailed behind me inside the stores, keeping his distance. It didn't take long for me to recognize him as the one from the photos he'd sent. Everywhere I went, his shadow wasn't too far behind. Driving an old maroon Subaru station wagon, he'd drive off when he'd had his fill of frazzling every last nerve in my body.

Besides, he knew where I lived. That was the scariest bit.

It took me a few weeks to tell my dad, who was pissed off I hadn't disclosed this info right away. But that particular day, Richard scared the shit out of me when he approached me right outside my house. Acting as though the shit was normal, he confessed his admiration for me, told me how beautiful I was, and would I go out to dinner with him?

I tried to be as cautious as possible in my response because I had no idea what a crackpot like him would be capable of. The man was in his late fifties but acted really weird and spoke fast. I'd never experienced fear like that before.

When I was finally able to get rid of him and he left, I entered the house shaking all over. It would have been impossible to hide my distress from Margie and my dad, so there I was, spilling the beans. No point in hiding the truth anymore. I was a twenty-six-year-old grown woman, but in that moment, I needed the support.

Dad insisted I take screenshots and show him all the emails and comments on my various social media posts and live streams. Just doing that proved harrowing to my emotional state. He was both shocked and furious at what he saw.

Despite my protests to wait it out a little bit, telling him the guy might back off, he dragged me to the police station to file a report, and then asked me not to go out alone until he'd figured out how to get me adequate protection.

Needless to say, that didn't go down well. I hated the feeling of being trapped. And all because of a douchebag who was apparently obsessed with me. A self-professed devoted fan who loved reading romance novels. I just didn't want to escalate things to the point this whole thing took over my life—but in truth, it already had.

"Well?" Dad said with a raised eyebrow. "Earth to Cathy."

"Oh ... sorry." I lobbed my gaze from him to the mountain of a man to his left who was now standing and confirming all my suspicions about his size. *Hot damn...* I forced myself not to stare at him too long.

"Dad, but I think this is unnecessary. I'm not planning on going anywhere alone anymore. Isn't that enough?" I argued, not sure why.

I weighed all of this in my head: hot man versus my freedom. And I wasn't entirely convinced I wanted the latter in that moment. If I could, I'd have slapped the common sense back into me.

Lennox's gaze settled on me again and my insides started to melt. It felt suddenly too hot in the office. Or maybe it was just me.

"I'm sorry, honey, but I already signed the contract with Lennox. I don't like relish the thought of you going through this. That man, Richard, is off his rocker and I don't believe he's going to stop just because you asked. I don't want to scare you, but he clearly has an obsession with you so we need to be proactive. The emails alone are cause for concern, but the fact that he's seeking you out in person now ... unacceptable. He's a nutcase."

Dad crossed his arms and huffed, which I knew to mean he'd made up his mind about this. "Besides, the holidays are coming up and that's the busiest time for me. I will be traveling a lot and I won't have you here without protection. Either this or I cancel all my commitments."

"No! Please don't do that on account of me."

"Well, these are the options."

"I have already spoken to my friends, Nina and Jessica, about this," I insisted as a last-ditch effort. "I can have them with me everywhere I go. Plus, the police already know about him and once they come up with more information, I can file a restraining order—"

My father raised his hand to stop me. "That's all well and good, but Lennox is non-negotiable."

I sighed. Maybe he was right and I was just being stubborn. On top of that, I couldn't burden my friends or Margie with constantly looking out for me. Over the past six years, I'd spent the holidays with my ex-boyfriend and his family, but this year we weren't together anymore.

Matt, my high school sweetheart, was relocating to New York to pursue his music career and I was staying in Miami, Florida. He wanted me to go with him, to commit to staying together forever, but at the time, although I loved him—and still missed him—I just wasn't ready.

"Cathy, we both know you need this, while I need to have my mind at rest that you're taken care of," Dad's voice was gentler this time. He'd probably registered I was giving in, as I should. I couldn't trade my own security for pride or any other lesser reason. He smiled at me, then at Lennox. "So, I'll let you two get acquainted. I need to make sure everything's packed for tonight."

He rounded the desk and gathered me in an all-enveloping hug, then kissed my cheek. Unfolding my arms, I hugged him back, taking in the soothing comfort he offered. "You know you'll always be my little girl…" Pulling back, he cradled my face and smiled, his eyes crinkling in the corners. "It's going to be okay. Please humor your old man. I couldn't leave if I thought you weren't in good hands."

I pursed my lips and nodded, swallowing past a lump in my throat. Although he was so absorbed in his life and manic schedule, I knew he loved me and worried about me. I couldn't deny him his peace of mind—or my own.

"Okay, Daddy." I smiled back, but again, the gesture didn't go deeper than my eyes.

I wanted to say something more, but he was already rushing out of the room. I wished that for once, he wasn't racing to get anywhere. The stress would get to him at some point, and *that* worried me. How long had it been since we'd taken a vacation together? Way too long…

It took me a few seconds to realize that I was alone with Lennox, who didn't try to hide that he was studying me. I did not like that. I did not like that one bit.

I turned to fully face him, allowing my reservations to show in my expression.

"Don't you worry, baby. You won't even notice me. I won't let anyone you don't know or trust near you," he assured in a rough, formidable tone.

Why did he have to be so intimidating? And did he just call me *baby*?

He took a step to the window and casually leaned against the frame, arms and legs crossed. He must have been over six foot nine. I suddenly felt overwhelmed by his presence and the way he seemed to fill the room with it. A little devil tapped me on the shoulder and whispered in my ear...

"Well, Mr. Carter, let's get one thing straight. First off, I'm not your baby, and second, I can take care of myself. My father is worrying about me and that's understandable, but I don't take unnecessary risks, so if you don't mind, in the coming weeks, try to keep to yourself and stay out of my business. I hate to be rude, but I have to set some ground rules. You can do your job from a distance and we'll be fine..."

I paused, standing from the chair, already regretting my bluntness because that wasn't like me at all. Despite my natural red hair that made people assume I always spoke my mind, that wasn't usually the case. I had no clue how to make a resting bitch face, I was definitely the wallflower of any group, and I cried when people died in scary movies. I actually watched Hallmark movies without cringing.

"Are we clear?" I added for good measure, that blasted devil egging me on.

At five foot seven, I wasn't considered short, but next to this guy I felt like a resident of Lilliput in Gulliver's Travels.

God, he's fine, fine, fine...

Peeling his form from the window frame, his face half light, half shadow, he stepped towards me and I instinctively backed away until I hit the wall of bookshelves. In a flash, he was standing so close to me, the air was sucked out of the room—and my lungs—in a whoosh. His bright green eyes shone with a definite note of challenge, but also something else I couldn't identify.

My heart began a frenzied gallop and for a moment, I was hypnotized by his heavy gaze. Then, my poor organ skipped a beat when he leaned down as though he wanted to kiss me. He raised an arm and rested his palm against the bookcase behind me.

Wait, what?

"No, we're not clear. You see, baby, I don't really work like that. It's my job to be in your business and in your space. Soon enough, I will become your shadow and you won't be able to go anywhere without me, so get used to it. Your father's paying the big bucks for this, and I'm damn good at my job. I could have sent an employee to handle this, but we're booked solid for the season," he said, his voice soft like a velvet. "I don't cut corners in *anything* I do."

Now there was a suggestive tone if I'd ever heard one. My cheeks heated up fast like flames on kindling.

My throat was so dry, I struggled to swallow. The air between us was charged with electricity. I squeezed my thighs together, feeling the heat that suddenly poured inside the pit of my stomach, then lower...

I seemed as though he wanted to consume me, fanning me with his warm breath and leaving me no room for escape.

Yup. Total bad boy. A character from one of my steamy reads come to life. One of my friends would call this her Wattpad moment.

I wouldn't give it a name just yet.

My life was perfectly organised and planned out. I enjoyed my freedom. I didn't want any other person—man or woman—to follow me everywhere. It didn't take much to make me happy. Even after Matt left, I was content with my work and my books. All of a sudden, everything was changing, my life turning upside down.

"You said it well. My father hired you, which means he's your boss, and so am I. So, I can do whatever I want and you can't tell me what to do," I said firmly, making myself cringe while feeling like a four-year-old in the throes of a tantrum. All I had to add was, 'Who do you think you are?' and I'd put the final accent on dramatic flair.

He smirked then. He actually did. I knew I was supposed to come up with something witty in a retort, but it seemed my brain had temporarily stopped working.

This was a disaster. I couldn't be fumbling for words. Not me—the person who made her living with them.

Lennox leaned even closer then. Totally inappropriate. As his cheek brushed mine, I did not move. Not a millimeter. Frozen was the word.

My throat burned with words unsaid, my hand stung with the itch to slap, if only I had control of my limbs. This feeling of arousal made no sense because this man needed an ass whooping, not a humping.

But dammit, it had been six months since I had sex and those books I loved to read … well, they were so steamy, they burned a hole in my bed at night.

I wondered what it would feel like if he kissed me. The near-caress on my cheek had my legs buckle and it took all the strength I had in me to stay upright. I sighed and inhaled sharply, taking in his musky scent. Clean man and pine trees...

I'd never felt like this before, even with Matt. And I'd just met the man. For goodness' sake, I thought stuff like this only happened in books. For a moment, I relished in his closeness, drowned in a whirlwind of sensations that took me under, and then…

I told my silly self to get off that train. Pronto.

"It seems you're going to be a handful," he whispered in my ear, then stepped back, putting distance between us as though he hadn't just reduced me to a puddle of mush. "Your father already sent me your schedule. You have a book signing tomorrow, and in the evening there's going to be some Halloween event, right?"

"Yes," I replied breathlessly, wondering what people were going to think if I showed up at the signing with a bodyguard.

"Great, so get ready because I will be watching you like a hungry wolf on the prowl," he said with a roguish grin. He certainly looked the part.

I shut my eyes, trying to control my whirling emotions but failing miserably. I couldn't believe how my dad could hire someone to watch me without consulting me first, as though I was some child.

When I finally opened my eyes, putting my anger in check, Lennox was gone.

I hated that I felt so hot and bothered by him.

Hated too that I couldn't act on all these unexpected fantasies that suddenly filled my mind.

Chapter Thirty-Eight

Lennox

This girl was going to be trouble. The moment I saw her walking into her father's office, I knew this job wasn't going to be easy. She looked so ticked off when I called her baby, setting her boundaries, and that amused me a little too much. I was treading dangerous ground, but I couldn't help it. The sooner she understood how things were going to be, the better.

She was much more beautiful in person. The picture her father had emailed me of her days ago didn't do her justice. She was a paradox—somewhat introverted and shy at times, extroverted in others, with a fiery personality simmering beneath the surface. Bringing that fire out of her, kicking and blazing, filled me with satisfaction.

The problem was, my fantasies of her were not professional in the least.

Visions of her lying on my bed, her glorious mane of hair spread across the pillows. She wasn't as tanned as so many women in Florida. I surmised, with her complexion, she spent a small fortune in sunscreen lotions. But she had a healthy glow to her, the barest smattering of freckles along her nose. In my fantasy, her cheeks were flushed and her eyes glossed over with desire. With fulfilment. Then her on her knees, her backside red and raw from a good bout of spanking...

My cock strained in my pants and I let out a curse under my breath, knowing I had to get it together or I was going to blow this assignment. I'd only seen this woman once and she already had my balls swelling with need. Hell, she had me all in a twist *before* I even met her. Things like this didn't happen to a grown man like me who was always in control. Pathetic.

I wished I could get one of my guys to take over and I would if we weren't bursting at the seams with work. Since I returned from Afghanistan and my relationship fell apart, first my work for my old boss, Sebastian Dimitrei, and then setting up my own company gave me purpose. We served wealthy clients and business was never slow. Besides, I got to help other veterans like me by giving them jobs—three of them, for now.

I built my reputation from the ground up, protecting wealthy people with a strict code of ethics and sheer hard work. My contracts came mostly through word of mouth at this point, including this one. LHC Security had come strongly recommended by an old client, who'd told me Dalton Rogers only wanted the best for his daughter. And he was paying top dollar, too. What was I to do except step up to the plate and take on the job?

Maybe it was time to hire more people.

I sighed.

After reading Cathy Rogers' file, I knew I couldn't underestimate the danger she was in. Her father was right, and definitely not overreacting. Some guy had developed an unhealthy obsession with this woman, a book blogger with a huge presence on social media. Fame came with a few nasty side effects—dealing with a stalker was one of them. Those kinds of people could be unpredictable.

Cathy Rogers. What was I going to do with her? I had an impeccable record. In my business, I was known for my professionalism. But this one here would be my downfall, I could just feel it.

We'd exchanged a few words after her father left—and those weren't ones I'd ever dare even think to say to a client. But somehow, her attitude egged me on and brought out the devil in me. She was supposed to be the timid librarian type, according to her father, yet she seemed anything but. She'd more likely be a pain in my ass from beginning to end.

She didn't like the fact I was going to be her shadow. Sparks flew from her eyes and she stared daggers at me. Her anger turned me on and that was not a good idea. She made me want to touch her, and the compulsion to corner her against that bookshelf had been impossible to resist. What the fuck? No one had ever made me feel this way, especially within moments of meeting—not even Eleanor, my ex-fiancée.

Letting out a ragged breath, I dragged my hand through my hair, then hightailed it out of the office, annoyed at myself for losing my temper. My grip on self-control.

I should stop getting all riled up about this though. As long as Cathy followed my rules and didn't do something crazy, such as ditch me or play me for a fool, things would work out fine.

I hurried to the open plan living room and found her father grabbing a bottle of water from the refrigerator. Good, because I wanted to have a word with him before he went on his trip. Rogers had been a single dad all of Cathy's life, and he'd never remarried after his wife died. Cathy was his only daughter, and he cared deeply for her. I'd brought myself up to speed with their family dynamic before I took the job. Such research was something I always did before accepting an assignment.

"Thank you, sir," I said. "I'll make sure to take care of your daughter."

He nodded. "I know she resisted this because she likes to keep to herself. But she'll come to terms with it, I assure you. She is not stupid, Lennox. She's aware Richard can be dangerous. She doesn't go out much, but her community means a lot to her. She doesn't want to disappoint her followers."

We walked outside and I helped him take his luggage out, where the cab driver placed the pieces in the trunk. He put his hands in his pants pockets and sighed. "I haven't told my daughter this, but I'm thinking about getting into politics. Senator Wellesley has been trying to get me involved for years. I haven't made my decision yet."

"I'm sure she'd support you, sir, if you told her."

He nodded, his expression thoughtful. "I need to figure things out first." He smiled then. "Please call me anytime, Lennox. I'm available twenty-four-seven if it has to do with my daughter."

"Sure thing, sir. Rest assured she's in good hands."

With a sad smile, Rogers patted me on the shoulder and shook my hand. Then, he got in the cab, headed to the airport.

I walked back inside the large house. Rogers had arranged to give me one of the downstairs bedrooms. Getting through the nights here, knowing Cathy would be upstairs in her bedroom, alone, was going to be a long, slow torture. I knew that right off the bat. I just hoped I didn't screw it up by letting my cock do the thinking, instead of my brain.

The décor here was tasteful and understated. Privileged clients could be difficult to deal with, but despite Cathy's initial attitude with me, I could tell she wasn't spoiled and disrespectful like that. Rogers was a self-made man, the kind I admired, and he hadn't forgotten how to deal with people. He'd likely raised his daughter with those same principles. Besides, I'd seen her social media posts. She was passionate about her work, down to earth, and I had a high regard for a person who put such energy and effort into what they loved.

I stopped in the living room, which was currently vacant, and took some time to study all the pictures of her that were set on the fireplace mantle. I could see she got her looks from who I guessed was her mother, in a framed wedding picture with Dalton Rogers.

Cathy was only a few years younger than me. She seemed mature enough and was truly beautiful, in the classical sense. She was petite but with curves, just the way I liked my women, and her delicate facial features and striking gray eyes drew you in ... along with a mouth that was made to wrap around a large, thick cock...

But as my client, she was off limits. I was here to protect her, not to have her on her knees ... crawling towards me...

Dammit. Lennox, stop!

Her body wasn't the only attractive thing about her. She was able to read from an early age, and in almost every picture I saw, she had a book in her hand. Such dedication.

After a few moments of contemplation, I decided to set up my laptop in the kitchen area for now. Perhaps the living room was a bit too intrusive and I didn't want to be in the way too much, but I wasn't in the room to go to my room just yet. Still, she'd already made it clear that she didn't want me in her space, and I had to respect that.

Blending in would be just fine, I figured, and she wasn't here right now, so I sat on one of the barstools by the countertop, right by the pantry. In a few minutes, I answered several urgent emails, checked the CCTV footage, and made a few phone calls. Richard hadn't been seen in this area since he'd confronted her outside the house. But guys like him didn't just give up. Sooner or later, he'd be back.

I then called my contact at the Marriott to check on security for the book signing event tomorrow, as well as the dance later that night. The venue had assigned a security team that seemed experienced at their job and most of all, didn't need handholding. This would make my work easier. Stressing on the need for discretion, I'd shared with them pictures of Richard and told them to be on the lookout throughout the day.

Although she'd blocked her stalker from her social media accounts, he would likely be aware about this event, so we had to keep an eye on all the possible entryways and exits. My biggest goal was making sure she'd feel safe at the Halloween party tomorrow.

For a long time, I was lost in my work until the back of my

neck prickled with awareness. Heat rushed through me, and I just knew she was there. When I lifted my eyes, I realized Cathy was in the kitchen, staring at me. She must have been there for a while.

"You seem busy," she said, leaning on the opposite side of the counter, across from me, forearms on the surface. Between her palms rested a mug of steaming tea, the bag still in there, steeping. She liked her brew strong, it seemed. I wondered if she felt the same about her men...

I rubbed my eyes and shifted on the chair. She'd changed her clothing to a pair of white shorts and a black t-shirt. Most importantly, she clearly didn't have a bra on.

Her round, full breasts commandeered my entire field of vision. Even though I'd never laid eyes on her naked, I knew a luscious pair of boobs when I saw them.

My mouth went dry and my cock stood at attention, straining against my jeans. She was petite, yes, but her breasts were magnificently large. And free. So very free. And bouncy. And pert...

She reminded me a little of Angelina Jolie in her Lara Croft getup. Only way more better looking.

Warmth flooded my groin and I was getting uncomfortably hard. This time, she didn't have her glasses on, but it didn't matter because she was such a turn on with or without them.

I told myself to keep it together and remember my place, but my imagination started to run wild.

"I got things set up for tomorrow, so you'll be safe," I said, then went back to my laptop, because I had to stop staring at her hard nipples jutting through the thin material of her shirt when she stood straight.

I clenched my fists when a flash vision of her unclothed, sensually crawling toward me like a wildcat, appeared in my mind. I needed to take a fucking cold shower, otherwise I'd be bound to that chair all evening. My cock was insistently pressing against the zipper of my jeans, making its presence known. Making demands. No surprise there since she was so hot, her hair in a messy ponytail, and no makeup on.

When I chanced a glance at her, she was standing by the sink, filling a glass with water and standing on her tiptoes in a pair of white Converse. I had to take another sharp breath at the sight of her ass that fit so snugly in those shorts.

My cock approved big time, of course. Her legs were long, her skin creamy, perfect for wrapping around my waist. Her dips and curves would move sinuously against me, rubbing, feeling, while I pushed her down on my hard cock, forcing her to take it...

Then I seriously considered clearing the counter, throwing her on it, and fucking the living daylights out of her.

What the fuck was wrong with me?

"I'm leaving in an hour," she said. "I'm meeting my friend at the Barnes and Noble for a coffee and book chat," she informed me after she drank her water and turned to face me.

The woman was giving me attitude again. Or maybe she was afraid I'd take over her life—which honestly, wouldn't be far from the truth.

The devil in me suggested that maybe she wanted someone to teach her obedience, and I was the best person for that job—but that was me thinking with my dick again.

"I will drive you there," I said, closing the laptop.

"Fine, whatever. I just want to make sure that you give me

some privacy in the store. I don't want others to notice I have a babysitter. All the staff there know me, so this place is safe enough," she explained, drumming her fingers nervously on the countertop.

Then, she walked off in a huff, but not before I noted the gleam of uncertainty in her eyes.

I clenched my fists, telling myself to stay calm. If she were my woman, my lover, I'd be punishing her for speaking to me in that tone. Right after I kissed her senseless, making her smile again.

Her file had stated she'd had a long-term boyfriend for a while, pretty much her first relationship, but I didn't think he was still in the picture. I hoped not, because I'd have to kick his balls and keep him away from what was mine...

I wanted nothing more than to see how far I could push Cathy Rogers. How easily I could claim her. My dark inclinations when it came to sex had to be alien to her and that was a real shame, because I could teach her a few things. She was probably inexperienced, especially if she had only been with one guy.

Fuck. There I was again with my thoughts going left field. If I couldn't keep it in my pants, I'd seriously have to consider resigning from this contract and hand it over to somebody else. But the idea of another man protecting Cathy made me sick to the stomach.

An hour later, I was driving her to the bookstore through the city. She'd changed again into jeans and a bookish blue top with the image of a black cat drinking coffee by a stack of novels printed on the front. It was a good size that hugged her torso, just tight enough for me to see the outline of her breasts, and she had me practically salivating. Stealing glances through the rear-view mirror while she was on the back seat, scrolling through her phone.

She met my gaze a few times, and I drowned in her gorgeous gray pools. But that connection was so fleeting, I wondered afterward if I'd imagined it.

"Tell me, Lennox, where are you from?" she finally spoke. "And how long have you been working in security?" She put her phone away and waited for my answer. No attitude or sarcasm in her tone.

I tightened my grip on the steering wheel. "I was born and raised in South Carolina and a few months ago I decided to move here to Miami to set up the business," I told her. I wasn't ready to talk to her about my past just yet and I could already tell that she was a curious little thing. "I returned from Afghanistan a few years ago. A friend of mine, Pedro, got me on board with his job. I worked for a man in Chicago called Sebastian Dimitrei. I respected him but he was involved in some shady stuff and after a while, I knew I wanted out of that gig."

She nodded and waited for me to continue. "I had to do something, so I contacted another friend, Bud, who suggested I set up a security firm. Felt overwhelming at first, but I got things going before leaving my job. Bud had some contacts here and at the time, it seemed like a good idea to move the operations here. The rest is history."

This conversation stirred some toxic memories—war, the end of love—but luckily, we arrived at our destination before she probed further. I was glad to get out of the car. I went around and opened the door for her. She seemed pleased with the gesture, but maybe her eyes were shining brightly because of the prospect of exploring the huge bookstore up ahead.

I followed her, acutely aware of our surroundings. After we entered the store, Cathy headed straight to the romance novel section, then informed me that she'd spotted her friend on a bench, perusing the books. That woman was the complete opposite of Cathy. She wore an oversized hoodie and a baseball cap, her hair cut short on one side, and the rest dyed purple. She kept glancing at me and giggling at the same time, like a thirteen-year-old girl at the first blush of puberty.

I stood several feet away from them, trying not to attract too much attention. Cathy wasn't happy that I entered the store and planted myself so close but tough luck—her safety was my prime concern. I looked around, making sure everything was copasetic.

"Shut up, Jess. He's my new bodyguard." She sighed. "He's going to be around, so let's just go look at what's new. We'll pay for our stash and then go to the Starbucks next door," Cathy hissed at her friend, then dragged her towards the book shelves.

"Oh my God, he's so hot. He looks exactly like one of our book boyfriends. No, I take that back. He looks like a total badass hero," Jess said, laughing out loud.

I followed them closely, sniggering to myself. Her friend was right. I was a fucking villain, because I liked having my women on their knees.

"Fuck," I snapped when I realised the girls had vanished. One moment they were standing between the bookshelves and the next, they were gone. It was probably Cathy's idea. She liked playing games, did she? I suspected she'd roped in her friend to hide with her.

As I searched among the shelves, cursing under my breath, a few people in the store were staring at me. My height and large frame weren't exactly conducive to me walking around unnoticed, and sometimes I hated that. Made it difficult to be discreet.

Cathy was going to get a good spanking later on if she wouldn't come to her senses soon. After running up and down the length of the store several times, ending up sweating like a pig, I was directed to a section at the back, decked with sofas and armchairs. I spotted them right away, not on any one of the seats, but trying to hide behind a large bookcase.

I inhaled sharply, putting a check on my temper as I approached them. This woman was going to pay for this.

In that moment, I decided that I had completely lost my mind because I was going to keep her on a short leash. Later on, once she was safely tucked in her bed reading one of her books, I would teach her a very important lesson. One that she would remember forever.

Chapter Thirty-Nine

Cathy

"Do you think he found us? He's gonna be angry with you, isn't he?" Jessica asked, still giggling like a schoolgirl nursing a crush.

We were looking at the new book by Carly Hoover, because we'd decided this was going to be our next read. I'd meant to get to that novel a long time ago, but my TBR pile was so long, I'd had to put it on the back burner.

"I have no idea. My dad means well and maybe I should be afraid, too, but I refuse to give in to that Richard creep. It's what he wants. To ruin my life and force me to pay attention to him. Now I have to deal with a guy who's supposed to follow me everywhere. It hasn't even been a day and I already feel suffocated," I said with a huff.

But at the same time, I felt petty and unreasonable. I'd also possibly gone too far. Yes, I had. Lennox was going to be pissed.

"But he's so gorgeous. You should enjoy this while it lasts…"

I looked at her as though she'd sprouted horns. "Enjoy what? Being stalked?"

"No! That's not what I saying!"

"Okay, fine. I'm sorry… been on edge lately," I said, feeling dejected.

"Oh sweetie. I wish I could suckerpunch that creep and get him off your back. I think Lennox will do that though. He's huge. Richard doesn't have a chance."

Lennox. I suddenly felt guilty for doing the disappearing act on him. I was putting a wrench in his game by not allowing him to do his job.

I had told myself I didn't care but that was a lie. This guy was different from anyone I knew. He was a pro, but at the same time he looked at me with fire in his eyes. Was he as stumped by this insane chemistry between us as I was? Just so fast, he brought out my inner wanton and made me bold. Daring. Nothing like my usual self. Every time he was near, I wanted to kiss him and … do so many other naughty things to him.

Crazy.

This little game I started with Jessica as an accomplice was a dangerous one. Deep down, I wanted to draw the devil out of him. I wanted him to chide me, get in my face … make me feel unspeakable things.

I had been so lonely since Matt broke up with me and I wasn't the type to go out to meet men. I also didn't care for dating sites. While everybody else swiped left and right, I turned the pages of an engrossing novel. Books were my escape because while I was reading, I didn't have to think about my issues or wallow in misery.

"He looks like Jameson. You know, that older guy from 'Praise'," Jessica pointed out with a lustful sparkle in her eyes. The girl was obsessed with that book. She must have re-read it at least five times. Although the young woman was currently single, she was much more experienced than me in the sex department.

"Yeah, but Jameson is much older than Lennox," I corrected her, thinking about those large hands and how much I wanted him to hold me close.

Lennox made me feel ... adventurous. Something Matt and I hadn't been, with our sex life tending to be somewhat one-note and predictable. My smutty books allowed my fantasies to go wild, the way they never were in real life for me. Lennox wasn't like Matt—I just knew—and that both scared and excited me.

I wanted to play games with him.

"I know but he does remind me of him and he was a fantastic character. Typical alpha male, yet incredible caring. Just a hunch, but I think this guy here looks like someone who would care for you," Jessica added with dreamy eyes.

If looks could kill, my friend would probably be burned to a crisp right now, a heap of ash on the floor. I knew what she was thinking but hell no, she wasn't getting him. Lennox was *mine*.

Wait ... what? Have I lost all my senses?

I'd only just met him, he worked for me—well, my dad but same thing—and I was trying to assert some claim of ownership on him. Yep. I was losing my marbles.

"Let's move. We need to pick up a few more books by Carly Hoover. We got so much to plan. I need to read one before my next livestream after today," I said, changing the subject. I didn't want her to sense that there was something going on between Lennox and me because there wasn't. Well, except for my inexplicable urge to jump him every time he came in my line of sight. She was a great friend, but no one needed to know absolutely everything about me.

"Oh my God, you are so boring. I think you need a good roll in the hay. Matt was such a loser. You must be so horny. You've read a mountain of steamy books in the past few weeks." She then gave me that "I know what you're trying to do by switching the conversation" look.

Jessica often encouraged me to go on dates, but I never listened. She could be over-the-top but I loved her dearly and she always looked out for me. She loved spicy romance books, too, but had only joined Instagram recently.

"Trust me, I'm fine," I lied. "Let's just get on with book hunting and see if we can find Lennox again. Maybe this was a bad idea. We shouldn't have pulled this on him," I told her as we started to walk away from the paranormal romance section.

Then I stopped in my tracks because Lennox was there, just beyond the seating area, and he was glaring at us. He looked furious. *Oh dear.*

I felt every step he took toward me in my head. Pounding. I was now nauseous, and feeling faint. Oh God, I wanted the earth to swallow me almost as much as I wanted to lick his face. And other things...

"Oh, look at these cute bookmarks. I think we should buy a few," Jessica said, pointing to a display beside the shelves, along with swag and other interesting merch for sale. Authors usually sent me a ton of such items so I never bought them, but any other time I would have enjoyed perusing the options anyway.

Lennox was almost upon us. Jessica must have seen him approaching, but it looked like she'd decided to ignore him.

"I like this one. I think it's from the AKOTOR series. Is that Hayden?" I forced myself to act nonchalant as I picked up a shiny laminated bookmark with an illustrated picture of the character from one of my favourite series of all time. Jessica reached out for it and as she grabbed it, a sharp pain sliced into my palm.

"Ouch!" I cried.

"Oh no! What happened?" she asked in a panic, dropping the bookmark.

"I'm fine," I replied, shaking my head, but then my finger started to bleed. It was a damn paper cut from the sharp laminated edge—how could a mere bookmark cause such damage? My finger throbbed and a drop of blood fell to the floor. I was so shocked, I couldn't move. This was ridiculous.

"Oh my God. You're bleeding!" Jessica started rummaging through her bag. "I'm pretty sure I bought some tissues but where the fuck are they..." she mumbled.

"It's just a small accident..."

"No, it isn't! Look at your finger, dang it."

Not a heartbeat later, Lennox was right there, grabbing the injured hand.

"Come on, Ms. Rogers. Let's go take care of that small injury," he stated gruffly.

"But it's just a small cut. Jessica here has some tissues. Right, Jessica?"

My friend mumbled something unintelligible, still searching through her enormous tote.

"I insist," he ground out. His tone brooked no argument and he looked as though he was just about to flip.

"Uh, okay. Jessica, I'll be right back."

I'd barely finished talking when he hauled me toward the restrooms.

We finally found them and I started to walk in the women's. When he didn't let go of me, I looked over my shoulder. "I know you're not going in here with me."

"I'm not letting you out of my sight."

"Where am I supposed to escape to from the restroom? There are no big windows or side doors in there."

"Doesn't matter."

Uh oh. His curt tone held a world of barely restrained ire.

"Please? I promise I won't be long."

"Hmmm," he grunted, but then pulled me back and steered me to a separate restroom marked with a disabled sign.

"What ... no!" I hissed as he opened the door and marched me inside.

He locked the door and waved his hand under the automatic faucet, then examined the damage to my finger.

"It's surprisingly deep and you have to run it under cold water for some time," he said, then put my hand under the stream of water.

At this point, the initial shock passed and I realized we were standing way too close to each other. His whole body radiated heat and instant desire welled in the pit of my stomach. The stinging pain was suddenly gone.

"You don't have to do that. I'm fine," I said, pulling my hand back, but my finger was still bleeding.

"Don't do that," he chided, grabbing my wrist again. For a

split second, I thought he was going to put it under the faucet again, but instead, he lifted my hand to his mouth.

Holy shit. What is he doing?

My breath hitched when he started sucking the blood off that finger, staring at me with those penetrating green eyes of his. Electricity sparked between us. Oh my God... I closed my eyes, my wits scattered all over the place.

I opened my eyes again and immediately, the intensity in his gaze reminded of Twilight and Edward Cullen.

I was too stunned to speak or even move. I had nothing to compare it to ... this incredibly erotic thing no one had ever done to me before. My mouth went dry and I licked my upper lip, losing myself in his gaze.

The sensual way he was licking my finger sent me into a frenzy of arousal. I let go of a small whimper and tried to convince myself this was wrong.

But how could it be when it felt so right? I was allowed to enjoy this.

I bit on my bottom lip when he slid my finger out of his mouth and kissed the tip once ... twice.

"Put your finger in the water again and leave it there," he said roughly. "Otherwise I'm gonna have to spank you."

"I'm not a child, Lennox. Do not speak to me like one," I said, pursing my lips.

I felt claustrophobic in this tiny space with him. I had to put some kind of distance between us because the attraction was both senseless and unbearable. Maybe he did see me as a spoiled brat and I'd gotten it all wrong.

While I wanted more ... so much more. I wanted to hop into one of my books and act out the steamiest, dirtiest scenes with him. Dance around each other in a game of seduction until we couldn't hold back any longer...

"I'm warning you again there will be consequences if you won't cooperate with me. Do you think this is a joke? I'm trying to keep you safe and you're acting like this is a game, Ms. Rogers," he snapped.

I kept my hand under the water, suddenly feeling like that child he was making me out to be. After all, I'd been acting like one.

"I know we're not playing, but this is my safe place. The staff know me and nobody's going to attack me in a bookstore. It's a public place... So I'm not allowed any fun is what you're saying?"

Lennox's eyes darkened and he shook his head, no doubt holding back a retort. Grabbing a piece of paper towel, he wrapped it around my bleeding finger. "We need a Band-Aid. Probably an antiseptic, too, just in case. Do you have any?"

"I do, at home."

"Fine," he said with a nod.

As I turned to let myself out of the restroom, he caught my elbow and swiveled me back to face him. He loomed over me, bending so his face was inches from mine.

"Just so you know, a stalker will get bolder each day. They don't care if it's a public place or not. You remember how he cornered you at your own house. Do you really want to underestimate an unstable person?"

"No," I breathed out after a slight hesitation. "No, I don't."

"Right."

The only reason I couldn't feel any fear or disappointment was the adrenaline rushing through me because of his closeness.

The devil on my shoulder reared its head and I lifted my hand to his t-shirt, finally breaking my gaze from his. "You have a piece of lint here." Removing the offending speck, I let my hand fall to my side but he caught it mid-way.

"It sounds like you need to learn a lesson, Ms. Rogers, but unfortunately, disobeying the wrong one might get you hurt or even killed," he said, drawing lazy circles on the back of my hand with his thumb. Can't you see that?"

I looked down at our joined hands, following the trail of his caress but he hooked his finger under my chin and made me look up again. I found myself unable to respond, feeling suddenly emotional. He said that not because he cared, but he was simply doing his job.

"As for your fun ... there are so many ways to have it, especially if you keep disobeying my instructions like this." He dropped his gaze to my mouth and I licked my lips, holding my breath. "I know I'll regret this, but I'm gonna show you anyway."

He lowered his lips to mine, but barely touched me. A whimper escaped my throat before I could stop it. This was wrong, but nothing in the world would have made me move away at that moment. I was frozen. Utterly.

I parted my lips, ready to deepen the kiss, but instead he pulled back and spun me around to face the bathroom mirror.

"What—"

I stared back at my flushed face and bright eyes. Lennox came to stand right behind me, flush against me, leaving me no room to wriggle out ... if I wanted to. In a daze, I felt his hard body against mine as he slid his hands down my arms, making me shiver from head to toe. His erection throbbed against my back and just then I realized ... it was all because of me.

I'd made him hard.

Was it my little act of rebellion that caused the excitement?

An unexplained chemistry between us?

His hands now at my hips, holding me steady, he grinded against me ever so slightly, making me jump. My entire body became a thunderstorm of pure want.

He moved his hands to the sink and gripped it, now in complete control, with me a prisoner between his massive arms.

"What are you doing?" I croaked out.

"I'm teaching you a lesson, my little librarian," he said, his words drifting softly in my ears, a mere caress... "I'm teaching you how it feels when you're completely helpless. Powerless. At someone else's mercy."

He traced the edge of my ear with his tongue and now, I was the one who needed to grasp the sink. I moaned again when all sorts of fantasies assaulted my brain. Of him flicking his tongue on my nipple, then my clit, over and over again, until he made me come...

"So let's learn a few things," he continued, "in a way you'll hopefully remember."

My head leaned back against him because all the strength seemed to whoosh out of me, starting from my legs. I whimpered, not bothering to hide it this time.

"Lesson one—never try to hide from me. I will always find you. Do you understand, Ms. Rogers?" he asked in a forbidding tone. "Do you understand?" he repeated when I didn't respond right away.

"Yes."

"Good." And just like that, he took a step back and I almost fell on my butt, were it not for his hand when he reached out to keep me steady.

I held on to the sink for dear life and gathered myself—not an easy task.

He dragged his hand over his chin, studying me through the reflection in the mirror.

"Just one more thing," he said, then smacked me hard on my ass, drawing a loud yelp from me. He did it again and to my eternal mortification, I enjoyed it immensely, just like the heroine Lydia in one unforgettable filthy romance I read a few months ago.

"I think that'll do for now…" I felt his breath by my ear again. "I hope you'll do what you're supposed to. Or not. Either way, I'm looking forward to teaching you more lessons, *baby*."

And with that, he exited the restroom, leaving me alone in a steaming heap of desire.

Chapter Forty

Lennox

Dammit. Why the fuck did I do that? I did believe she was going to be trouble and here I was, proving that theory right.

When we returned to the house, Cathy refused to talk or even look at me. The moment we entered the door, she bolted upstairs without a backward glance. After that, I didn't see her for the rest of the day. I just hoped she wouldn't tell her father what happened.

Hell, I was doing this all wrong. Cathy Rogers made me forget my entire code of ethics, professional decorum, and every single word of my interpersonal skills rulebook!

I distracted myself with work, checking for the millionth time that all was set for the next day. I didn't want any surprises. After checking the CCTV of the last few hours, I sat up straight on the sofa and worked out a kink in my neck. This time, I hung out in the living room because I doubted anyone would need to use it. Margie wasn't there, the house cleaner wouldn't be in today, and Cathy was giving me the silent treatment.

Done with any work I could possibly think of getting done, I guessed it would be a night of jerking myself off to sleep. I felt like a pervert, unable to help himself. Disgusted, I headed to my room, wondering what the next day would bring.

In the morning, she came down to the kitchen and I overheard her talking to a friend on the phone while she acted like I wasn't even there.

I should be feeling constant shame for I'd never dreamed of doing something like this with a client. But fact was, I had no doubt in my mind she wanted it as much as I did. The bumping and grinding, the spanking, the near kiss... When I left that bathroom, I was so frustrated, I thought I was going out of my mind. Masturbating in the en suite shower in my room had taken some of the edge off, but just for a little while.

Cathy Rogers was messing with my head, and I suspected there was only one way to get her out of my system.

To take what she offered, even before she knew she wanted to offer it.

Her ass was made for spanking, and her responsiveness only confirmed she had a dark side hidden somewhere deep within that she might never have explored before.

I shouldn't crave a client. I shouldn't want this. It wasn't my modus operandi.

But when she whimpered and moaned that first time, I was done for.

After she'd had a cup of coffee and a breakfast bar, it was time for me to drive her to the book signing at the Marriott.

This was going to be a busy day. After we arrived, I walked inside with her and made a quick scan of the lobby area. We checked into the hotel first. I got a room next to hers because the party would take place at the same location tonight.

We went down to the signing and I planted myself inside the large banquet hall by the entrance. Author tables took the space all around the room, with an enthusiastic, mostly female crowd milling about and gushing over their favorite authors.

I watched her fill her tote with signed books and taking pictures with a bunch of authors and readers, who were probably her fans. I noticed she was taking her time to acknowledge everyone. Her kind, open demeanor and smile were so genuine, she drew people to her like a magnet all the time.

To say Cathy loved books was an understatement. She was a passionate fan of smut literature, as she called it. We'd only just met, but in some ways, I felt like I knew her, just by observing her in her natural habitat.

She was not a spoiled brat—she was natural, honest, and hardworking. As much as I wanted to keep her at arm's length, to see her as just another client, every moment in her presence stripped me of my resolve.

We hadn't spoken since that incident in the bathroom, and my palm was itching to touch her again. Staying away from her did nothing to temper this need I felt for her. It didn't even make sense. And now, watching her here, laughing and carrying on, so happy and carefree … I just wished she could be that way with me.

Of course, it was silly for me to envy a bunch of books and strangers. Who did that?

I tried to distract myself again from spiraling thoughts of

her by keeping an eye on everyone that entered. Particularly the men. It wasn't many of them, thank goodness, but enough that I had to remain alert at all times.

I had an excellent view of the hall from where I stood. A few women noticed me, sparing me curious looks and flirtatious smiles or winks. Some whispered between themselves and I knew they were talking about me. But right then, I didn't care.

During the event, I acted like I was part of security team, and not specifically with Cathy. It was easier that way because she didn't like bringing too much attention to herself. The last thing I wanted to do after what had happened was rile her up further. I could tell she was nervous having me around at times.

Last night when I realised that she wasn't coming back downstairs and I'd taken my infamous shower, I settled in bed with my laptop. I went online, logged in to TikTok and searched for her name. She was streaming live from her room.

This was a completely different Cathy. The woman on the screen was confident and simply adorable, talking about her favourite books and showing her limited edition covers. She had no reservations talking about some pretty steamy scenes. I was fascinated by how many people were actually watching her. I kept an eye on the comments, but luckily nothing stood out in a negative way.

Of course, I had to see to my demanding cock one more time before I was even able to catch a wink.

The Cathy I was seeing now was pretty much the same. Comfortable and cheerful. Charismatic.

Around lunch time, she headed to the restaurant with a few of her bookish friends. I found a small table tucked away in a corner, within view, and settled there. When the sandwich and fries I ordered was brought to me, I downed it as fast as I could. I wanted to be done when Cathy decided to move elsewhere.

After the meal, she went to the bathroom and I followed her at a respectable distance. The day dragged on and I was slowly becoming addicted to her. That was the word: addicted. I just couldn't take my eyes off her. It had been three long years since I'd felt this way for anyone. At least since things went south with the woman I was supposed to marry, and even then, it wasn't like this.

Around eight o'clock, the signing event was over and Cathy told me that she was going back to her room to get ready. She must have ordered room service because I heard someone knocking on her door, and she opened it right away. I hoped she didn't just do that without first checking who it was.

Soon, I would need to talk to her. We couldn't keep going like this forever. Fleetingly, guilt ate at me once more for going too far with her, but in the next moment, I thought about her face in the mirror. The desire I'd witnessed in those beautiful eyes of hers. Sometimes there was no rational explanation to things. They just happened, as sudden and forceful as lightning in a clear sky.

Half an hour later, I changed into a black shirt and pants and knocked on her door. We needed to discuss my involvement during the dance and a few other important details about safety protocol.

"Lennox. We need to talk," Cathy said curtly, opening the door. Her room was much bigger than mine. Her light citrusy scent lingered in the air and when I finally looked at her, I cursed silently. My cock strained in my pants.

"You should always ask who it is first before opening the

door. There's no keyhole here. You must be more careful," I blurted out right away.

"Oh, yes. You're right." She waved a hand as if to dismiss me. "I'll do that from now on."

I grunted in response because what I really wanted to do was throw her over my lap and spank her silly. But the power of speech was briefly yanked from me when I saw what she was wearing.

She stood by the bed wearing a revealing black and silver witch's costume with a tight strapless corset and a full, above-the-knee tulle skirt that exposed a good bit of her stunning legs. Her bountiful breasts threatened to pop out of her bodice, and on top of her bouncy red curls sat a tall, pointy hat. Smoky grey eyes and plum-colored lips completed the look, along with high-heeled ankle boots on her feet and fishnet tights.

Would there be many men at the Halloween event tonight, I wondered? If so, I might have to kill every last one of them when I caught them staring at her.

"Wow, Cathy, you look ... amazing."

"Thank you," she said with an air of dignified sophistication. "Not very creative, I suppose. But I love being a witch." She smirked.

"You do, don't you?" A loaded statement, and she didn't miss the intended meaning.

"Well, sometimes a situation calls for such a persona," she countered. Her eyes crinkled at the corners and for a moment, her mood seemed to lighten. "But back to what I wanted to say..."

She put her hands on her hips and gave me a coy pose—totally unlike her.

"Being like this ... in costume ... I feel different," she stated, her head held high. "But I'm not stupid. I promise I won't create problems tonight, make your job difficult..." She bit on her bottom lip, as if hesitating to say more.

"Is something wrong?" I pressed.

The silence stretched for a while.

"I ... I've been thinking about yesterday," she finally admitted. "A lot. I just wasn't expecting that. You took me by surprise. You were a little rough, but..."

"But what?"

"But ... Jessica will kill me if I don't tell you this. And... oh, for fuck's sake!" Releasing a huff, she plopped down on a chair and hung her head.

Walking to her, I picked up a strand of her hair and worked it between my fingers. She finally looked up at me. "I liked it. What you did. I ... want more."

I didn't respond for the longest, more out of shock than anything else. Was I imagining things?

But more importantly, what was the right thing to say? That I wanted to fuck her senseless, or that it was wrong and improper in our circumstances?

"I don't think you know what you're asking for, Ms. Rogers—"

"Seriously, you want to keep calling me Ms. Rogers after yesterday? My name is Cathy."

"Ms. ... Cathy, you are my client and I promised your father I'd keep you safe. We both know we can't be intimate with each other," I explained, but each word coming out of my mouth was bullshit. Cathy was a grown woman and could make her own decisions.

Still, it was a matter of ethics—a reason that was fast losing importance.

Cathy wanted more from me.

She wanted me to touch her ... dominate her.

She wanted to be my submissive. She didn't say that in so many words, but that's what she meant. It was right there, in her eyes. As clear as day.

Standing, she put her hand on mine while I kept playing with her hair. Her gray gaze told me so many things without a single word from her lips. The air was suddenly thick with tension. She placed her other hand on my chest and smiled seductively.

Clearly, her costume was giving her a confidence boost.

"How about we play a little game?" she suggested.

I wanted to taste her, manhandle her, but I stood still, waiting for her to continue.

"Tonight's going to be all about turning the negative into the positive. This is my world, and when I'm in it, I feel like a queen," she said. "So just for tonight, I want to be who I'm normally not. I'll be happy to have you play a part in it."

"How?" I rasped.

"Hear me out. We'll play a game. You're going to pretend to be my stalker, so when I go downstairs to the dance, I'll spot you in the crowd. I'll find you terrifying so I will run and you'd have to catch me. If you do, then I will do anything you ask me to. I will become your ... plaything for the night." She paused, swallowed, then added, "It would help me deal with the real stalking situation, too. Having this game on my terms."

"Why do I get the sense that you're acting out some kind of

scene from one of your books?" I said, stunned she'd even propose such a thing.

"Maybe I am." Her smile lit up the room. She inched closer to me until our bodies touched.

"You have no idea what you're asking for," I said again, wanting nothing more than that, but trying to do the right thing. Desire rushed through my veins, the need to please her and make her come like no one had ever done before.

I had to have her.

"No, I had a long time to think about this. Yesterday and today. I know exactly what I want. I'm single and I'm available. I could pretend I'm pissed at you but I'm past those kinds of games. I want a different kind of game... I want to have the night of a lifetime. Maybe this will be my only chance," she said.

Well, she was certainly honest. She knew what she wanted and had the guts to ask. It might have been the costume, Halloween night, the bold spirit of the season—whatever it was, she wasn't afraid to go for it.

"So, you're eager to learn how to please me?" I asked, still finding it hard to wrap my head around her bizarre request. My thoughts tumbled out. "This is a very dangerous affair you're proposing and I am doubting myself. Thinking about consequences. You can run, but can we get away from those? There's undeniable attraction between us and that's a fact, but is it enough? I don't think I would be able to control myself when I catch you. What if I push you too far?"

"I trust you. I don't know why and I've got no explanation for it but I do. I am asking you for one night only. After that, you can go back to being my bodyguard," she said, then laughed nervously, glancing quickly at the stack of books that she must have put on the floor earlier on. There were a lot of shirtless men on the covers.

It seemed I wasn't the only one doing insensible things.

"I understand, but this is the real world, not fiction. I don't think you're ready for the kind of game I have in mind." I dragged my hand over my face, trying to remove the image of her on her knees, choking on my cock, from my mind. Fuck, I was already so unbelievably hard for this maddening woman.

"Of course I am ready. I have read countless books about BDSM, for example, and I know what to expect. This may be the real world but as I already said, we are now on my turf. The party downstairs ... it's all about fantasy. And I do want to play with you." She moved her hand over my lower abdomen, then farther down. I wanted to grab her, pull her to me, and claim her lips over and over, but I resisted. "Maybe you're the one who's scared, Lennox? Maybe you're not up to this challenge."

Exasperating woman. Bat shit woman...

I remained still when her fingers brushed the waist of my pants because I wanted to hold tight to my weaning self-control. She could feel how aroused I was, almost on the verge of wiping that smirk off her face with my cock. Savage heat enveloped me with her touch, as well as the sight of her creamy mounds pouring from her corset. This costume would have any man sniffing around her skirts, and that wouldn't do.

Just that moment, I finally acknowledged there was no way I'd say no to her proposal.

"Fine, we will play this game but first of all, Cathy, take off your tights and panties. I want to have free access to you all the time," I ordered, roughly grabbing her neck and bringing her closer to me. Her pupils dilated when I put enough pressure on her flesh. She swallowed hard and nodded, then I let go of her so she could take off her boots to slide her fishnets down her legs.

"What are you going to do to me once you catch me?" she asked, her voice vibrating in anticipation.

I leaned against the wall, watching her strip. "Something that will stay in your memories forever. You will have a minute head start before I start the chase. And once I track you down, I won't show you any mercy. I will want to punish you for your smart mouth and earlier defiance. I will make you do things that will be painful and uncomfortable. It's Halloween and you will see the monster within me. This game is going to be scary and frightening, but since you asked for it, I am willing to play it."

She licked her lips and nodded.

When she was done, her boots back on, I grabbed her by the neck again. "So, I will ask you one last time: Are you one hundred percent sure of this?" I added.

"Yes," she said. "I am."

I let go of her. Despite her answer to my question, she was still hesitating and for a second, I thought she might change her mind. But then she bolted out of the room so fast, I thought she might trip.

I laughed to myself as I set the timer. I had to stop overthinking this and just accept that my fantasies from the previous night were coming together. Ms. Cathy Rogers, the quiet librarian, wasn't so shy when she came to certain things. And hot, dark fantasies were one of them. She craved some dark, depraved things and I was ready to give them all to her.

When the timer rang, I walked out of the room. There was nowhere she could hide from me because her fans were everywhere and I used to spy on people for a living. Maybe after tonight, she would finally understand that there were evil men in this world who wanted to harm her, and if they wanted that badly enough, she'd be in some serious danger.

This night was going to be interesting and I was so excited to see how this whole thing would pan out.

I was already imagining her cuffed to my bed, alone in my apartment, hopeless and needy with desire. She had no idea how much I wanted to tease her with all my sex toys, until she begged me to make her come. Then I'd spray my cum all over her tits and that dirty mouth. *My* fantasies were down and dirty, bottom-barrel, no holds barred shit.

I was downstairs in record time, and I noticed Cathy hadn't gotten very far. She was standing in the hotel lobby, talking to some guy, and didn't seem pleased. I stopped in my tracks and decided to watch her, trying to figure out who the asshole was. It seemed that she knew him because she let him hold her hand. Or, more accurately, he wouldn't let her shrug him off.

I pulled out my phone and looked at the photo of her stalker, confirming he wasn't the one. This blond man was much younger and softer looking. Besides, despite what I told her, I didn't think the stalker would risk appearing in such a crowded place at this juncture. The young guy was looking at her as though he wanted her, and that made me fucking furious.

I walked as close to them as I could, planting myself behind a wide column. From here, I could listen in to the conversation, as well as watch them.

"Matt, I really haven't got time right now. I need to go. We can talk about this later," she said, almost pleading. I knew she'd spotted me before I found my hiding place. "Let me go."

She pulled her arm back but the bastard held on as though playing a motherfucking game of tug of war. I reared to go break all the bones in his body but she gave me a brief look of warning, to stand back.

"No, we need to talk now. We have unfinished business, Cathy. I miss you. I can't stop thinking about you," the weasel said, reaching out to snake his hand around her arm.

I inhaled sharply as jealous rage filled my system. He was touching what was mine and I couldn't allow it. Cathy glanced at me, now begging me with her eyes to give her a little more time. I shook my head slightly.

She needed to get rid of that loser now. I had never been a patient guy and this asshole was too fucking needy for my liking. From the name, it had to be her ex-boyfriend who left her a few months ago and moved to New York.

"We will talk later. Right now, I really have to be somewhere else," she snapped at him. "Besides, we have nothing to talk about. We are over, and I have moved on."

She finally broke free from his grasp, and then took off running.

"Smart girl," I muttered to myself.

"Cathy! Cathy!" he shouted after her, but luckily, I caught up with him and grabbed his arm before he could go after her.

"I think the lady said that she wants to be left alone," I said.

A few people were staring at us and I told myself I should calm the fuck down. The scrawny boy looked at me, his face contorted in anger.

"Let go of my hand, you idiot. Who the fuck are you?" he yelled, trying to pull away from me, but I squeezed him harder.

"I am her new bodyguard, so you better think before you

say another word," I growled. "Now walk away or I am going to kick your ass in front of all these people."

"All right, man. Chill. I was leaving anyway," he said, looking like he was going to piss himself.

A moment later, I was walking away, determined to show my little librarian how truly angry I was with her.

I was already picturing her on her knees, staring at me with her big gray eyes and begging for my cock.

Chapter Forty-One

Cathy

I had no idea what had gotten into me, but I had never been more excited in my life. I had always wished I could be more adventurous in the bedroom and I couldn't believe that I'd just shared with Lennox one of my wildest fantasies. Matt had been reluctant to try anything new in the sexual realm, he was mostly a vanilla guy, so I never suggested anything.

I had been thinking about this long and hard. I'd be a fool to deny the chemistry I and Lennox shared that hit me with brute force every time I laid eyes on him. How often did such a thing happen in life? A sensation so overwhelming, you simply *had* to act on it. It had certainly never happened to me. Jessica was right: This had to be the beginning of my own Wattpad romance, and I wasn't going to let it pass me by. There'd be regrets.

After he spanked me in the bathroom, I could sense the power in him, the energy that practically oozed off him. He was a natural dominant, and that both excited and terrified me. The feelings he awakened were so strange and new, I just couldn't face him after that. So, I locked myself in my room and proceeded with my live streaming session, trying to act as normal as possible.

But then I noticed him watching me—I recognised his grumpy face on his profile picture. No matter what I did or where I went, he was there. I couldn't avoid him, not only physically but in all ways.

I was barely able to sleep that night, tossing and turning for hours. When I eventually drifted away, I had all sorts of erotic dreams about him. In my six years with Matt, since college, this sort of thing had never happened. We had a straightforward relationship that was supposed to lead to marriage one day. I thought my life was sorted for the next fifty years or so.

Despite having a massive following on TikTok and being very social when it came to discussing books and tropes, I didn't really know how to talk to men—especially since my whole adult life, I'd been with one guy only. Reading about such situations in books gave me hope that I could do it, but when I finally found myself standing in front of a cute guy, I was lost. Let alone one of Lennox's caliber.

The man was watching me from a distance. He pretended he didn't know me, and that was sweet. He was giving me some space. I noticed how other women were staring at him, admiring his incredible physique, ever since we'd arrived here this morning. I wanted to shout out to everyone that he was mine, but that would have been ridiculous, wouldn't it? We'd only just met and technically, he was a stranger.

But when he showed up in my room and I looked into his eyes, I didn't want us to be strangers anymore. So I found the courage to tell him what I wanted. And he agreed.

Ask and you shall receive.

In one small moment, everything changed between us. For this night, we would allow our fantasies to take center stage. Things were moving fast, but I'd never felt more certain of anything in my life—because I had complete control of the rules of this game, as opposed to the situation with Richard, my stalker, who wanted to take my power away. Lennox found me attractive, and he wanted this, too.

He gave me a head start, so I ran downstairs, which was where I bumped into Matt. It took me a moment to overcome my shock at seeing him after so long.

He tried to talk to me and just then, Lenox showed up, of course. He didn't look pleased when Matt grabbed my hand, which secretly filled me with satisfaction. Was he jealous? I realized all I wanted to do was to make Matt stop talking about how much he missed me and couldn't stop thinking about me, and get on with my game with Lennox.

It was hard for me to believe Matt, who'd never reached out to me since we parted ways, was standing in front of me. I'd finally gotten over him and I wasn't about to go down that road again with him. So, I said my piece and left him in the lobby.

The Halloween dance was taking place in a lounge bar located in the hotel basement, surrounded by a network of rooms that granted me myriad possibilities to hide from Lennox.

I headed down a flight of stairs, bypassing the elevator. After passing the ticket booth manned by a couple of my friends, I entered the lounge, which was decorated in rich wood and royal blue velvet. The dim lighting gave off a suitably eerie aura, accentuated by the Halloween décor all around. The ceiling was covered in spiderweb and ghostly decorations and shadowy images moved around the walls thanks to the clever use of a projector.

Soon, the dance floor would be filled with partygoers under the strobe lights, and people would be drinking and engaging in general shenanigans. I should be feeling a strong sense of FOMO but strangely, I did not. Lennox was a much more exciting opportunity that would be a one-time-only deal. Use it or lose it, the saying went.

I wished I hadn't worn these heels because my feet were killing me already. Lennox was a vet, so he no doubt had some killer people tracking skills. My outfit would hinder my efforts, but maybe the idea was for him to catch me pretty fast so we could act out our fantasies asap...

My pulse pounded in my ears when I thought about him fucking me against a wall, or on the desk in my hotel room upstairs. Damn it, I had to get a hold of myself. This just wasn't a fantasy anymore—it was happening for real. Fact was, we only had this one chance. I couldn't think beyond that. Lennox was here to protect me from Richard. Once the stalker wasn't a problem anymore, there'd be no reason to be around each other anymore.

A publisher rep approached me. We'd discussed working together earlier today, so I quickly set up an appointment for next week and put it on my phone calendar. Then, I proceeded to look for the perfect hideout.

I spotted a couple of maids entering a room at the end of a corridor labeled 'Staff Only,' past the restrooms and 'round a corner. I waited until they left and turned the knob, happy to see they hadn't locked it. Perhaps they were planning to return soon.

I went inside what appeared to be a laundry room, with a line of washers and dryers across one wall, some of which were going through their cycle. I quickly took off my heels and massaged my left foot, making a mental note to wear flats next time.

There was a pile of clean sheets to my right and I counted at least five large washing machines. I wasn't sure where else to hide, so this would have to do for now. It would likely take Lennox a minute to find me here. I hid by the wall next to one of the dryers, sitting on a low stool. Adrenaline flowed threw me, filling me with anticipation as the loud hum of the machines droned on.

I fished my phone out of my corset and opened the Kindle app. Might as well be productive and read while I was waiting, hoping he'd locate me soon so I could let him have his way with me. I wondered which of the two novels I was currently reading I should resume. There was also a dark fantasy I was dying to start—always my favorite genre. I opted for the fantasy. Tonight was for doing all the things I wanted, without reservations. It was about letting go and not thinking my way out of things, letting reason take over.

Charlotte, one of the PR people who'd organised the signing, had also arranged a fun ghost hunting tour for later. Apparently, the top floor had never been renovated, so she'd planned and created a spooky paranormal world in the different rooms. It had to be the perfect place to end this amazing Halloween night, being chased around by monsters and ghosts.

And then there was Lennox...

I'd barely read two pages when the door opened. Probably another maid to retrieve some clean linens, I figured. Heavy footsteps moved purposely around the room and my heart stopped. *No—not a maid.* My gut told me it was Lennox.

"Come out, little birdie, wherever you are," he said in a terrifying sing-song voice. I cursed under my breath and braced myself, my heart now almost beating out of my chest. "I have to admit I haven't been playing fair. I tracked your phone all the way here. I just didn't want to waste time searching for you, but I did take my time."

Dammit! Why didn't I think of that? One of the first things he'd done was link our phones, just in case any number of unthinkable Richard-related scenarios happened.

I covered my mouth with my palm, trying not to give up my hiding place just yet, but I was ready to scream. He'd totally one-upped me.

This was it.

I wanted him to fuck me so hard, I forgot who I was. I wanted him to spank me, tie me up, and use me like a dirty whore. These thoughts were scaring me a little, but for once I wanted to be honest with myself. Just let go, forget about other people's expectations of me. I had never felt like this about anyone else.

"Very interesting choice, little birdie. We're going to have so much fun together here. I have locked the door, so no one will interrupt us while we catch up on things. Get acquainted. I have a confession to make. I've looked you up and learned so much about you. I know you don't have a man in your life right now, so you must be feeling pretty horny. And lonely," he said, each step bringing him a little bit closer to me.

His crude language amped up the excitement level to the max.

I bit my bottom lip, thinking that he was playing the role of my stalker a bit too well, and feeling concerned about how much I wasn't in the least bit worried about it.

I never had the chance to ponder that because I was grabbed by my hair and dragged out to the middle of the room, past a couple of rows of shelves laden with cleaning products. I kicked and screamed, calling him all sort of names, panicking a little because all of a sudden, the realism became overwhelming.

The bastard laughed. I ranted and raved, told him that he was hurting me, that this was painful, but none of my appeals got through to him. I remembered I didn't have any underwear on because he'd asked me to take my panties off earlier on and this room wasn't particularly warm. A draft from a small window brushed against my bare skin.

He picked me up and sat me down on the top of one of the operating dryers.

"What the fuck are you doing, you sick son of a bitch? This hurts!" I shouted, anger turning me into a nasty hag. I wasn't seeing straight. "Besides, we're in a hotel. You have no right to lock this room. The cleaning staff will know something's wrong." I winced because he wasn't letting go of my hair.

"Shut your fucking mouth and don't you tell me what to

do. You have no idea what you got yourself into, little birdie," he growled, getting in my face.

Tears welled in my eyes. Although I knew he was acting, his ruthlessness felt so tangible and real. Real enough to break me.

But I reminded myself once again that I wanted this. I asked for it, so I had to play the part and toe the line—or digress and face the consequences.

Fear and arousal warred within me. For a fleeting moment, Lennox and Richard felt like the same person.

But then, Lennox let go of my hair and his mouth curved in a smile. He caressed my cheek, his expression softening—not for long though because he then wrapped his hand around my neck and squeezed. His grin darkened when I gasped. The perfect villain bad boy. A bully in the flesh. He was a natural...

"Well, well, well. Who would have thought that Little Miss Perfect had such a filthy mouth?" he scoffed, increasing the pressure around my neck. "What would your father say if he saw you like this, all hot and bothered?"

"Fuck you," I spat, and his eyes sparked with fire. Green, full of shadows and dangerous.

I inhaled his masculine scent that was making me lose my mind.

Terror and sensual stimulation kept on wrestling in their brutal match—such a heady mix.

"You must learn how to be obedient, little lamb. You shouldn't have tried to run away from me and hide with your slutty friend. But first, let's play a new game. My rules now. Let's see how long it will take you to beg me to finish you off," he ground out.

"I'm not one to beg," I said firmly.

The dryer rattled on beneath my bare ass, making me more aroused and hot.

"Oh, you will when I start sliding my cock into your slick pussy," he said crudely. I wanted to wipe the self-assured smirk off his face. "Now stay here and don't move."

Lennox cradled me with his huge body, then produced a pair of handcuffs from his pocket, dangling them in front of me.

"Someone might try to get in here at any moment," I said. "I don't want you to put those on me."

"Put your hands behind you or I'm going to have to punish you." He sounded like a stern army general—a man to be taken seriously.

With a sigh, I put my hands behind my back, and Lennox made quick work of handcuffing me.

"You are not being gentle," I remarked when he adjusted my position on the edge of the dryer and instructed me to lay my palms flat on the machine.

"Such a good girl," he murmured when I let him spread my legs wide.

"Is this when we have to discuss safe words?" I asked.

"Hmmm ... not yet," he said with a glint in his eyes, then kneeled in front of me and released a breath against my most intimate spot.

Oh my God, this was so fucking hot. My breath caught in my lungs when he trailed his hands up my legs, from my calves to my thighs.

I shut my eyes and enjoyed his touch. I was already dripping wet for him.

"You have such soft skin. I want to eat you up. I want to

have you naked on my bed," he said, moving his hand up until his fingers brushed my clit.

"Oh fuck," I gasped when he caressed me there. The sensations were already so intense and my whole body vibrated with need.

"Damn, woman, you're soaking for me. Tell me you have been thinking about me? Have you thought about how would it feel if I used my tongue to fuck your tight pussy?"

His crude language again made my core throb with yearning. No wonder he said I'd be begging for release soon enough. I wasn't sure how long I could hold on, and he'd barely touched me so far.

Fucking hell. I was in trouble.

Chapter Forty-Two

Cathy

If he kept talking like that, I might climax purely from the sound of his husky and sexy voice. After drawing lazy circles around my clit, he sank his middle finger deep inside me for a brief moment—just enough to send me to another dimension of pleasure. I leaned back on my palms, seriously doubting I had the strength to keep myself upright for long.

I gasped for air, silently praying that he'd continue doing what he was doing, because it felt so wonderful.

"Now spread your legs wide for me and don't say a word," he ordered, pulling his hand away.

I wanted to scream in protest but instead, I obeyed his command.

I wanted his fingers on my folds, rubbing over my throbbing clit. Incredible pressure built in the pit of my stomach.

This was all alien to me because I'd never felt like this before. Not even with Matt. My pussy was so wet for him, my juices were probably dripping to the floor.

I spread my legs wider and then he lifted my dress further up so he could bury his face in my crotch, drawing a surprised cry from me. Lennox inhaled deeply and groaned, like one did when taking in the aroma of a wonderful perfume. I was suddenly self-conscious about the fact that I was so exposed to this man I didn't know very well.

I whimpered when he started assaulting me with his mouth, his tongue licking me everywhere, sucking on my clit. At this point, I was struggling to remain in a seated position. My legs felt weak and when he blew warm air onto my engorged pussy, I thought I was going to lose my mind. Then he licked me, gently at first. Once, twice, more times until I lost faculty of my brain and could no longer count.

My whole body was a trembling mess and soon, it was going to give up on me. My heart was pounding deep inside my chest. This was all too much. He was pushing me to the edge of the most mind-shattering orgasm of my life.

Grabbing my hips with both hands, he pushed his face into my crotch as if he couldn't get enough. Soon, he was feasting on my pussy like a starved man, licking me everywhere, then fucking me with his tongue. I moaned again and again and didn't bother to control myself at this point. I wished I could tangle my fingers in his hair, and I hated being restricted by the handcuffs.

Matt had never made me feel this way. Never went down on me or made me orgasm like this, and I never said anything because I thought this was normal. I didn't want to rock the boat. Many women, I read, found it difficult to climax. I had been so wrong though. I liked masturbating, I liked coming on my own, but this felt simply incredible.

He sucked on my clit as though it was a lollipop. My body kept shaking uncontrollably as I reached the edge of the precipice, so damn close to breaking apart.

I threw my head back, dropping my witch hat behind me, and moaned his name as he hungrily fucked me with his tongue, over and over. He moved my tulle skirt out of the way several times to get in there and give it his all.

The orgasm loomed close but then, just like that, he suddenly stopped.

Horrified, I let go of a loud whimper and glanced down at him, in a daze. He was staring back at me, breathing hard. His whole face was covered with my juices.

"What are you doing? I was just about to come," I said breathlessly, overwhelmed with the need for release. I thought I might just slide down to the floor and then order him to uncuff me so I could make myself climax.

"You're not allowed to come until I say so, flower. Tell me, how much do you want to climax? How much more time do you need?" he asked, tilting his head to the side and looking directly into my eyes.

I shook my head.

"I don't know. Just do it... Just keep fucking me like that. It felt so good," I mumbled, not sure why he was stalling.

"Then beg for it, pet. Beg me to keep fucking you with my fingers and then with my tongue. If you do that, then I will gladly oblige and trust me, you'll come like you've never come before," he said, casually getting to his feet.

I shook my head again, refusing to beg. There was no way I could do that, even though I burned for him to touch me.

"No," I said, then licked my lips.

"So proud... but I can already tell you're about to give in. Once I sink my cock into your tight hole, you'll change your mind," he said.

Lennox was like a demon that had come straight through the gates of Hell to taunt me. He totally turned me on but for some reason, I felt compelled to resist him. However, he wasn't going to let me come until I begged him for it, so we were at an impasse.

Before I could say anything, he picked me up off the dryer, set me on my feet, and spun me around, making me lean against the rattling machine with my dress hitched up—my hands still confined, my ass exposed to him. Not the most comfortable of positions.

"Let go of me then!" I protested. "You promised me I'd be enjoying myself, but this is no fun."

I struggled but he pushed me down.

"Oh, this is going to be so good," he said, laughing, and before I could take another breath, or at least brace myself, Lennox spanked my backside three times.

I screamed every time the weight of something—not his bare hand—landed on my flesh. The pain was raw and my skin burned with raw fire. I felt like I was going to pass out and then, he unzipped his trousers. I looked back to find him holding one of my trade paperbacks in his hand—and he was spanking me with it!

"What ... where were you hiding that? That book's mine," I said in a pained tone. I didn't remember him carrying that when he found me. Maybe he was hiding it in his shirt, or he'd placed it somewhere and retrieved it while I was in the throes of pleasure just a moment ago. But when did he do it when he was focused on my punani the whole time, eating his heart out?

"Hmmm... You need to be punished for staring at all these shirtless cover models," he said. "I feel this is an appropriate and fair punishment."

He pushed his pants down and I started to panic because we hadn't discussed the logistics. Was he using a condom or not? When I was about to ask, he was tearing open a wrapper and sheathing himself. I felt my eyes go wide when I realized just how big he was.

And then, finally, he thrust his huge erection inside me, making me scream for I wasn't ready to be stretched to the limit like that. His sheer size took my breath away. For a short while, I thought he was going to rip me apart as he pounded into me like the beast that he was.

"Take my cock like a good girl. I'm going to fuck you so hard that you won't remember your name afterwards, flower. But you won't come because I won't let you. This is for my pleasure only," he growled, panting with every lunge. His hands dug into my hips and his grunting sounds filling the space with the exertion of it all.

My body was wound tight like violin strings. My limbs existed solely to be manhandled by him. The handcuffs prevented so much movement, and my breasts ached as they were crushed on the dryer surface every time he sank into me. He filled me to the brim, taking all of me, and I knew I was going to come soon. Once again, I was on the edge of orgasm.

Sweat gathered on my brow, my mind was spinning.

Lennox needed to fuck me a few seconds longer—just a few more thrusts and I would explode. But then his phone started ringing and he suddenly paused.

"Hello?" he said gruffly.

What the fuck? Is he actually answering the fucking phone? Asshole!

He sounded like he was out of breath and I was so shocked, I froze. I was falling apart and he was still inside me while talking to someone on the phone.

"Oh, hello, Mr. Rogers. Yes, everything is all right. I have my eye on her. She's resting at the moment. It was a busy day you see, so she's recharging right now."

I swallowed hard, feeling like someone had slapped me hard. He was talking to my father while buried deep inside me.

Fuck me sideways. I hit him on the chest.

"Hold up, Mr. Rogers... Yes, Ms. Rogers?" I glared at him. "Oh, it's nothing, sir. I thought your daughter was coming."

My jaw dropped to the floor, and I started hitting him with my fist, but he soon caught my hands and held them in a vise grip, all the while sporting a stupid grin.

"Yes, so far everything is fine and no sign of anything wrong. You don't have to worry. I'm looking after her and not letting her out of my sight. Will keep you posted. Goodbye, Mr. Rogers. Hope you have a great night."

Lennox

. . .

This woman was going to be the death of me. I was already losing my head for her. She was so slick and perfect—perfect for my cock. Her pussy was throbbing for release but I wasn't ready to give it to her just yet. And I knew she was so close. She smelled incredible, and the noises of pleasure she was making were driving me absolutely insane.

She'd asked for one night only, but it wouldn't be enough. There was so much more I wanted to do with her. Dark and twisted things that only possibly lived in her imagination.

Training her as my submissive would require a lot of patience and discipline, and we didn't have the time to do this in just a few hours. I would need this to be a full-time position so I could spend days, weeks, months with her. The likelihood of this happening was a stretch.

But we had the now. The present.

I pounded my cock into her dripping cunt, and I too was on the verge of coming. I wanted her to remember this day forever. She was whimpering so damn loud, begging me for more, begging me to fuck her harder, but she had to earn her orgasm.

I wanted to hear her screaming my name right before she came, too.

I slowed down a little because I was precariously close to losing control. She was so fucking tight, her pussy milking my cock like there was no tomorrow.

"Why did you answer the phone? What if my father heard me?" she questioned in a panicked voice. She tried to get up but I pushed her down so her face was flat on the rattling dryer.

I continued to fuck her over that machine, adding a little

intensity to her torture. I could barely stay sane myself, but I wanted to stretch the pleasure for as long as I could.

"Be quiet," I barked, then sped up the pace. Harder and faster. *Do not come, do not come, do not come,* I kept telling myself as she mumbled incoherently.

In that moment, I knew she was just about to explode, so I thrust once more, savoring that moment before pulling out.

She cried out then, protesting, cursing me out. She sounded so desperate, but I wanted her to beg me for my cock and she wasn't willing to do it. The two of us could play this game for a bit longer.

I purposely didn't talk to her about safe words. Everything happened so fast and I wanted to play the game as realistically as possible. She truly wanted to experience something magnificent during this Halloween evening. She wanted to be terrified, but satisfied, so tonight there'd be no limits.

I never liked playing by the rules anyway, and besides, I had no doubt that in the end, she would beg me to stay longer. I couldn't imagine never seeing her again after my assignment was over, or even after tonight. My dick was pulsating, so swollen it hurt.

Reluctantly, I pulled my pants back up, thinking about her ass and wondering if she would scream for me if I thrust my cock into that tight hole, too. Red and raw, it was made for spanking. I glanced at her book that I'd thrown on another dryer and smiled. The possibilities were limitless...

"Look how much mess you made with your dripping pussy," I chided. "Disgraceful."

She flinched, lifting her head slightly. Her eyes were hooded, glossed over.

Then I was beside her, caressing her backside, around her hole there, and she shuddered. She craved this.

"Please, Lennox, fuck me. It felt so good to have you inside me," she practically whined.

I hummed in satisfaction to myself, dragging my hand through my hair. Her juices and scent were all over my mouth, seducing my senses.

A few minutes later, I removed the handcuffs from her hands, finding her skin slightly bruised. I kissed all around her wrists, gently, slowly. Were those tears I saw in her eyes? She frowned when I put the handcuffs back in my pocket.

"What are you doing?"

"We have so much left to experience," I replied. "Now get on your knees, my love. Let's start our first proper lesson of obedience."

I called her 'my love' and it felt right. I was past questioning the sanity of all this. Since my fiancée Eleanor and I had drifted apart years ago, I'd never felt anything remotely close to this.

After a year of dating and a marriage proposal, our bond didn't survive my deployment to Afghanistan. She wrote to me for a few months but after a while, her missives became more and more infrequent. Until I stopped hearing from her. When I came back, I found her dating one of my old college buddies. My heart broken, I was left to pick up the pieces. I'd waited for her and she hadn't—plain and simple.

In the years after that, I wasn't interested in a serious relationship anymore.

Until now because Cathy made me feel things I couldn't describe. Such feelings couldn't bloom in mere days, could they?

For a while as I waited, she stood still, a hint of defiance in her eyes. Would I need to punish her again?

As I mulled this, she finally listened and kneeled right in front of me. She took her time getting on the floor, her gaze full of heat and curiosity.

I stepped back to the opposite wall and ordered, "Crawl towards me."

Cathy looked so sexy on her knees, her cheeks flushed and her eyes bright. Much like a dream come true. My dream.

Hesitantly, she went on all fours and did as I instructed. Her cat-like movements mesmerized me, her breasts swaying, cradled by her corset. I was yet to suck on them—a foresight I had to remedy. When she made it all the way to me, I smiled.

"Since you passed this test, I think we are going to change things up a little. We're going to head upstairs to the top floor where the hunting is going to take place later on. Your friends have arranged a little party up there, as you know. It's pretty spooky but I think it will be fun. After you suck my cock and take all of me, then you will be allowed to come. Do you understand?" She nodded and I slid my finger between her lips. "Now suck on this. Show me how much you want to have me in your slutty mouth."

Again, she hesitated at first, but then started sucking on my digit. Grabbing the back of her head, I pushed my finger through to her throat until she gagged. Her eyes glistened with tears.

"That's it. Now imagine you're sucking on my shaft. You're such a good girl," I praised, and her eyes lit up. It was going to take some time for her to understand what was expected of her, but I was up for the challenge. Saliva dripped down her chin as she sucked on my finger, so I pulled my hand out, giving her a little break.

"Do you want me to fuck you again?" I asked.

"Yes," she said breathlessly, but I shook my head.

"No. We haven't got time to get messy in here and trust me, if I fuck you, I won't be able to stop..." Her face fell, showing pure disappointment. "But I'm glad you're dressed as a witch. We're going to have a lot of fun."

She wasn't too happy with me denying her, which tickled me because she looked so sexy when she was pissed.

"Here," I said. "Put this on. Goes well with your costume." I pulled out a mask I'd brought for her from my pocket. You make the perfect witch."

I'd also brought a cape and mask for me, which I promptly grabbed from one of the shelves where I'd placed them and put them on. I grabbed her hand, then unlocked the door and we headed outside.

Cathy was very quiet as we rode in the elevator, and no doubt frustrated as hell. She had no idea what else I had planned for her. Her eyes sparkled through the mask. She looked so mysterious and enticing in this getup. This was going to be a Halloween night she would always remember.

She had to learn that I wasn't planning to let her come if she didn't follow the rules. Her obedience turned me on, but so did her defiance. Whatever the case, I knew I had my work cut out for me. When we got to the top floor, the whole space was dark and gloomy with spooky music playing in the background. I overheard a few women talking about the ghost hunting game that was planned for later, after the dance. The event downstairs would go on for another few hours, so we had time.

I let go of Cathy's hand and gave her a predatory look. It was time for her to get in the mood.

"Run, little birdie. Run as fast as you can because when I catch you, no one will come to save you," I whispered in her ear.

She took a sharp intake of breath and then she was gone, bolting across the room. The adrenaline and thrill of this game was going to make her even wetter and I was looking forward to sinking my cock into her warm, welcoming pussy once again.

A few heartbeats later, I went after her. She was giggling pretty loud, so I had no problems locating her in one of the rooms. She tried to dodge me, but I was faster and wasn't wearing heels, so I tackled her to the floor. Instead of landing on a hard surface, we ended up bouncing on something soft. It took us a moment to realise that we were probably lying on an old mattress someone must have placed there to add to the shady ambiance, along with random pieces of vintage furniture.

Chapter Forty-Three

Cathy

"Let's take the dress off and the mask and hat, too," he said.

I was so high on adrenaline, I could barely feel my body. My pulse pounded in my ears. This floor was huge, but he was fast and I didn't have a chance against him.

I couldn't believe we were on the top floor, playing hot, nasty games while everyone else was partying downstairs. And it had all been my idea, while Lennox sorted out the logistics. What was more astounding though: I was ready to miss one of the most significant book events of the year to be chased around by a six-foot-nine ex-military hulk of a man.

"Yes, sir," I replied, getting well into the zone now. I disrobed, soon completely naked before him.

"Hmmmm... you're stunning," he said softly. "Especially

these." Bending down, he flicked his tongue over a nipple, and I jolted in response.

"We have a few hours and you will miss the entire event most likely, but I promise I'll make it up to you. By the time I'm done with you, Cathy, your pussy will be well used and you won't be able to walk at all," he promised.

I knew he wasn't joking. After all, he'd already given me a taste of what was to come, right downstairs in the laundry room.

My mouth felt deliciously achy after sucking on his finger. Matt didn't care for oral sex in general so I rarely got to practise on him—and never in such a manner. Lennox had such dark, sexy fantasies that drew me in, and I fast discovered I loved servicing him, just like the heroines did the heroes in my smutty books. At last, I felt just like one of them.

He made me want things I never knew I wanted. Pleasuring him was at the top of my list, as well as finally getting the release he'd been teasing me with.

I mildly worried about people asking questions if I didn't show up at the dance. But then I looked into his eyes and all my reservations melted away. Andrew Gold was singing about scary skeletons while Lennox lay on top of me, covering me with his huge body.

"What are you going to do to me? Maybe I should run again?" I teased. For one, I was looking forward to sucking his cock.

Bending down, he left a trail of kisses on my shoulder, down my arm, then back to my neck. "I'm going to tie you up with these ropes someone left here and then I'm going to use you the way the way I see fit. So get back on your feet," he said, getting up and reaching out to help me up. "And then when you do well, I'll let you suck my cock later."

I put my hand in his and he pulled me back to a standing position. This whole place was not made for sex, but it was Halloween after all and we were both on a mission, so we just had to make it work.

Lennox grabbed the ends of the ropes off an old, scary-looking suspension, then started looping them around my wrists.

He seemed to be an expert in tying knots.

"This will do for now," he muttered, securing the ropes with my arms raised so I didn't have much wiggle room. He was irresistible when concentrating hard on a task, the frown on his face creating ridges that pronounced the sharp angles of his face.

I wanted to ask him about his time in Afghanistan later on, once we were done here. He seemed like a focused individual and did everything with precision. More than that, I wanted to get to know *him*.

Unlike so many other couples, we led with the sex first. Less talk, more action. But this was only spurring my interest more. Everything else just had to come later.

But wait a minute—why was I thinking of us as a couple? We weren't one.

We were purely having fun.

The thought of him fucking me while I was tied up and helpless made me shudder with anticipation. I could only hope he'd actually locked the door to this room because if not, anyone could just walk upon us.

He stood behind me, tracing the length of the rope while trailing his tongue on my shoulder, then, he trailed a hand down my side, over the curve of my bare hips, to my thighs. My anger at his relentless teasing dissipated, and I wobbled on my feet. Gripping my hips, he steadied me, bringing me flush against his hard body.

I didn't think I could wait any longer. I wanted him to fuck me until I couldn't take it anymore. My mind was already imagining all sorts of scenarios.

"You smell so good, I want to imprint you all over me."

I leaned against him as he suckled on my skin, releasing a little whimper.

"You know," he continued after giving me a little nip, "I could just leave you here for others to find you." He pulled on the rope. He was right—I wasn't going anywhere. "And what would they think then? Maybe they will see you're not the shy and naive girl you pretend to be in real life."

"I have never claimed to be shy. I am an introvert, but on social media I become someone completely different," I replied, breathing hard.

I was still having a hard time wrapping my mind around the fact that Lennox had agreed to explore alternative sex with me. That he'd asked me to become his submissive.

"I could hardly believe you," he said.

"I always wanted to try these things we're doing ever since I could remember, but my boyfriend was never too keen. He just didn't think it was a good idea," I admitted. I didn't much feel like talking about my ex, but I wanted to be honest with him. "So, are you going to punish me, Daddy?"

I remembered a book called Consumed, written by a pair of author sisters under one pseudonym. The hero in that story loved when his love interest called him daddy.

I bit on my bottom lip, wanting nothing more than to pleasure him with my mouth, but by now I'd figured out I had to earn that privilege.

"You are such a teaser, Cathy, but I still don't think you have any idea what you're asking for." He chuckled, but I could tell he was tense. He needed this just as much as I did. I wished I could see his face right then.

The Ghostbusters movie theme song drifted through the space, making me chortle. Then he wrapped his arms around me, breathing in my ear, reducing me to putty.

"Or ... I could keep everyone away from here to make sure we won't be interrupted. You drive me insane with need, Cathy," he whispered.

My skin was so sensitive to his touch. He moved his large hand down to my stomach, taking his time.

I shut my eyes, trying to keep it together, but it was all too much. My skin became hypersensitive to his touch and my pussy ached. I was filled with anticipation and eagerness to be consumed by him. When I thought I couldn't hold on any longer, he lowered his hand to my pubic bone and brushed his fingers over my clit.

He strummed his fingers over my delicate nub.

"So how much do you want to come, flower?" he asked.

"So, so much, Daddy. I want you and only you," I replied, nodding frantically. I wanted this release so fucking much, I could barely speak. And then, he finally dipped his finger into my folds, letting out a sexy half growl.

Lennox was driving me crazy with the lazy movements of his fingers. I panted for air while he held me close, his lips barely an inch from my cheek. He was cruelly teasing me, gently moving his finger over my clit and then retreating.

"You are loving this…"

I never thought a deep, husky voice talking dirty would bring me so close to the edge.

And then, before I capitulated and started begging in earnest, he pushed his fingers in and out of my throbbing pussy, going deep. I cried out, my voice echoing in the room.

With one hand, he ministered to my clit and with the other, he thrust into me.

"Lennox!" I screamed, my hips and legs trembling. My bound hands were almost numb.

"What is it, baby?" he asked, keeping up the pace. I was seconds away from reaching the top.

"Please don't stop, just keep going," I moaned.

"Beg me to make you come. Ask me nicely, flower," he responded.

I shook my head, yet was ready to say anything at this point. I was too anxious that he might stop and leave me high and dry.

But he kept going, increasing the pressure with every heartbeat. My mind was refusing to obey, but the sensations were too strong and if he stopped, I'd go mad.

I swallowed and took a deep breath while Lennox kept on taunting me. Touching me. If he didn't give me what I needed, I would scream in frustration.

"All right, all right! Please, Lennox, please do it! I'm begging you to make me come. Now!" I yelled.

He was breathing hard in my ear, pressing his erection against my ass. I needed to have him inside me.

"I figured you'd end up begging me, but are you sure about this? Are you certain you're ready?" he asked.

I nodded frantically and he sped up the pace, while pressing his thumb over my clit. I closed my eyes as my whole body vibrated with energy. My core was on fire. Then, when I was right there, about to fall, Lennox smacked me hard, right between my legs. I cried out because this was so painful yet so arousing at the same time. My clit started pulsating with a strong beat and Lennox rubbed it fast then, increasing the pressure even more.

And that was all it took. I let out a keening moan as haunting music played in the background. Wild pleasure flooded my core, spreading to every cell in my body. Inside of me it felt like a fireworks explosion, bright lights drawing me in and sparkling with warmth. Lennox kept going, rubbing his fingers over my pussy. The orgasm dragged on, tearing me asunder, and I truly thought I might pass out.

My vision blurred and I could barely see as I was coming down from the heavens. This orgasm felt like it lasted for hours and I had lost track of time. By the time I was able to think, I didn't know what was happening. I discovered that I was literally dangling from the ropes because my legs were too weak to support me and gave under me.

Everything hurt. My breaths were labored and at some point, Lennox must have let go of me because when I opened my eyes, he was standing right in front of me.

He cradled my face with both hands and bent down to kiss me tenderly on the lips, lingering there for a while. When he pulled back, his thumb drew lazy circles around my jaw. He stared at my breasts, the nipples standing at attention. Juices were running down my legs, sticky and hot.

"You're a little firecracker. You went through an explosion," he said, closing the distance between us. A huge erection was straining his trousers.

"You need to let me go now, Lennox. My wrists feel sore..."

This man was a beast, and I didn't think he was even close to done yet.

"I'm not done with you. This is just the first orgasm, but I expect you to experience plenty more tonight. Trust me, I'm just getting warmed up. You'll leave everything to me." His grin was nothing short of evil.

I didn't think I understood what he was saying, but I knew I couldn't stand in this position for a moment longer. Now that I was quieting down from the climax, I could feel the discomfort way more acutely.

Exiting my line of sight, I felt him behind me, loosening the ropes. At last, I could put my arms down.

"Now, flower," he said, running his fingers through my hair. "Are you ready to die and go to heaven all at once? Again?" he asked before placing me on the mattress on my knees, my ass in the air. "Spread your legs wide slowly. Be careful with those wrists. They're a little bruised."

Then, he slid under me, diving right between my legs, and started feasting on my pussy once again. His tongue was *everywhere* and he was licking me with a passion I'd never been the recipient of before. The familiar pressure grew and I was fast losing control of every part of me.

I didn't think I could survive another orgasm. But then, he

licked me all the way from my clit to the crack of my ass. This was wonderful. exhilarating, unbelievably arousing.

My body hadn't yet recovered from the first climax but the overwhelming sensations took me under again, tugging at me.

"You're so addictive. I can't get enough of you and when you come next, I want you to scream my name out loud," he growled, pausing for the briefest of moments.

He sucked on my clit and then thrust two fingers inside me. My breasts were bouncing back and forth, up and down. Another climax was upon me and I begged him to stop because it was all too much to bear. I was surrounded by stars, whizzing about my vision, spinning and dashing forth.

Pleasure took wings and I could feel it at the tip of each finger, each toe, in every nook and cranny of my body.

"Lennox!" I shrieked out his name as though I was being tortured, and I was surprised no one had tried to barge in here, trying to rescue me.

I didn't know how much time passed, but when I finally came back to the world of the living, Lennox was talking to me.

"You have no idea how hot you were just then. Your moans are music to my ears and I can listen to you coming for me like that every day."

He must have caught me in his arms because I was pretty much numb.

"Lennox… This … this was amazing."

Slowly, I started coming around, sinking into a gentle lull in the comfort of his arms. I could feel his heart beating where I was resting my head. And it was in that moment, on a random mattress on the top floor of a hotel that I realized, there was no place else I'd rather be. No one else I'd rather be with.

I swallowed, deciding to take the plunge and share my thoughts. "Where have you been all this time? You must be my ideal book boyfriend," I said with a light laugh, tinged with disbelief. "You can't exist."

His eyes bore into mine.

"I couldn't ask for more..." he said, playing with my hair. For a moment, I convinced myself we were a real couple, as normal as can be. "But I will," he added.

No, not normal. Nothing about Lennox could come across as ordinary or mediocre. Already, I wanted him again. What was he doing to me?

"Lie flat on your back, flower," he said before I had the time to work in a response. "I need to be inside you. Brace yourself," he demanded.

I didn't know how I managed to move, but I did. This wild night was nowhere near over, and I had no gripe with that. Who knew what the next hours would bring?

Chapter Forty-Four

Lennox

This woman was like a volcano of passion and her scent, her very essence, had seeped into my system, branding itself into me.

She'd already come at least three times and I knew I should let her rest, but I couldn't stop touching her. I wanted to hear her screaming for me again and again. I wanted to see her exploding when I was filling her up with my cock. She clearly hadn't experienced a guy like me before, felt sensations like this, and I was slowly becoming obsessed with how she said my name and the wanton way she orgasmed, throwing herself in the feeling with abandon. Her scent, her laugh, the little noises she made affected me on a visceral level. I'd been with many beautiful women, but Cathy wasn't like any of them. And that included Eleanor.

As irrational as it sounded, happening so fast, I felt like I was connected to her soul. I was so fucking screwed. There was no way I could just walk away from her after tonight. I had never engaged in a game like this before. Sure, I'd had my own favorite kinks and didn't care for casual vanilla sex, but as far as commitment went, I'd never considered it since Eleanor.

This was supposed to be only a one-night stand, a game as she called it, but for me, it was somehow developing into something else.

I was ... invested in her. I wanted romance with her. Flowers and slow loving on black satin sheets. Making out under the stars. Dark, twisted kinks on stormy nights ... with her.

Sooner or later, I would take her to my apartment. I wanted her to see my world, which was nothing like hers. I mean, my place was nice, but nothing like the mansion she was used to. Somehow, I didn't think she'd care ... and that was the clincher. I liked her as a person. I imagined more with her... The thought of her being with someone else already didn't sit well with me.

Once I had her on my turf, I'd show her what else I could do to her, give her the most pleasure she could experience ever.

I discarded my clothes and mounted her, wrapping her legs around my neck, the position allowing me deeper access. She'd feel every single inch of me. Then, I drove into her and sighed. It felt like coming home.

"Lenox, please, I can't take it! I can't..." she sobbed. I had been pretty rough with her, taking her to the limit, but I was nowhere near done with her.

I had to mark her. I had to make her remember me —forever.

Earlier, she'd been filled with defiance and anger. I pressed her buttons, wanting to discover how much I could push her, and she didn't disappoint. This whole situation was slightly complicated and I had to be sure these risks were worth taking.

Cathy was made not only for my cock, for my tongue, my mouth or my hands.

Cathy was made for me. Period.

"A little more, baby. I can't let you go just yet."

I gripped her ass cheeks and moved her into my thrusts so she'd feel me even more. She trembled in my arms, and I relished the strength of her desire. She said she couldn't do this anymore, but I had to disagree. The woman was insatiable.

This time, I didn't even bother with a condom. I'd asked her and she let me know she was on the pill. Besides, I regularly checked myself for STDs, and I was clear.

I slowed my pace, fucking her slowly and trying to prolong this for as long as I could. She felt incredible and wet—all for me.

She kept begging me to stop, but I knew she could take it. Besides, I wasn't going to last long. I was ready to explode deep inside her, fill her with my seed. I'd told her I wanted to cum all over her tits, but the feeling of her wrapped around my cock was too good to end too soon. She was my Procaine, my heart's anesthetic.

Panting for air, I slowed down a little and caressed her soft skin, then massaged her breasts. She looked into my eyes, her hair framing her exquisite face like a fiery crown. She shuddered, tightening herself around me. Reaching down between our bodies, I started massaging her rear hole while I fucked her. She tensed around my finger but from the sensual noises she made, I had no doubt she loved every second of it. She loved being teased.

"No, please..." she protested as I kept pounding my shaft into her, now a bit faster.

"Just relax, my love. Trust me." I slipped my thumb inside her asshole while I fucked her with my cock. She gave out a long moan, and I felt her walls squeezing my girth once again.

I pushed harder as the pressure built in the pit of my stomach. Scorching heat filled my veins. She became my virus, a disease that came unexpectedly out of nowhere, getting right into my system and infecting every healthy cell in my body. But instead of destruction, it brought immense joy.

I kept fucking her in both holes, and when she shouted out her release, I came hard at the same time, filling her up with my load.

Moments later, we both collapsed on top of each other. I pulled her close to me, embracing her tight. It took us a long time to come back to reality. The orgasm had drained me in more ways than one. I was so fucking done for.

"I think it's time to get dressed, baby. People might be up here soon," I said, shaking her gently, but her eyes were closed. She must have fallen asleep and I didn't want to wake her just yet, so I lay there thinking about the uncertain future ahead. How was it all going to play out? Cathy was intelligent and independent. She loved books and didn't need a man in her life, but having someone to look after her would make her happy.

At the same time, this was a completely unprofessional thing to do and her father would probably kill me.

I could get out of the contract, and then make sure Cathy

was safe, anyway. So then, I wouldn't be a hired contractor anymore and there'd be no barriers to us having a thing going.

Whatever the solution, I just couldn't let her go. Besides, she still had the stalker to be dealt with. I had no intention of allowing someone else to protect her. Nobody could do that as well as I would.

I let her sleep for ten more minutes, then woke her up.

She slowly came around, disoriented, but then smiled when she spotted me beside her.

"Hello, how long have we been here?" she asked.

"Long enough. Baby, we need to sort ourselves out and get going," I urged her. I handed her the witch costume and we both got dressed.

"What have you done to me?" she asked when it became clear she could barely walk. She looked pretty worn out, a sight that made my dick hard again.

"Well, I hope I showed you heaven," I quipped.

She looked like she wanted to say something, but was hesitating.

"What is it?" I pressed.

"Lennox, I just … I want to do this again. I want more … and I want to get to know you better," she admitted, biting on her bottom lip. "Maybe this … what we have … it might go somewhere. You see, my ex, Matt … he was never like this. He didn't know how to … how to…"

She looks so cute when she stammered. Her cheeks had gone ruddy, and she shyly averted her gaze.

Me, on the other hand— I was fucking angry.

That loser had never made her come? Was this what she was trying to tell me? What the fuck was wrong with that man? I would have liked to know more, but right now I was filled with righteous fury. If I ever crossed paths with the fool again, I'd tear him a new asshole and give him a wedgie. Just like they did in middle school and high school because in my mind, he wasn't any older or more mature than a schoolkid.

"Fuck, Cathy ... your father probably won't be happy if he ever finds out what happened here. We cannot take this lightly," I said, but this wasn't what I wanted to say at all. I was subconsciously sabotaging myself, giving myself and her all the reasons why we couldn't be together.

She was right though and she had the courage to admit it. What I needed to express was that I was more than happy to keep this going, extend this game, whatever she wanted, but although I wanted to think I didn't care and take what I wished, when I wished—I really couldn't do that to Cathy. She deserved much better than a low-key relationship.

Her face dropped and I hated myself in that moment. I remembered how she was telling people we were an item just before we got into the elevator. She had no reservations about her connection with me.

"So this is it? You want to say goodbye? Do you still want to be my bodyguard?" she asked, her voice so sullen, it nearly broke me apart.

I sighed, scrambling for words. Language was her specialty, not mine. I didn't know how to soothe and make us better. I was a man of action. Yet, I was chickening out.

I had to get a grip and accept the truth. The truth of all these feelings I wanted to explore with Cathy Rogers, Booktoker extraordinaire.

"When you said you wanted to play a game with me, I knew

I was fucking screwed. There was no way I could just let you go after one time, flower," I confessed. "There is so much more I want to teach you. And that's just the sexual part. Even more, I want to … spend time with you."

She looked initially shocked by my words, confused, but then her face brightened up like a thousand suns.

"Do you really want more? I want to learn … and to be with you more, too," she said. "It's like I know you but I don't know you."

"That's right, my little birdie. And that won't do."

I walked up to her and placed my hands on her arms, then slid them down and intertwined my fingers with hers. She was beautiful, funny, full of heart and damn smart. Was this what they meant when they talked about love—or lust—at first sight?

Already I felt she was mine to take care of. Mine to play with. Mine to touch and protect. So I leaned down and kissed her. A kiss into which I poured all of my longing for her. Without hesitation this time, she kissed me back, returning the gesture with the same intensity. She tasted like roses and chocolate. Hope and seduction. I devoured her, relishing her as a man on death row would his last meal.

When I pulled away, I was fucking hard again, and breathless. Her cheeks were rosy and she was beaming.

"Yes, baby. Let me show you the world. You're my little slave, my dirty little whore who loves to be punished in the bedroom. And my supersmart, sexy librarian outside of it," I said.

Holding hands, we started walking towards the door. Then the elevator arrived and when the door opened, a small group of women poured out. Cathy went all shy when a few of them suddenly surrounded her and started asking questions.

Most of them wanted to know if we were a couple and how long we knew each other. To my surprise, she smiled and told them that we'd only just started seeing each other. That this whole thing was still very new.

When we got into the elevator, I put my arm around her shoulder. She could probably see I hadn't expected her answer.

"They will keep asking about you, so I had to give them something," she explained.

I nodded, and secretly loved her response to those women. She was mine. She needed to remember that I wasn't going to share her with anyone else. But we had plenty of time to discuss this again and discover more about each other.

From the top floor, we went back to our room. I unlocked the door and she strolled inside. This was going to be one of the hottest Halloween nights I had ever experienced. We were about to rock this bed, and we had many hours left to explore our fantasies.

She dropped on the bed with a sigh, and I went to the bathroom to wash my face. I tried not to show it, but she'd truly exhausted me. My body was aching in several places, but I was so fucking satisfied.

As I dried my face with a washcloth, a shadow moved in the periphery of my vision and I realized I wasn't alone. Someone was standing in the bathroom with me, and that someone wasn't Cathy.

I turned around abruptly to see a man standing by the shower. He was staring at me with such unadulterated hatred, his eyes wide and bloodshot. In that moment, I recognized him right away. It was Richard, Cathy's stalker.

Dread flew down and sank its claws into my shoulder.

He raised a hand in which he held a gun. "She's mine. She'll always been mine. So you better get the hell out of here, or I will kill you."

Bonus Scene Halloween Games

Lennox

When I heard the doorbell ring, I got up from the sofa where I was catching up with a few emails. The Rogers' house was blissfully quiet, so I could actually hear my thoughts as I mulled several gameplans to handle Cathy's stalker situation.

Cathy was currently pissed off with me after I punished her in a bookstore bathroom with a good spanking, after she played a game of hide and seek there with her friend, Jessica. She'd promised me she'd never do it again, but she'd earned herself a solid punishment.

She was probably more furious about the fact she enjoyed my rough treatment of her a little too much.

The woman in question flew down the stairs like a bat out of Hell and opened the door. I didn't know how she could run like that in flipflops without tripping all over herself. I frowned, making a mental note to let her know about the dangers of opening front doors before checking who is on the other side beforehand. Fucking hell.

"Oh, I've been waiting for this!" she chirped to the guy who delivered a large, long rectangular box. Wasn't she charming to anyone but me? "Would you mind help me bring it upstairs, pl—"

"Never mind. I'll take it from here," I cut in, sneaking in behind her and thoroughly loving how she jumped in surprise, her unrestrained breasts bouncing with her. She was wearing a short gray dress that looked more like a long, tight tank top, leaving little to the imagination. No bra.

I had to have yet another conversation with her about opening doors to strangers half-naked or too-enticing attire. I wondered when I noticed no panty lines: was she wearing any? Her nipples stuck out, the outline clearly visible through the fabric.

Damn.

My cock said 'hello there', but I wasn't in a position to adjust my junk. I had to physically stop myself from grabbing her ponytail and dragging her inside like a possessive caveman.

She glared at me in a way that made me feel as if I'd been struck by lightning. "No, you won't."

Her tone was firm but so was mine when I said, "Thanks, buddy. Here's a tip." I handed him a ten, then grabbed the unwieldy box from him, hauled it over the threshold, and closed the door before she could protest further. "Okay, where do you want this?"

She pursed her lips and crossed her arms, mouth twisted around some sort of expletive, I was sure.

"Where?" I repeated. "Or are we going to stand here and get into a staring contest."

Rolling her eyes, she walked to the stairs. "My room. But before I put that together, I need to fix the broken bed."

Bed. Cathy Rogers. Naked. Dirty ... hot ... sweaty ... sex...

"What happened to the bed?" I asked, more than eager to repair something that might come to a lot of use for something other than sleeping in the future. If it wasn't sturdy enough, perhaps it should be replaced?

She looked over her shoulder at me, her eye on the package—the one I was holding, not the one in my jeans. As she climbed, her delectable ass swaying back and forth, I could see the very top of her thighs, but her dress just about concealed the ultimate prize.

"Please be careful."

"I'm good. Now tell me about the bed." *Stick to the important things.*

"Well, it's quite new, but I put it together myself and I think I made a mistake getting something from a low-cost manufacturer. The leg broke when I sat down on it last night and I had someone bring me a replacement from the store. It was too late to overnight it."

"When?"

"A little earlier." She studied her cuticles then finally caught my questioning gaze. "I went out the back, through the garage..."

...Thus avoiding the living room. She must have crept around real quiet like.

"Who?" My head was about to explode with annoyance. How did I not know this?

"A friend of my dad's who actually owns the store I bought it from. He personally posted it in the mailbox. Do I have to explain everything to you?" Irritation punched through her tone.

"You went out to the mailbox on your own when your stalker knows were you live? Are you out of your frigging mind?"

"Oh, for fuck's sake!" she exclaimed, stomping on the last few steps to the second floor, swinging her arms and increasing her pace. I thought I could actually see steam coming out of her ears.

"So, what's this I'm holding?" I asked, changing tack.

"Oh, it's bookshelves. I'm running out of space for my books and a new unit is very much needed. My plan is to cover an entire wall eventually."

We got to her bedroom and she went in, holding the door open for me to walk inside. What was the story about evil vampires? That if you invite them in, you're fair game. She should know, with all her reading...

"I suppose you need someone to help you with this, too?" I said, setting the box against the wall near a corner. Her room was huge and I could see a separate sitting area off one side, along with floor to ceiling bookshelves lining one of the walls.

"I can assemble those myself another day." She could easily hire someone to do this job, yet she chose to handle it herself. I liked that. I liked that a lot. "But, tonight, I need my bed."

Oh yes, you do...

The damaged, lopsided bed caught my eye. "Did you sleep on that last night?"

She shook her head. "I took the lounger in the living area. I actually like sleeping in that, and often drift off there while reading..." she said, then stopped when she probably realized she was supposed to be mad at me and not ramble on with TMI.

"Well then, let me get this sorted for ya."

She nodded, then said, "Oh," with a finger raised as though remembering something. Opening the door to her closet, she pulled out a small box and plastic package.

"Here's the replacement leg and the tools you need."

I stared in confusion at the small package that contained what seemed to be a tiny L-shaped thing.

"What's that?"

She wiggled the bag. "It's a screwdriver."

"Huh. Looks more like something you'd use to poke holes in paper. Do you have other tools? Real ones?" I asked.

"I do." She went back to the closet. "But that's all you need. Promise." She handed me a pink toolbox.

Bright pink. With Betty Boop stickers all over it.

I took it from her by hooking one finger around the handle, making my disgust visible.

"There's a small drill there, too. And wood glue," she said, disregarding my reaction.

"Uh-huh."

I'd deadlifted close to nine hundred pounds and bench-pressed over two-fifty, so I figured screwing in the leg while lifting the bed should be a piece of cake.

She sat down gingerly on a small upholstered armchair while I pulled up the duvet to assess the damage. Taking the leg out of the box and lining up everything else I needed, I opened the toolbox to find the cordless drill. A pink one, too. I suppressed a groan.

Taking my t-shirt off, I got to work, lifting, drilling, screwing... and all I could do was feel her eyes burning into my now sweaty back and fantasize about drilling into *her*.

In minutes, I was done. I stood, downed the entire bottle of cold water she'd brought me from her mini-fridge, and threw it in the waste bin in a slam dunk.

"Okay now, let's get started on those shelves, shall we?" I said, pretending to ignore how she was gaping at me when I flexed my muscles. I chuckled inwardly. This was going to be fun.

"There's no need to—"

"Just tell me where you want them, and I'll get them set up in no time." I grabbed the box from where I'd put it and carried it to the living area.

Nice. A wall of shelves, desk, floor lamp, curtains drawn to showcase a huge bay window. Everything was white with gold and pink accents, with hints of blue-green. Her laptop had a pink and gold design on it.

The large chaise she was talking about sleeping on reminded me of a 1930s style with a curved back, but larger and more comfortable looking in teal velvet with gold legs, decorated with cushions in the same color, trimmed with gold, and a blanket with kittens on it. I didn't normally care about décor and such, but I liked how her personality shone through in this space. Elegant, understated, yet fresh and slightly whimsical.

One hundred percent feminine.

How fucked was I when a bunch of furniture reflecting a woman's taste turned me on? Maybe I needed a shrink, even.

"This?" I asked, pointing to the one wall that had nothing on or against it.

She nodded. "But—"

"I won't be long."

"Do you need help?"

"No."

She quickly realized I wasn't about to stop and leave this room until I was ready. Her shoulders slumped in resignation, she sighed and picked up a book from the desk, the one I wanted to throw her on, lift her dress up to her waist, and fuck her from behind.

"Fine, I'll just sit here then."

She lounged on a stack of cushions against the arm, removed her flipflops, and crossed her bare legs on the lounger, book on her lap. I had an inexplicable urge to lick her pink painted toes. Hmmmm... starting with the big one, kissing my way down, then taking them in my mouth and sucking...

"Lennox? Are you there?"

"Huh ... what?"

"I was asking if you'd like some coffee or tea," she said, sitting up off the cushions.

"Ah, no. The water from the small refrigerator here will do."

I removed the contents of the box and checked out the instructions while she got me another bottle and handed it to me. On the way back to her lounger, she trailed a hand on my shoulder, leaving a trail of pinpricks on my skin. Purposely or an accident?

As I toiled away, occasionally swiping the sweat off my forehead, I threw a few discreet glances her way to take in the sight of her reading and sucking on a small pack of gummy bears, her magnificent fiery red hair framed by sunlight. She looked like an avenging angel on a snack break. Rather than covering herself with the blanket, she'd spread it beneath her, leaving her legs exposed for my viewing pleasure.

I was doomed to building this bookshelf with a constant hardon.

Fuck this shit.

Putting all my sexual frustration into the task at hand, I had the base done in a flash.

I stood and stretched, exaggerating the movements to catch her attention. Her nose was still in the book but her eyes kept darting back and forth between me and the page.

Yes, baby. I see you want a piece of me, in the Biblical sense. I got a long, thick sausage for you to suck on, darlin'...

I took a sip of water and looked out the window, meandering a little closer to it. A landscaper was trimming the hedges outside. He'd probably get off work soon, before dusk.

"How's that book going, baby? How'd you like the read?"

She bit on her bottom lip. "It's good. Stop calling me baby."

"That's cool, baby..." Walking closer to her, I reached out to grab a loose strand of her hair. She jolted again, her breasts bouncing. This woman was being super skittish around me today, poking the devil in me. "And I'm especially impressed that you can read upside down. Where and when did you pick up that skill?"

Immediately, she closed the book and looked about ready to burst.

"It slipped to my lap and I picked it up and it was upside down," she said quickly, avoiding my gaze.

"You're a bad liar," I said, pulling on her ponytail and

getting on my knees in front of her. "And you're a bad, bad girl, too. Ogling me with my shirt off." Her cheeks were now the color of a red liqorice. Leaning closer, I licked her ear then whispered into it, "You thought I wouldn't notice?"

I sucked on the lobe, never releasing her hair. Rather, I sank my hand under the band and got a better grip. She whimpered—music to my ears.

With my free hand on her knee, I started a trail up her thighs to the prize I'd been hankering to see and touch all damn afternoon. Hell, since I'd laid eyes on her.

I pushed my fingers into what seemed like a flimsy thong. "Did you wear this for me?" I asked.

"No!"

"Well, that doesn't matter. I still like it," I lifted her dress to take a look, "but I'd appreciate it more if you didn't wear any." With that, I tore the sorry excuse for underwear off her, exposing her delicious pussy.

She screamed. "What is wrong with you? Are you—" she shouted.

"I'll buy you another one. Now let's cut to the chase so I can give you what you want."

Pulling her up by the arm, I dragged her to the window and had her face it. The landscaper hadn't finished yet, but he was focused on his task and wasn't paying attention to anything around him.

"Place your palms against the window," I ordered.

"But if he looks up, he'll see me!"

I slapped her hard, and she yelped. "Let's pretend he won't. And stop questioning me."

Reluctantly, she did what I told her to do.

Then I slapped her again, her butt cheeks turning attractively ruddy. So sexy. "That's for hesitating in following orders."

I caressed the offended skin, taking my time as she put her forehead to the glass pane and gulped down deep breaths. Sliding my finger down the crack, I teased her hole there before traveling farther down and slipping two fingers in her pussy.

Heaven had to be worse than this. Couldn't possibly be better, in any universe.

Her juices dripped down my fingers, betraying her arousal.

"Hmmmm, baby, I see you're so wet for me. You can say you don't like it rough all damn day, but I know you do. See that? That's the fucking truth." I removed my fingers and lifted them to her face, so she could see them glistening with moisture. After putting the tip of my index in her mouth so she could taste herself, then dragged it down over her lip, I put the fingers back home—back in her pussy.

I started a slow, even rhythm at first, paying close attention to her breathing. When a slow whimper escaped her, I chuckled. "Oh yes, I can't wait to fuck you now. But first things first."

"I hate you!" she said breathlessly while gyrating her hips and pushing her groin into my hand.

"More lies. You want more. Your body doesn't tell tales," I growled, and then started pounding her with a fast rhythm, moving my fingers in what felt like the speed of light. Her movements got more frantic, more sinuous, and soon, she was moaning loud, her irritation with me clearly a thing of the past.

"Ahhh ... more ... Lennox. I can't ... almost..." she went on.

My hand would be sore after this but it was oh so worth it. I went all out, maintaining the highest speed I could, like a human vibrator, brushing against her clit with every in and out motion.

Soon, her legs started to tremble and she scrambled for purchase against that window as the yearned-for orgasm loomed. Her ass moved in rhythm with me, while her pussy sought to swallow me whole. I honestly thought that if we practiced enough, I'd be able to slip my whole fist inside her, but I didn't want her so wide open. I wanted her pussy to be narrow enough to get a good hold of my dick when I fucked her senseless. For her walls to close in on me, squeezing and milking me.

She was there ... so close.

"Lennox ... Don't stop."

I laughed and covered her free breast with one hand, teasing the nipple through the ribbed, stretch material of her dress. "So rude. Don't you know how to ask nicely? C'mon, beg me. Beg me to get you off."

"N-no! Just keep going!"

"That's not what I want to hear," I said, maintaining the rhythm until I felt her about to explode.

But in that crucial moment, my cellphone rang. I released her breast and slowed down, drawing a frustrated moue from her.

Her father's voice came on the line. I put him on speaker phone, but kept my other hand inside her, barely moving.

"Hello, Mr. Rogers, great to hear from you. Hope you're having fun."

"I just wanted to thank you for the report you sent me. You're very thorough."

"That I am, sir. Thank you."

"Well, I don't want to keep you. I hope Cathy's doing well. I will call her later tonight."

"No worries, sir. I'm downstairs expecting her to get here so we can eat supper together." I suddenly resumed my rhythm in her pussy. Fast, faster, until I got her right where I wanted her. On the edge. Then, I added, "In fact, I think she's coming right now."

"Oh, that's great! I'll talk to you later."

"Have a good one, sir."

"You, too!"

As I ended the call, I could see her lips twisting, and she made a faint hissing sound as if it took her all the strength in the world not to turn around and sock it to me.

I put the phone in my back pocket and gave her breast a final squeeze, then stopped and pulled out.

"Lennox! You're such an asshole! Don't *ever* touch me again or I'll cut your balls off."

"I guess I should go back to those shelves now, and you to your book. Hopefully you'll get some serious reading done this time."

With a chuckle, I cleaned my hand with a washcloth but didn't use soap and water because I wanted her scent to stay on me for as long as possible.

I resumed working, tuning out her angry, frustrated ranting as she called me everything but a child of God.

Until next time, my flower.

Newsletter

Thank you for reading! We appreciate you.
If you enjoyed this book,
the next in the series, Her Surrender (Men of Sin Book one), is available on pre-order today. Click here to get it now!
Also, please consider joining our lists to get notified of all our hot new releases (promise we don't spam!):

Sign up here